BUDDHISM THE
LIGHT OF
ASIA

by Kenneth K. S. Ch'en
PRINCETON UNIVERSITY

BARRON'S EDUCATIONAL SERIES, INC.
WOODBURY, NEW YORK

TO WILLIAM HUNG
TEACHER AND COUNSELOR

Table of Contents

Foreword

"THESE DOCTRINES, monks, comprehended and taught by me, you should learn, follow, practice, and cultivate, in order that this religious life may be permanent and lasting, that it may be for the profit of the many, for the happiness of many, out of compassion to the world, for the good, profit, and happiness of gods and men." (*Mahaparinibbanasutta*)

In the two and a half millennia since the Buddha uttered these words, his disciples have well heeded the admonition of the master, and have disseminated their religion to the far corners of East and Southeast Asia. Everywhere the religion spread, it has served as a civilizing influence. Truly it is the light of Asia. Within the covers of this book, an attempt has been made to trace the origins of the religion in India and its journey to win the hearts and minds of such diverse peoples as the Ceylonese, Burmese, Thai, Tibetans, Chinese, and Japanese. It is the modest hope of the author that this little volume may furnish a little understanding of the complex and variegated currents present in the Buddhist world, so that such events as the exodus of the Dalai Lama from Tibet to India and the involvement of Ceylonese and Burmese monks in politics may be viewed in their proper historical perspectives.

The author wishes to take this opportunity to thank the following publishers for much appreciated permission to use their copyrighted materials:

Oxford University Press, for selections from

F. L. Woodward and E. M. Hare, *Gradual Sayings*, London, 1932, Vol. 1, p. 128.

Lord Chalmers, *Further Dialogues of the Buddha,* London, 1926, Vol. 1, pp. 53-54.

Rhys Davids, *Dialogues of the Buddha,* London, 1923, Vol. 1, pp. 280-282.

Harvard University Press, for a selection from

H. Warren, *Buddhism in Translations,* Cambridge, 1947, pp. 117-123.

John Murray, for a selection from

L. Barnett, *The Path of Light,* London, 1947, pp. 44-45.

Royal Asiatic Society of Great Britain and Ireland, for a selection from

G. P. Malalasekera, *The Pali Literature of Ceylon,* London, 1928, p. 103.

I wish to take this opportunity to thank my son, Mr. Leighton Ch'en, for his diligence in typing the manuscript, and my wife for her able management of our home, thus affording me the leisure to finish this book.

Kenneth Ch'en

Princeton, 1967

The Background

BUDDHISM, THE RELIGION founded by Gautama Siddhartha who was born in India in the sixth century B.C., has been referred to sometimes as the great aberration from the Indian tradition. While there are certain elements of truth in this charge, it must also be admitted that Buddhism did not depart entirely from the prevailing Indian systems. For an understanding of the forces that led to the emergence of Gautama and his teachings, it is necessary to devote some time to the religious and social background as well as to contemporary conditions in India. For want of a better term, we shall call this the Vedic background, after the Sanskrit word *Veda,* sacred lore, derived from a root which means to know.

Sometime during the millennium 3000-2000 B.C., a race of people known as the Aryans began pouring into India through the mountainous passes in the northwestern part of the land. It is still very much of a puzzle as to where these people came from originally, but the view most widely held would put this original home somewhere in the vicinity of the Kirghiz steppe south of the Ural Mountains. After they settled in India, they produced what is commonly referred to as the Vedic literature, a body of lyric poetry, hymns, and verses that furnish us with a considerable amount of information about the life and beliefs of the early Aryans before and after they arrived and settled in India. It is

1

impossible to date this body of literature accurately, and we shall find as we proceed along that this same problem of chronology will plague us continuously even as we study the events in Indian history and thought during eras much closer to our own. For this deficiency, we shall probably have to blame the lack of historical sense among the Indians. In the past, they have refused to record the dates of events or the names of authors of important literary works, and when they are confronted with the vast body of historical literature which the Chinese kept, with recordings of day to day happenings together with the names of the principal characters, they are simply dumbfounded. However, the Indians argue that Europeans and Chinese place too much emphasis on the historical treatment of ideas and art, that in a piece of literature, what matters is whether or not the ideas presented are true to human experience, and not the name of the author or the date of composition.

Of the *Vedas,* the most important is the *Rig-Veda,* or *Laudatory Verses,* a collection of hymns addressed to the gods who were created largely by personification of various powers, such as the fire, sun, and wind, praising their mighty deeds and in turn asking them to bestow beneficial effects on mankind, such as wealth, numerous offspring, long life, victory in battle, and abundance of material possessions. The most important of these gods was Indra, described as one of stupendous prowess and physical proportions. When he issued forth into battle against the enemies of the Aryans, he usually fortified himself with copious quantities of an intoxicant called soma, which enabled him to overcome his adversaries without fail, so much so that he earned the reputation as destroyer of demons. He was invoked by the Aryans whenever they engaged in battle. Another important god was Varuna, described as the upholder of the physical and moral order in the world. The Vedic poets looked upon nature with wonder and astonishment, and the regularity of the appearance of the sun and moon and the seasons suggested to them an unchanging law that prevailed in the universe. Later this unchanging universal law was interpreted to embrace not only the natural but also the moral order, and Varuna was the deity conceived to prevent the world from falling into physical and moral chaos. The hymns to Varuna are predominantly ethical and devout in tone, and describe him as the god of righteousness, guardian of all that is good and worthy, the knower of truth and falsehood in man. As guardian of the physical world, he supports the heaven, leads the sun across the sky, bestows rains, regulates the seasons, and causes the ocean not to overflow, in spite of the continuous flow of rivers into it. Besides knowing the sins of man, Varuna is also able to forgive sin, and many of the hymns are indeed prayers for forgiveness.

On the whole, the hymns in the *Rig-Veda* are not much interested in what happens after death. There is no mention of the doctrine of rebirth, although some hymns indicate belief that a righteous man would go to the realm of the gods to dwell in immortality.

Rituals also played a role in the life of the Indians during the Vedic period. The ritual was probably just a simple ceremony in front of an altar consisting of a single fire in the domestic hearth, carried out morning and evening, and on the occasion of such events as birth, marriage, death, worship of ancestors, and so forth. The purpose of the ritual was also very simple: to invoke the gods to grant their favors to the inhabitants of the house. In time, however, such rituals became more and more complicated and elaborate, entailing many altars and numerous presiding priests. In this later development, the purpose of the ritual also changed. Instead of prevailing upon the gods to grant some special favors, the purpose was now to compel or coerce the gods to do what men wanted them to do. In the light of this change, the ritual now was looked upon as a sort of sacred science, possessing mysterious powers capable of controlling the universe and the gods. The method to achieve this control was by the scrupulous observance and performance of the ceremonies, and since only the priests were able to carry out the complicated rituals correctly, their positions as the dominant element in society became enhanced and consolidated. Indeed, so powerful did they become that they could destroy even their patrons by deliberately committing errors in the performance of the ceremonies. Moreover, since the ceremonies themselves were endowed with so much power, they were conceived as being identical with the universal order, so that the punctilious observance of them would bring about good results in the form of power and prosperity to the officiating party.

During this period of the supremacy of the rituals, we see the beginning of the idea of *samsara*, or the cycle of repeated births, according to which an individual would be reborn repeatedly as a result of good and evil deeds performed. To attain rebirth in the company of gods, a noble and virtuous life on earth was necessary, while the wicked would be reborn in another world to suffer the punishment for their evil deeds. However, such rewards and punishments were not considered to last eternally, for it was thought unreasonable that the limited good and evil which man committed during his brief span of life on earth could affect endlessly his pleasure and pain in the future. Thus the enjoyment of good rewards must come to an end, and the individual must face the prospect of rebirth.

This excessive ritualism inevitably led to reaction. It was held that the correct performance of the complicated rituals could not be expected of all people. There must be some other way of attaining emancipation from worldly bondage, and in response to this quest, there arose what might be called the intellectual approach, stressed in a body of literature called the *Upanishads*. The word means to sit at the feet of another and listen to his teachings. Such teachings were considered to be secret, to be carefully guarded from the unworthy, and to be taught in private to those ready to receive them. The term *Upanishads* therefore came to mean secret doctrines or knowledge. Knowledge instead of the correct performance of the rituals was to be the key to emancipation. Rituals were pushed aside, and speculations became all important.

This speculation probably arose as the Indians pondered certain questions when they carried out the rituals and contemplated the cosmic order they attempted to control. Is there a unity behind the universe? Is there one absolute truth behind all the phenomena around us? If there is this unity, what is the nature of it? What is the relation of this absolute to the individual self? The Indian search for this unity went through several stages. In the beginning, the Indian seers saw that all the gods had certain features in common, that they all enjoyed the same attributes of might, light, goodness, and wisdom. So there arose the belief that omnipotence was the characteristic of all the gods, and this omnipotence was personified in a deity called Visvakarma, the All-doer, the architect of the universe. Following this, there arose the conception of the common fatherhood of all the deities, and this was embodied in Prajapati, the Father-god, who was called the lord of all created things. Finally, the idea arose that the various gods were but different aspects and different names of the same supreme being. This monotheistic trend was to culminate in the *Upanishads*, which expounded the view that behind the diversities of the phenomenal world, behind all creation, gods, men and nature, there stands one absolute unity, the supreme Brahma. This Brahma is said to be the whole universe and everything in it, animate and inanimate. By thus identifying the universe with Brahma, the *Upanishads* see Brahma in everything, and everything in Brahma. At the same time, while acknowledging the immanence of Brahma in all objects of nature, the Indians also reflected on his transcendence of the created world, for Brahma is said to cover the world all around, and yet exceeds it by a span, or he stands pervading the whole universe with but a single segment of himself.

While this quest for the absolute unity in the universe was going on, there was a similar quest aimed at the discovery not of a cosmic but of a psychic principle, the inner essence of man, the *atman* or self. At first, the *atman* was taken to mean breath, but gradually it came to mean self or soul. A progressive definition of this self could be found in the *Upanishads*. At first, the *atman* was taken to be the bodily self, the body that was born, grew up, and died. Objections were raised against such a self being the inner essence of man, for the bodily self could be blind, or maimed. It was next thought that the *atman* was the empirical self, the self that moved in dreams, that floated about untrammeled by space and time, free from the accidents of the body. However, it was objected that this empirical self was subjected to the whims of experience and changed every moment. Dream states were not self-existent, but were tied to a local and temporal environment.

The third step was to regard the *atman* as the self in dreamless sleep, reposing and at perfect rest. It was pointed out, however, that while the self in deep dreamless sleep was indeed freed from fear and pain, it could not be taken as the real self because in deep sleep we are conscious of nothing, neither ourselves nor of external objects, so that we are no different from a log. The speculation then proceeded to the fourth stage, which held that the *atman* was pure consciousness, freed from all bodily and mental limitations. As pure consciousness, the true self was realizable through self-intuition, a mystical state that transcended wakefulness, sleep, and dream. When man realized his true self in this mystical state, his only experience was that of pure bliss.

Having discovered the inner essence or the psychical principle of man, the Upanishadic thinkers then drew the parallel that the universal principle of the universe, Brahma, the ultimate reality, must be related to the physical universe in the same manner that the individual self or *atman* is related to the physical body. With this parallel in mind, they propounded the fundamental truth of the *Upanishads,* that Brahma, the inner essence of the universe, is the same as *atman,* the inner essence of man. Through a long process of training, consisting of study under the guidance of a *guru* or preceptor, reflection, and meditation, one becomes enlightened in the sense that one comprehends intellectually the view that all is one, and realizes that unity in his own experience. All differences and diversities disappear, and the individual realizes that his own individual self is identical with the universal self. In this identity of Brahma and *atman,* the long quest of the *Upanishads* for a fundamental principle underlying the universe comes to an end.

The writers of the *Upanishads* resorted to numerous metaphors to illustrate this identity. As a lump of salt thrown into the water would dissolve and could not be taken out again, while the water when tasted would be salty, so would the individual self merge into the great universal self without leaving a trace. As a river would flow and disappear into the great ocean, losing its name and form, so would the sage released from name and form be merged into the divine spirit. This union is probably best expressed in the phrase, *tat tvam asi,* "that art thou." The "tat" or "that" refers to the perfect Brahma, the universal cause and the supporter of the universe. The "tvam" or "thou" refers to the same Brahma, now in his function as the inner ruler of the soul or self. By this expression, the Indian seers sought to enunciate the truth that the Supreme Being which is the universal cause and source of all existence is also the inner ruler of man.

When after a long period of training, meditation, study, and speculation, the individual comes to the realization of this great truth taught in the *Upanishads,* that one is said to have attained liberation, or release from the cycle of rebirth. This goal could be achieved while still alive. However, the *Upanishads* also pointed out that a large majority of the people would be unable to do so in this one life, though they might be able to attain the goal in some future existence, depending on the nature of the deeds performed. Thus the chief doctrine of the *Upanishads,* that knowledge led to emancipation, was closely related to the theory of transmigration. According to this theory, a being would be reborn again and again until such time that the deeds which he had performed would enable him to break through the cycle of repeated rebirths and attain deliverance.

In the western end of the Ganges Valley, the area was more fully Aryanized and the Vedic tradition was prevalent, but in the eastern reaches, this Aryan element was not so powerful, and consequently, the king and the people were more important than the priestly class, and men were less speculative. When the priestly or Brahman class attempted to impose their religion on these peoples in the east, they ran into opposition, which took the form of new teachers who taught novel ideas about the path to deliverance. The followers of such teachers were called *samanas,* or recluses, as opposed to the brahmans, the followers of the priestly class. Some of these teachers were ascetics, and since they relied on self-mortification as the means to emancipation, they tortured their bodies by taking as little food as possible, or they did not sit, or they sat on thorns. They wandered about alone or in groups clustered around their masters, always engaged in debates with one another, very much like the Sophists in ancient Greece or the peripatetic philosophers of ancient China. However, there was one great difference; these ascetics were mendicants, men who had renounced the world and had no secular interests like the Sophists and the Chinese philosophers. In general, the vows made by these ascetics were similar: non-violence, search for truth, avoidance of theft, sexual continence, and renunciation of property. By adopting the vows of chastity and poverty, they sought to rise above the bondage of physical desires, home, family, and society. However, it cannot be said that they were anti-social, for they respected life and property of others.

Besides these ascetics, there were also six teachers who were contemporaries of Siddhartha, and against whom the latter directed some of his sharpest barbs. The first of these, Purana Kassapa, held to a theory of fortuitous origin, for he believed that whatever good or evil one did had no effect on that individual. Another was Pakudha Kaccayana, whose doctrine of non-action held that the four elements that composed an individual, earth, fire, water, and air, were permanent and imperishable, and therefore there was nothing that one could do about them. Consequently, an act of killing such as chopping off the head was not a bad act, for all that the killer did was to insert the sword in the space between the elements. The third was Ajita Kesa-kambalin, who was a materialist in that he did not subscribe to the doctrine of rebirth and transmigration, for he believed that when a person died, the four elements that composed the living body merely returned to their original places, earth to earth, water to water, etc. Good deeds were therefore of no avail. The fourth was Makkhali Gosala, an upholder of the doctrine that fate controlled everything, and that there was nothing a person could do to interfere with the operation of inexorable fate. The fifth was Sanjaya Belatthiputta, classified as a skeptic who took delight in evading the problems of the day and suspending judgment on all issues, hence he and his followers were characterized as eel-wrigglers. The last of the six was Nigantha Nataputta, leader of the Jains, a group which taught that one could alter the effects of past deeds by deliberate acts, especially austerities. The Jains therefore emphasized restraint of the senses, freedom from passions, aloofness from society, renunciation of property, and indulgence in such practices as naked-ness, penance, and confession. All these teachers were branded as heretical by the Buddhists chiefly because they held to non-Buddhist ideas.

Turning over now to the contemporary political and social con-ditions pertaining to India during the sixth century B.C., one finds that the area was divided into a number of states, the most power-ful of which were Kosala and Magadha. The latter was located on the eastern portion of the Ganges Valley, ruled by a king named Bimbisara at the time of Gautama. It appears that the people of Magadha were not yet entirely Aryanized, and this might be the reason why the teaching of Gautama found such a ready response among the Magadhans, from the king down to the common people. North of Magadha was Kosala, the most impor-tant of all the kingdoms, ruled by a king named Pasenadi at the time of Gautama, who though not converted was friendly.

Besides the kingdoms there were a number of republics, whose existence and form of government were testified to by numerous references in the Buddhist literature. These republics were gov-erned by a supreme assembly, which met frequently to discuss matters of state, and to elect the head of state who held office for a number of years. The members of the assembly were very likely representatives of smaller administrative units. In this sense the assembly was a popular body whose proceedings were regulated by definite rules concerning the passing of resolutions, the con-stitution of a quorum, and the establishment of committees to transact business. For example, in the passing of resolutions, it was generally the practice to repeat the proposal three times, and if no objections were raised, the resolution was considered passed. In the event of opposition, however, a majority vote would ensure passage, but if the matter under discussion was complicated, then it was often referred to committees for further study. There is reason to believe that when Gautama organized his monastic com-munity, he modeled his organization after the pattern of these republican assemblies.

As for social conditions, the most important feature of Indian society at this time was the caste system, according to which society was divided into four broad castes or groups, the brahmans or intellectuals, the kshatriyas or warriors, vaishyas or merchants, shudras or laborers. Membership in a caste was determined by birth, confirmed by initiation, and lost only by expulsion. The food eaten by the individual, the clothing that he wore, the religious practices that he performed, the social life that he led, the occupation which he followed, and the girl whom he married, were all determined by the particular caste to which he belonged. In the matter of food, for instance, the restrictions covered not only the kind of things to be eaten, but also the persons preparing them, and the persons with whom the food was to be eaten. Since a person was born into a caste by birth, he was not free to leave it on his own free will; there was no such thing as social mobility.

Controversy has raged for a long time among scholars as to how and when the caste system originated in India. Some have contended that the Aryans originated the system to protect themselves from absorption by the indigenous peoples whom they faced after invading India. Others have surmised that it was created by the priestly brahmans in order to preserve the purity of the Aryans. Still others would have us believe that the system was due to occupational differences among the different guilds who wanted to protect their own secrets. According to a view now widely held, the system arose after the Aryans migrated from northwest India to the east. In the campaigns that ensued when the Aryans fought against their enemies, centralized authority was needed to ensure efficiency and purpose, and so there emerged a powerful monarch. Around him now clustered the nobility, made up of the lesser kings and princes. From the rank of these kings, princes, and lesser nobility, the army was recruited to carry on the fight, to defend the kingdom, and to suppress revolts. Thus was formed the warrior class. The great masses of the Aryans, now freed from the necessity of fighting, and protected by the warriors, lost interest in military affairs, and settled down in peaceful pursuits, trading, commerce, industry, and agriculture, and they became the vaishyas. In an earlier age, when the sacrificial rituals were simple, everyone performed the ceremonies, but such rituals soon became more and more complicated, necessitating the emergence of a special group to preside over them. The intellectuals among the non-fighters answered to this need, and they became the priestly brahmans, men who devoted their entire attention to the performance of the complex ceremonies. As for the shudras or laborers, they were probably drawn from the inhabitants of the aboriginal villages or tribes in the hills who acknowledged the overlordship of the Aryans. Beneath these four classes were the outcasts, made up of people who were engaged in such menial occupations as scavengers, refuse gatherers, butchers, barbers, leather workers, etc., and whose status was so low that they were not permitted any contacts with the members of the four classes, and hence were classified as untouchables.

At the time of the Buddha, the dominant position in Indian society was held by the brahmans. They held the key to knowledge, and the power that went with that knowledge. The life of the brahman was passed in solemn routine. His youth was spent as a religious student, studying the Vedic literature and the *Upanishads* in the home of his teacher, whom he served as a personal attendant. Upon the completion of this period of study, which normally lasted twelve years, he entered the next stage of his life, that of a householder, during which period he married, brought up a family, and performed his duties in society. When his children were old enough to carry on by themselves, and when his hair began to turn gray, he then left the household life to begin a new phase, that of going forth into the forest with his wife to live a life of meditation. Or he might become a mendicant, a recluse who abandoned all his property to live a life of poverty, and who immersed himself into a self-made world of meditation, in which he allowed his fancies to soar far above mundane considerations into the realm of the abstract speculations.

It was out of this religious and social background that Gautama Siddhartha emerged during the sixth century B.C. to establish a new religion called Buddhism. He repudiated the brahmanical claims that the *Vedas* were the sole and infallible source of religious truth. He also rejected correct performance of the rituals as means of salvation, and he disapproved of the Upanishadic emphasis on intellectual means to attain emancipation. He also protested against the iniquities of the caste system, especially the high pretensions of the brahman class, and welcomed among his followers members from not only the four castes but also from among the outcasts. In all his sermons, he preached the middle way, rejecting austerities on the one hand and gratification of the senses on the other. For Gautama, salvation was to be attained by following a rigorous code of personal behavior, with the greatest emphasis on personal conduct and individual ethics. It was because of these deviations from the traditional Indian pattern that Buddhism was sometimes referred to as the great aberration. In spite of these differences, however, Siddhartha was still a child of his age and could not divest himself entirely of the intellectual and religious baggage of his times. In his system, he still followed the Indian doctrine of deeds and rebirth, that a sentient being was to suffer repeated rebirth in the endless cycle of life as a consequence of the deeds that he had performed. He adhered also to the prevailing view that the goal of religious life was release from this endless circle of rebirths; likewise he believed that this religious life could best be lived by cutting off ties with family and society. In the light of these similarities there are some who would object to branding Buddhism as an aberration, and who would argue that Gautama Siddhartha still belonged to the great Indian tradition. The following pages will be devoted to the study of the religion founded by this famous Indian sage, as it unfolded not only in his native homeland, but also in Southeast Asia, Tibet, and the Far East, where it was to become one of the great civilizing forces of mankind.

CHAPTER **2**

The Life of the Buddha

THE FOUNDER OF BUDDHISM, acclaimed by some of his fellow countrymen as the greatest Indian teacher who ever lived, is known by a number of names. Since he was a member of the Gotama clan, he was sometimes referred to as Gautama. The name given to him at birth was Siddhartha, meaning "he who had accomplished his objectives." In later Buddhist literature he was often designated as Sakyamuni, the sage of the Sakya tribe. After he became enlightened, then he was called the Buddha (one who had attained bodhi or enlightenment), or the Tathagata (one who had reached the culmination of enlightenment and realized it himself), or Bhagavan (The Blessed One). Before he attained enlightenment, he was often referred to as a bodhisatta, a being destined for enlightenment.

When did the Buddha live? This is a simple question, and for such a famous individual, one should be expected to supply the answer with a fair degree of certainty. However, chronology never comes easy in India, for we come face to face again with that ever-recurring problem of the Indians' not keeping historical records, a situation that forces us to turn to records and events outside India if we wish to determine the chronology of the Buddha.

Our first recourse is to the chronicles kept in Ceylon, which inform us that 218 years after the nirvana or demise of the Bud-

13

dha, the great Indian monarch Asoka was consecrated. Now this is a very definite piece of historical information, but it is valuable only if we can relate it to some event or incident in history which can be dated. Fortunately this is the case concerning King Asoka and his consecration. The Ceylonese chronicles inform us further that Asoka reigned four years before his consecration, and that he was preceded by King Bindusara, who reigned for 28 years, and who in turn was preceded by Candagutta, whose reign lasted 24 years. Candagutta thus would have ascended the throne roughly 162 years (218 minus 4 minus 28 minus 24) after the nirvana of the Buddha.

For the date of Candagutta's accession to the throne, Greek records come to the rescue, as the event is connected with the invasion of India by Alexander the Great. The latter died in 323 B.C., and after his death the Indian empire which he conquered began to disintegrate. Out of that breakup emerged Candagutta, the founder of the Maurya dynasty of which Asoka was the third in succession. Assuming that it must have taken a year or two before Candagutta could have consolidated his strength to establish a new dynasty, it is reasonable to date his accession at ca. 321 B.C., and if we use this figure as the basis of calculation, then we would place the nirvana of the Buddha at 483 B.C. Since the Buddha died in his eightieth year, his date of birth would be 563 B.C.

It must be emphasized that the date 563-483 B.C. are only approximate, for there are several factors which are doubtful. In the first place, the entire calculation rests on the assumption that the number 218 is authentic. Some scholars have expressed skepticism on this point, but on the whole, the tradition appears to be trustworthy. In the second place, the date of Candagutta's accession being only approximate, it may be off by a few years. In the third place, there is the supposition that the duration of Candagutta's and Bindusara's reigns is authentic. It is because of these uncertainties that the nirvana is variously dated at 477 B.C., 486 B.C., or 487 B.C. by different authorities.

While this chronology has been accepted by most western scholars at the present time, it must be pointed out that there are two other calculations which have claimed support in recent times. One of these is based on the list of kings from Bimbisara, king of Magadha and a contemporary of the Buddha, to Asoka as found in the Jain traditions. According to the Ceylonese chronicles, roughly two hundred years elapsed between these two rulers, but according to the Jain chronology, only one century elapsed. This would put the nirvana of the Buddha at ca. 386 B.C. The other calculation is based on data found in Buddhist literature written in Sanskrit, the classical language of India and one of the two fundamental languages of Buddhism. This literature reported that the accession of Asoka took place either 100 or 116 years after nirvana. Instead of relying on the data furnished by the Ceylonese chronicles to calculate the date of Asoka's accession, the proponents of the Sanskrit tradition resorted to the contents of one of the Asokan inscriptions, which recorded that King Asoka sent missions to various contemporaries in the Mediterranean world. Since the names of these royal contemporaries were given, their dates are known through the Greek records, and calculations based on these dates would place Asoka's accession at roughly 271 B.C. Taking the upper limit, 116 years as given in the Sanskrit tradition, the nirvana of the Buddha would therefore be ca. 386 B.C.

Thus there are three traditions concerning the dates of the Buddha that must be considered. The fact that the Jain and Sanskrit traditions arrive at approximately the same conclusion independently would be a point in their favor, but serious objections have been raised against each, and hence they have not been as widely accepted as one would expect. To complicate matters even further, the Burmese government in 1956 celebrated what they said was the 2500th anniversary of the nirvana, in which case the date of nirvana accepted was 544 B.C. The Burmese Buddhists derived their chronology not from the Ceylonese chronicles but from the traditions of the Ceylonese Buddhist church which have no historical basis. If we assume that the nirvana took place in 544 B.C., then the consecration of Asoka, which occurred 218 years after that according to the Ceylonese chronicles, would be dated 326 B.C., obviously impossible since at that time Alexander the Great was still living. If we follow the Jain and Sanskrit chronology, the historical discrepancy is even greater.

With the discussion of the dates of the Buddha out of the way, the next problem is, what do we know about the life of the master? Curiously, no complete biography of him was compiled until centuries after his passing away; indeed it was only in the fourth century A.D. that such a complete biography appeared in Sanskrit. Before this appeared, there had existed two types of biographies, neither of which gave a complete life of the Buddha. The first and the earlier of these was certain suttas or discourses written in Pali, the other fundamental language of Buddhism, which furnished information covering certain episodes in the life of the master. One group of such discourses dealt with the period from renunciation of home and society to the attainment of illumination. Another account covered the period from illumination to the conversion of two important disciples Sariputta and Moggallana. The longest of these suttas, the Discourse on the Great Decease, was a detailed record of the last three months of the master's life on earth. Other than the fact that the Pali canon was reduced to writing in the first century B.C., it is impossible to determine clearly just when these suttas in the canon were compiled; one can only say that they were not drawn up during the lifetime of the master.

The second type of biography appeared at the beginning of the Christian era, written in Sanskrit and purporting to be lives of the Buddha, although in fact this is not true. One such account, entitled *Lalitavistara,* or *Detailed Narration of the Sport (of the Buddha),* is a continuous recital of the master's life from his decision to be reborn down to the first sermon after illumination. Another, entitled *Mahavastu* or *The Great Story,* starts with the master's life during a previous rebirth and carries the narration down to the time he established a monastic order with his first conversions.

Obviously, since these various accounts of the Buddha's life are separated by such long intervals of time, they must be assigned different values. Chronologically, the fragments found in the Pali canon form the earliest stage, and for this reason must be accorded the highest consideration as far as reliability is concerned. For instance, if we compare the treatment of the events immediately before and after illumination in the Pali discourses and the later Sanskrit versions, we will find that the former recorded just a matter-of-fact description of the master's experience, with no attempt at adornment and embellishment, whereas the latter included numerous details embroidered with interesting and miraculous episodes. However, in the case of the pious Buddhist reading the biographies of his teacher and master, he would make no distinction between early and late, between the prosaic and the miraculous. To him, all the biographies are trustworthy. The descriptions of the miraculous feats performed by the sage of the Sakyas would not strain his credulity, for he believes the master was such a powerful and extraordinary individual that all things were possible with him. It is with this Buddhist point of view in mind that the chief episodes of life of the Buddha shall be presented here.

In the Calcutta Museum there is now a medallion which once decorated the balustrade of the famous stupa at Bharhut in central India and which contains just the proper information to illustrate the legend concerning the birth of the Buddha. Maya, the mother of the Buddha, is presented lying down, head to the left of the spectator, surrounded by her attendants. Above their heads floated an elephant much larger in size than Maya, about to enter the left side of the future mother. Thus was pictured in concrete form the prevailing Indian view of the conception, which was to be immaculate as in the Christian tradition. According to the Buddhist legends, the future Buddha, whom we shall now call the bodhisatta (meaning a being who is destined for enlightenment), surveyed the world, and when he found that conditions were ripe for his descent to earth to be reborn for the last time, he changed himself into a white elephant and entered the womb of Maya while the latter was sleeping.

After ten months in the womb, the bodhisatta was born, to the accompaniment of flowers blooming out of season and of happiness pervading the world. All struggle, all hatred, all jealousy, sadness, selfishness and fear disappeared, sickness was healed, hunger satisfied and thirst quenched.

On the day of birth, a sage named Asita, dwelling in the Himalayas, saw the gods dancing in glee, and when he asked them the reason for their delight, he learned that a bodhisatta had been born in Lumbini Grove in the town of Kapilavatthu, at the foot of the Himalayas near the present Indian-Nepal frontier. Asita surveyed the land with his divine sight (one of the attributes of a sage) and saw the bodhisatta in the home of his parents, whereupon he flew through the air to where the bodhisatta was. When he saw the child endowed with the thirty-two major and eighty minor marks of a great man, he immediately realized that this child when grown up would either become a universal monarch ruling over the entire realm, or an enlightened one, the Buddha. At this thought the sage wept.

The father of the bodhisatta, Suddhodana, was naturally surprised to see the sage weeping, and fearing something wrong, asked the latter the reason for his queer behavior. Asita replied that he wept because he would not live long enough to see the infant grow up to become the Buddha and to hear his teachings.

This story of Asita predicting the future of the bodhisatta is usually paralleled with the story of St. Simeon in Luke II, v. 25ff., a parallel that has been accepted by many scholars as one of the most important pieces of evidences to show the interchange of ideas between the Christian and Buddhist traditions.

Seven days after the birth of the bodhisatta, Maya died and ascended to one of the Buddhist heavens to be reborn there as a deity. Upon her sister, who was also Suddhodana's second wife, devolved the duty of bringing up the baby. Was this death due to some complications arising out of childbirth? We do not know. At any rate the later Buddhist theologians provided some interesting explanations, apparently to sublimate this simple fact. First, they stated it was the absolute rule that the mother of a future Buddha must die seven days after birth. Such a law would imply that the Buddha in his omniscience would know what woman would die within seven days when he surveyed the world and thereupon took rebirth in that woman. Second, it was held that because the womb which contained the future Buddha must not have another occupant, the mother must die for fear that she might have another child. Third, the theologians also explained that since the bodhisatta upon becoming of age would leave the household life and thus would break his mother's heart, it would be better that she were to die early and avoid such a heartbreak. Such were the three reasons advanced by the theologians, inexorable fatalism, theological convenience, and the clemency of destiny.

As the father, Suddhodana, was the king of a petty kingdom, he surrounded his young son with a life of extreme luxury in the palace. For example, there is the following description in one of the suttas. "Monks, I was delicately nurtured, exceedingly delicately nurtured. For instance, in my father's house, lotus pools were made thus, one of blue lotuses, one of red, another of white lotuses, just for my benefit. No sandlewood powder did I use that was not of Kasi; of Kasi cloth was my turban made; of Kasi cloth was my jacket, my tunic, and my cloak. By night and day a white canopy was held over me, lest cold or heat, dust or chaff or dew, should touch me. Moreover I had three palaces: one for the winter, one for summer, and one for the rainy season. In the four months of the rain, I was waited upon by minstrels, women all of them. I came not down from my palace in three months." [1]

The education that the young prince underwent included not only the usual studies in the Indian languages and classical literature, but also the practice of physical exercise such as footracing, throwing the discus and lance, etc., and training in the four arts necessary for a gentleman, horsemanship, art of mounting an elephant, conduct of chariots, and deployment of armies.

During this boyhood there was one incident worthy of mention because it was referred to later by the bodhisatta in his quest for enlightenment. One day, while his father the Sakyan king was participating in a state plowing ceremony, the young prince was taken along to witness the ceremony. He was placed under the shade of a rose-apple tree, and under the influence undoubtedly of a warm afternoon sun he fell into a trance. When his nurses came to take him away, they found that the shadows of the other trees had moved, but that of the rose-apple tree remained still for the purpose of shading the youth.

At the age of sixteen, he married a girl named Yasodhara.

The life in the palace, amidst all the ease and luxury and entertainment by female minstrels soon palled on the young prince, who must have been a sensitive person, dissatisfied with sensual pleasures and ambitions of the world. The early Pali sources described him as being troubled and disgusted also when he found that he was subject to old age and death, sickness and sorrow. This repugnance for worldly pleasures and the knowledge that life was just endless misery, inspired in the young prince the thought of renunciation of the household life to seek peace and tranquillity in the religious life. No mention is made of the circumstances surrounding the renunciation in the early Pali suttas, but later commentaries furnish elaborate details concerning this momentous event.

These commentaries take the story back to the birth of the Buddha. According to them, brahmans were invited by Suddhodana to foretell the future of the newly born baby, and they prophesied that the youth would leave the household life when he saw the four signs, the old man, the sick man, the dead corpse, and the mendicant. In order to prevent the son from seeing these signs, the father initiated elaborate measures and precautions to keep the boy in seclusion amidst the luxurious life of the palace. However, the gods have a way of fulfilling the prophecies, and one day, when the bodhisatta was riding in the pleasure garden, one of them appeared in the disguise of an old man, with broken down body, gray hair, trembling, and stick in hand. Never having seen such a sight before, the young prince asked his charioteer what this sight was, and was told that it was old age, a stage which must come to all living beings. On succeeding days, the gods provided the sick man, the corpse, and finally the mendicant. When he saw the ascetic with his calm and serene mien, he decided that such a life would provide the escape from the disgusting and sorrowful and meaningless luxury he was enjoying. After making this resolution, he returned to the palace, only to find that a son had been born to him, thus providing one more link to home and society. However, he decided that even this event must not deter him from his resolution. At the time he was twenty-nine years of age.

On the night of the renunciation he awoke to find the female musicians sleeping in the most loathsome attitudes, "some with their bodies wet with trickling phlegm and spittle; some grinding their teeth, and muttering and talking in their sleep; some with their mouths open; and some with their dress fallen apart so as plainly to disclose their loathsome nakedness. This great alteration in their appearance still further increased his aversion for sensual pleasures." [2]

From the time he departed from the household life to the time he attained enlightenment, there elapsed a period of six years, during which time he subjected himself to the severest austerities to determine whether or not he could gain his goal of release from the cycle of rebirth through such means. This resort to austerities was in accord with prevailing Indian ideas that sagehood could be achieved when the physical senses were disciplined and the passions calmed. To quote his own words, "To such a pitch of asceticism have I gone that naked was I, flouting life's decencies, licking my hands after meals, never heeding when folks called to me to come or to stop, never accepting food brought to me before my rounds or cooked expressly for me. . . . I have visited only one house a day and there taken only one morsel; . . . or one every two days, . . . or one every seven days, or only once a fortnight. . . . In fulfillment of my vows, I have plucked out the hair of my head and the hair of my beard, have never quitted the upright for the sitting posture, have squatted and never risen up, . . . having couched on thorns, have gone down to the water punctually thrice before night fall to wash away the evil within. After this wise, in diverse fashions, have I lived to torment and to torture my body, to such a length in asceticism have I gone." [3]

Even after such austerities, the bodhisatta was not able to obtain the goal that he sought, so he decided there must be some other methods. He resumed eating and drinking as a normal person, went to Bodhgaya and sat under a tree on the banks of a river.

As he sat there, he recalled the trance that he achieved during his boyhood, and thinking that that method might be fruitful, he decided to practice concentration. One of the early Pali suttas recorded just what happened. During the first part of the night, he attained the supernatural faculty of remembering his past rebirths, reaching back to hundreds and thousands of his previous lives. During the middle part of the night, he attained to the knowledge of the coming into being and passing away of other beings according to the deeds which they had performed. Finally, during the last part of the night, he achieved the knowledge of the four noble truths and of the destruction of the cankers that hinder deliverance, namely, sensual desires, desire for existence, ignorance, and false views. With these attainments he reached enlightenment. Henceforth he was to be called the Buddha, or the enlightened one.

The remarkable feature of this Pali account is the very prosaic description of the Buddha's experience, with no mention of a tempter and with no embellishments of the miraculous. For this reason, it is often regarded as being probably the earliest version of the enlightenment. Later accounts, however, have filled out this momentous event with a host of interesting details to make it more dramatic and romantic. From these versions, we learn that when a girl named Sujata went to milk the cows, miracles began to happen, for the milk flowed from the cow on its own accord. She then cooked rice with the milk, and though bubbles arose, the milk did not overflow the brim of the pot. Thinking that some tree deity must be bestowing favors upon her, Sujata now called upon her servant girl to go to the holy place to make the preliminary preparations for an offering. Now on the previous night, the bodhisatta had dreamt that he would attain Buddhahood the very next day, so early in the morning he awoke and sat under a tree. There he was seen by the servant girl, who thought that he was the tree deity behind all the miracles; hence she hastened home to inform her mistress. Sujata immediately prepared food in a golden dish which she offered to the bodhisatta. The latter, having just renounced the practice of austerities, accepted the food, went to the river to bathe himself, after which he ate the food with relish. When he had finished the meal, he said to himself that if the dish were to go upstream against the current, then he would attain Buddhahood that very day. When he threw the golden dish into the stream, it began to sail upstream. The bodhisatta then returned to his seat under the tree to begin his concentration.

At this point, according to the later versions, Mara the tempter entered the picture. The introduction of this figure could be interpreted to mean that a severe mental struggle was raging within the bodhisatta. In Buddhist folklore, Mara was the spirit of evil, the personification of the abstract concept of evil. He was the lord of the world of desires, and was the father of three daughters, Desire, Discontent, and Passion. The aim of Mara was to thwart the bodhisatta from attaining his goal of deliverance from the cycle of rebirth. To this end, Mara brought onto the scene his huge menacing army equipped with all the weapons imaginable. He first attacked the bodhisatta with whirlwind, rainstorm, showers of hot rocks, live coal, sand, and mud, but all these lost their strength and power when they reached the vicinity of the bodhisatta. Mara then tried darkness, but this was turned into light. His hordes now attacked with spears, clubs, axes, discus, arrows, etc., but these miraculously turned into heavenly scented flowers falling harmlessly at the foot of the bodhisatta. The latter now called upon the earth to witness that the Buddha seat really belonged to him, whereupon the earth responded with a deafening roar of assent that frightened and scattered the hosts of Mara. When Mara finally acknowledged defeat, the bodhisatta resumed the concentration that had been interrupted, until he finally realized omniscience in the last part of the night.

With the attainment of Buddhahood at the age of thirty-five, a serious question assailed the Buddha, would he go out to preach his doctrines to others? Apparently he felt some doubts as to whether mankind would listen to and understand the revolutionary principles he was going to preach and only after the promptings of Brahma, the chief of the gods, to the effect that mankind needed his message did he consent to spread his teachings.

After his decision to embark on a missionary effort, the Buddha made his way to Benares where he preached his first sermon, entitled "Discourse on the Turning of the Wheel of the Law," which contained the fundamental doctrines of his system. Now began a life of wandering in the eastern portion of the Ganges Valley, preaching the law and establishing a community of monks, a period that was to last for forty-five years until his death at age eighty. Success crowned his efforts from the very beginning, for within three months, he had converted sixty monks to his cause. Those who joined the community of monks came from all classes, brahmans, merchants, warriors, even outcasts. The various cities named in the discourses indicated the places which he visited often and were mostly the capitals of the important states, Rajagaha of Magadha, Vesali of the Licchavi Confederacy, Savatthi of Kosala, and Kausambi of Kasi. It is interesting to note that after the enlightenment, Bodhgaya was seldom mentioned anymore. Tradition has it that during the first twenty years of his ministry, the Buddha did not have any fixed abode, but in the last twenty-five years, he resided in Savatthi, in the garden Jetavana donated to him and the community of monks by the rich layman Anathapindada.

From the period of enlightenment to the last journey to Kusinara, where the Buddha entered nirvana, there is no connected account in the Pali discourses. There is however a rather detailed record of the last three months of his life in a sutta entitled "Discourse on the Great Decease." The discourse starts with the Buddha leaving Rajagaha for Vesali, and upon arrival there, he became dangerously ill, but he suppressed it, saying that it was not fitting for him to leave without having addressed some message to his community of monks. Ananda, the personal attendant of the master during the last twenty years of his life, was alarmed by this illness, but consoled himself with the thought that the teacher would not attain nirvana without making some determination about the order of succession in the community. The Buddha replied by asking Ananda what the order expected of him, since he had taught the doctrine without the idea of a closed fist, i.e., that he had not kept any secrets from his followers. He then exhorted Ananda with a few sentences which summed up his doctrine, that each man is the master of his destiny and that each one has but himself for a refuge. "Be ye lamps unto yourselves. Be ye a refuge to yourselves. Hold fast to the truth as a lamp. Hold fast as a refuge to the truth." After these words to Ananda, the Buddha was once again visited by the tempter Mara, who urged him to enter nirvana at that moment. The Blessed One refused, however, saying that he would not do so until his religion should be prosperous and flourishing. When Mara admitted that this had indeed come to pass, the Buddha then made the prediction that he would attain nirvana three months hence.

On the road from Vesali to Kusinara, the master and his retinue stopped at Pava to stay at the mango grove of Cunda the smith, who provided the travelers with some excellent food, including some generous portions of a dish named *sukaramaddava*, literally pig's soft food. The Buddha told Cunda to serve the excellent food to the rest of the retinue but to reserve the *sukaramaddava* for him. After eating it, the Buddha experienced sharp pains and the flow of blood, but he again endured them without complaint and continued the journey to Kusinara.

The question arises, just what is this *sukaramaddava*, or pig's soft food? Is it food made out of pig's flesh, or soft food eaten by pigs? If the latter, it could mean some form of mushroom or fungus growth. Either type of food would have caused the food poisoning which the Buddha apparently suffered. At any rate this was the last meal eaten by the Buddha, and all the events that followed were to happen within the same day.

After arrival in Kusinara, Ananda approached the Buddha to ask for further instructions. To this request the master replied that there were four places which should be honored after his death: Lumbini Grove where he was born, Bodhgaya where he attained enlightenment, Benares where he preached the first sermon, and Kusinara where he entered nirvana. These four spots have become the four holy sites of the religion. These remarks were then followed by some further instructions on behavior toward women. In response to Ananda's question, "How are we to conduct ourselves with regard to womankind?" the following exchange took place, "As not seeing them, Ananda." "But if we should see them, what are we to do?" "No talking, Ananda." "But if they should speak to us, what are we to do?" "Keep wide awake, Ananda."

After this exchange, the Buddha instructed Ananda to announce to the people of Kusinara that he would enter nirvana during that very same night, and to invite them to see him for the last time. So many of them came that Ananda had to announce them by families instead of individually. Now the Buddha asked the assembled monks whether or not they had any questions to ask him, and when they all remained silent, he uttered his last words to them, "Subject to decay are all compound things. Strive with diligence." He now entered into mystic contemplation and the trances, and then into final nirvana amidst the shaking of the earth and the peals of thunder. The body was then wrapped in one thousand layers of the finest Benares cloth and cremated, after which the relics were divided into eight equal parts and distributed to eight cities, each of which erected a stupa or memorial mound over its share.

Such is a brief outline of the life of this great teacher of mankind as recorded in the written literature compiled by faithful and devoted followers centuries after the event. Though these records are separated from one another by a few hundred years, they are in fundamental agreement concerning the main events in the master's life, the world he moved in, and the form of his teaching. Hence there is considerable reason to accept as reliable what these accounts tell us about the important episodes in the life of this profound Indian sage.

Does archeology offer any clue to support the evidence of the literary records? In 1898, an archeologist excavated a stupa at Pipravakot, one-half mile from the Nepalese frontier and fourteen miles from the ruins of Kapilavatthu. In the interior of the stupa chamber were found some relic bones and numerous artifacts, among which was a stone vessel which contained an inscription around its rim. Every word in the inscription was clear, but the interpretation was diverse. The first translation made of one portion of the inscription read, "This is the relic treasury of the

Blessed Buddha of the Sakyas." If this translation were correct, then the bones which were found in the stupa could be said to be the actual relics of the Sakyan sage. However, later and more careful study of the inscription, especially the letters which resembled those of the Asokan inscriptions in the middle of the third century B.C., led scholars to modify the translation to read, "This is the relic treasury of the kinsmen of the Blessed Buddha." Such an interpretation would mean that the relic bones were not those of the Buddha but of his kinsmen who lived during the time of King Asoka.

The second group of relics consist of teeth said to be those of the Buddha, two of which were reported in India, one in Gandhara and one in Dantapura. The former was the one probably referred to by the Chinese traveller Hsuan-tsang in the seventh century, while the latter was taken to Ceylon during the fourth century, where it figured prominently in the later history of Buddhism in that island.

The third group of relics comprise three small pieces of bone, discovered in 1909 in a stupa near Peshawar in northern India. The relic-casket containing the pieces bore the name of King Kanishka, a Scythian monarch who ruled over northern India either during the latter half of the first century or the first half of the second century A.D., and it is believed that the original relics were deposited in the stupa by the king himself.

There is yet another piece of bone-relic discovered in 1913-14 in Taxila and later presented to the Buddhists in Ceylon. Coins found together with the relic have been used as evidence to indicate that the latter was enshrined in the first century before the Christian era.

The teeth and the pieces of bones mentioned above are probably the relics that have the greatest claim to antiquity. It is impossible, however, to ascertain whether or not they are genuine. Devout Buddhists contend that the bone relics are genuine, since they were excavated from stupas which from the very beginning of Buddhist history had been designated to serve as reliquaries for the relics of the Sakyan sage.

Besides the archeological finds mentioned above, we might refer once again to the medallion giving a pictorial representation of the conception of the bodhisatta. This medallion was originally a part of the balustrade surrounding the Bharhut stupa, which dates back possibly to the third century B.C., and certainly to the second century B.C. If we put the Buddha's nirvana during the fifth century B.C., then the artist who carved the medallion must have lived at a time when the memory of the Blessed One was still very fresh in the minds of the people. It is likely that he drew his inspiration not from the written word but from the oral traditions which were being circulated among the followers of the Sakyan sage.

Finally there is the column set up by King Asoka during the middle of the third century B.C. to mark the spot at Lumbini Grove where the Buddha was born. On this column, which is still standing, there is an inscription left by the king which reads, "When King Devanampriya Priyadarsin had been anointed twenty years, he came himself and worshipped (this spot), because Buddha Sakyamuni was born here. . . . He caused a stone pillar to be set up (in order to show) that the Blessed One was born here." [4] Living at a time just two hundred years removed from that of the Buddha, and before the life and teachings of the master were reduced to writing, Asoka thus furnished concrete corroboration of the written records concerning the birthplace of the Omniscient One.

Though we now accept the Buddha, the central figure in the whole body of Buddhist literature, as a historical character, there was a time when students of Buddhism were not so sure that the person known as the Buddha ever lived. These students of course did not question the existence of a founder of Buddhism, for a religion must have a founder. They did argue however that the Buddha in Buddhist traditions never lived, and that his birth, his struggles, and his death were not those of a man. The principal protagonist of this view was the French student of Buddhism and Indian history, Emile Senart, who put forth his views in an essay entitled *Essai sur la legende du Buddha* that first appeared in 1873. In this essay Senart referred to the early allegorical tales of the Indians that spoke of a sun-god being born from the morning cloud which vanished before the illuminating rays of the sun, of his struggle against the dark demon of the thunder cloud, of his march across the sky, and of his defeat finally by darkness at the end of the day. Senart attempted to prove that the story of the Buddha was none other than an adaptation of the story of this sun-god. The Buddha was born from the womb of Maya, like the sun-god issuing forth from the cloud of the night. Maya died after the birth of the Buddha, just as the morning cloud disappeared before the rays of the sun. The Buddha then defeated Mara in combat, as the sun-god conquered the demon of the thunder cloud. When victory over Mara was achieved, the Buddha set into motion the wheel of the law; this was the sun-god revolving his luminous disk across the sky. In the end the Buddha died, as at sunset the rays of the sun vanished into the evening clouds. The funeral pyre on which the body of the Buddha was cremated was extinguished by streams of water which poured down from heaven, just as the last flames of the sun on the horizon disappeared in the evening mist.

This was indeed a most ingenious theory, and Senart was able to win quite a number of followers. However, the elaborate structure which he constructed was based entirely on the *Lalitavistara* (*Detailed Narration of the Sport of the Buddha*), which was a relatively late biography of the Buddha. He disregarded entirely the accounts as found in the Pali suttas which are generally acknowledged to be of a much earlier vintage and therefore more reliable. For this reason, Senart's theory is no longer given serious consideration.

Though Buddha lived and died over 2500 years ago, he still stands before us a strong and plausible personality, of unsurpassed spiritual profundity and moral strength, who left an indelible imprint upon those whom he met. Even today, we are impressed with his tolerant intellect toward divergent views, his universal compassion for all sentient beings, and his penetrating wisdom and intuition concerning the nature of the individual and the external world. He is indeed a teacher for all mankind of all ages.

CHAPTER 3

The Teachings of the Buddha

AS IN THE CASE OF the other two great teachers who were roughly contemporaneous with the Buddha, Socrates and Confucius, no records were kept of the teachings of the master while he lived. He merely traveled from place to place preaching the doctrines orally to all those who came to listen, while his disciples also transmitted them orally after having memorized them. We do not know exactly just when and where the teachings were first reduced to writing. In the middle of the third century B.C., the Indian monarch Asoka issued an edict calling upon his subjects to abide by the teachings of the Blessed One, and suggested certain titles of discourses which they should study. This might suggest that there were written texts at the time, but this is by no means certain. The only sure thing is that the earliest written compilation of the Buddhist scriptures was made in Pali (an Indian literary language) during the first century B.C., and it is on the basis of this Pali canon that we shall now base our discussion of the Buddha's teachings. We use the term Hinayana or the Lesser Vehicle to designate these teachings, but a more appropriate term would be Theravada, or Doctrine of the Elders. In our discussion we shall on occasion use the Pali word dhamma to refer to these teachings of the Buddha. The Sanskrit spelling of word is dharma. The Sanskrit spelling will be used whenever Mahayan Buddhism and Sanskrit literature are involved.

The Buddha often said that he offered his teachings in the manner of a physician, who had diagnosed the condition of the patient and then prescribed the method of cure. The therapy had worked in his case, and he assured his listeners that it would work in others also, if only they would follow the course of action he prescribed. In following his therapy of an arduous self-ordained discipline, there was to be no recourse to the supernatural for assistance. Very often he characterized his discipline as being that of the middle path. He steered a course that avoided the extremes of austerities and self-torture on the one hand and the pursuit of sensual pleasures on the other. Another set of extremes that the Buddha avoided consisted of nihilism, everything is not, and materialism, everything is; instead he stressed that everything is a becoming. The goal of the therapy is the cessation of the ceaseless rounds of rebirths, and the way to do this is to extinguish the fires of lust and desire that generate karma and kept the individual hankering for continued existence.

The word karma means deed. The doctrines of karma and rebirth were already present in India before the Buddha was born, and when he formulated his system, he incorporated them into it. The doctrine of karma provides for a moralistic and rationalistic explanation for the diversity of living beings, for good deeds are rewarded and evil deeds punished automatically, with no room for a mystical or theological agency to intervene. As a result of the deeds performed in the past or present, a living being would continue in the cycle of rebirth and assume a different form in each rebirth. To the Indians, therefore, life is usually symbolized by a circle, the circle of life with no beginning and no end. The aim of Buddhism as with all Indian religions is to break this circle at some point, so that the living being no longer continues to transmigrate. Once this is achieved, the individual is said to have achieved emancipation. Since the form of each successive rebirth is determined by karma, the greatest importance is attached to it.

The Buddha accepted the prevailing views concerning karma, but also added a significant point. He taught that not only the deed but also the intention or volition behind the deed is important, and that karma is generated only when intention is present. Here we see why in his system the Buddha attached so much importance to the discipline of mind. The Buddhist definition of karma is intention or volition plus bodily action. Every thought or act leaves behind some traces which could not be erased. Now this definition has a bearing on the Buddhist confession, which does not remove the sin of wrongdoing but merely is a repentance or affirmation that the doer would not repeat the offensive act. The traces of karma would be manifested in the present existence, or in future existences. Thus a living being, after performing some evil deeds in his present life, would require numerous lives in the future to work out the consequences of that act, and some of the consequences might be rebirth in a lower form of existence.

In the Buddhist scheme of life, there are five states of existences, deity, man, animal, hungry ghost, and denizen of hell. A hungry ghost is described as a creature continually tormented by hunger because he has a head the size of a pin-head sitting on top of a huge belly. The first two are considered to be meritorious states, the last three, evil. Rebirth as a deity is not everlasting, however, for the deities are still subject to karma, and once the fruits of meritorious karma have been exhausted, the deities will fall from their high state and be reborn in a lower one. Rebirth as a man is considered the most desirable, because it is only man who can achieve salvation and nirvana. However, to be reborn as a man is extremely difficult, as illustrated by a favorite simile of the Buddhists. Imagine a limitless expanse of the ocean, on which a tile is floating, with a hole in it just large enough for a turtle's head to go through. Now imagine also a turtle which comes up to the surface of the ocean just once in a century. How difficult it is indeed for that turtle to come up just at the right time and the right place to put his head into the hole in the tile floating aimlessly about. Yet the Buddhists say it is easier for the turtle to do so than it is to attain rebirth as a man.

If, as the Buddhists say, we are what we are through the operation of karma, is there any room for volition or intention? Would not our intention and volition also be predetermined? To these questions the Buddhists give no definite answer; they only teach that we are not only the heirs to our previous existences, but also the creators of our future, for the doctrine of karma leaves room for personal volition and action. Through the operation of karma, man need not look outside himself for assistance to reach the goal of the religious life, only he can save himself, only he can walk the path that the Buddha had pointed out. Because of this emphasis, the Buddhist would do away with all distinctions of peoples based on birth or caste or wealth. No matter what one may be, he is just as privileged as any other to join the monastic community and strive for the highest goal of religious life.

While accepting the prevailing doctrines of karma and rebirth, the Buddha also set out on paths of his own. In the very first sermon that he preached at Benares after enlightenment, he proclaimed the fundamentals of his system in the four noble truths: Life is suffering. Suffering has a cause. Suffering can be suppressed. The way to the suppression of suffering is the noble eight-fold path, which consists of right view, right intention, right speech, right action, right livelihood, right effort, right mindfulness, and right concentration. These eight are usually divided into the three categories that comprise the whole range of Buddhist discipline; *sila,* morality or moral conduct, embracing right speech, right action, right livelihood; *samadhi* or concentration, embracing right mindfulness, right effort, and right concentration; and *panna,* intuitive wisdom or insight, embracing right view and right intention.

Since moral conduct stands at the head of the three-fold discipline, it may be taken as the starting point of Buddhist culture. The kernel of the Buddhist discipline is expressed in the words, "Not to commit any sin, to do good, to purify one's own mind, that is the teaching of the Buddha." [5] As to what constitutes sin, the Buddha taught that any act that is harmful to oneself or to another is a sin. The Buddha looked upon sin not as a transgression of some divine law, but as originating in the minds and deeds of man, hence he was most anxious to prevent the arising of evil thoughts and actions. To help in such preventions, he drew up elaborate enumerations of human weaknesses and vices which act as fetters to the mind, and among these weaknesses, he considered the worst to be egoism, which gave rise to passions manifested in lust, hatred, and wrong views. Sometimes moral conduct is defined as cessation from sin, as seen in the commandmants and prohibitions. By right speech is meant refraining from falsehood, malicious talk, abusive language, harsh and frivolous words. By right action is meant to refrain from killing, stealing, and unchastity. Right livelihood means to abstain from such occupations that take the lives of living beings, make astrological forecasts, or resort to magic and fortune-telling. However, some positive virtues are emphasized, such as *metta* or loving friendship, and *karuna* or compassion. The Buddhist makes a careful distinction between the emotion involved in *metta* with that in *pema* or sexual affection. The latter is exclusive whereas the former is inclusive, for it extends to all sentient creatures. The other virtue, compassion, is the feeling that is shown to the unhappy and the afflicted, the feeling that suffers all the agonies and torments of others.

Loving friendship is not genuine unless it is accompanied by charity. The best example of such charity is illustrated in the Vessantara Birth-story, one of the most popular of its kind in Ceylon, Burma, and Tibet. A birth-story is a narrative of one of the previous rebirth of the Buddha. The Vessantara Birth-story tells of a young prince by that name who owned a white elephant that possessed the power to produce rain. A neighboring kingdom suffering from drought asked for the use of the elephant, and Vessantara in his generosity complied with the request. This infuriated his fellow citizens who gave vent to their anger by driving him and his family away. On his way to the mountains, Vessantara met brahmans who asked him for his horses, carriage, and furniture, and got them. Finally he found a resting place in the mountains where he lived on roots and fruits. One day a brahman appeared who asked for his two children as servants.

The children refused to leave, but Vessantara gave them away just the same. Finally another brahman came and asked for his wife, and Vessantara gave her away also. Now the great god Indra, presiding deity over one of the Buddhist heavens, revealed that the various brahmans were none other than he in disguise, that he was merely testing his (Vessantara's) charity, and since he was satisfied that Vessantara was genuinely sincere, he returned to the latter his wife, children, and belongings.

In later Buddhist history, this spirit of charity was to inspire the establishment of such institutions as hospitals, dispensaries, fields of compassion the income of which was used to care for the poor and indigent, and comfort stations on the way to famous shrines and mountains.

This consideration of vices and virtues leads us to the methods by which virtues are to be cultivated and the vices eradicated. The main institution organized by the Buddhists to carry out these objectives is the monastic community, established to guide the moral conduct of the monks in accordance with the rules of discipline laid down by the Buddha. In the monastic life, all the rules of discipline can be carried out. Since the Buddhists have a propensity for numerical categories, they have listed ten fundamental rules of good conduct, namely abstention from taking life, stealing, unchastity, speaking falsely, slandering, abuse, foolish talk, covetousness, malice, and harboring wrong ideas. In addition to these, monks are also forbidden to drink intoxicating liquor, eat between meals, attend secular amusements, use perfume and jewelry, use luxurious beds, and accept and use money.

The second of the tripod of Buddhist discipline is concentration. Concentration has for its objective the control of the mind. According to the Buddhists, one of the greatest of evils is *tanha*, usually translated as craving. Craving requires two things, a sense organ and an external object. Now Buddhism discourages asceticism or torture of the senses. Again the exterior objects are too numerous to be annihilated or ignored. While we cannot destroy the multitude of external objects, we can control the mind, so that it will not make the mistake of looking upon impure, impermanent, and unpleasant things as pure, permanent, and pleasant. This control of the mind is attained through concentration.

The mind is usually likened by the Buddhists to a monkey, jumping hither and thither, and not dwelling on one point for any length of time. This is the behavior of the mind when it is engaged in discursive thinking. The purpose of concentration is to bring the mind to a single point and hold it steady on that point, so that there is no wavering or wandering. According to the Buddhists, when the mind is concentrated on one point, it is not troubled by external disturbances, and it can attain states of bliss and ecstasy not obtainable otherwise. Listen to the words of one monk as he wrote of his experience:

"My heart stands like a rock, and swayeth not,
Void of all lust and things that lust beget,
And all unshakened in a shifting world,
My heart thus trained, whence shall come ill to me?" [6]

Because concentration requires long and arduous practice, its technique is worked out in elaborate details in the Buddhist manuals, the most important of which is entitled *The Path of Purity*. If a candidate wants to master the practice of concentration, he first presents himself to a monk whom he has chosen as his spiritual preceptor, and vows to follow his instructions. The master first chooses a place where the candidate can practice, a quiet place not too far, not too near, easy of access, not too crowded during the day and not exposed to mosquitoes or gnats, the winds or burning sun. He then prescribes a course of action to assure that the candidate can acquire the ability to pinpoint his wandering mind on one object and hold it there for a lengthy period. This he does by preparing a disk of a certain color, blue, red, or any other. The candidate is then asked to seat himself at a proper distance away from it; if too far, then he cannot see the disk, and if too near, he can see the imperfections of the disk. The chair must be of the proper height too; if too high, then he would have to bend his neck to look at the disk, and thus create a pain in the neck, if too low, then his knee would ache through the prolonged bending. With conditions just right, the candidate is then told to look at the disk as long as possible, until such time as he can have a clear mental picture of the disk even when he is not looking at it. When that mental picture is clear and steady, the candidate will have passed the first step.

Now the master will study the mental leanings of the candidate so that he can prescribe a proper subject for concentration. He studies his movements, his actions, his diet, and his attitude toward things. For instance, if he finds that the candidate is subjected to the passion of lust, the standard prescription calls for concentration on the ten foul things, or the ten stages of a corpse in decomposition. The candidate is told to repair to the charnel grounds and pick out a corpse on which to concentrate. However, he is not to do so at random, and the restraints that are put on him in his manner of going to the cemetery and his choice testify to the carefulness, practicality, and wisdom of the Buddhists. In going to the charnel grounds, he should first notify his fellow monks, for a very practical reason. Thieves have a tendency when pursued to drop their loot in the cemetery near a meditating monk, thus implicating him, whereas if he had notified his brethrens that he was going there, he would be freed from any suspicion. He should not go against the wind also, for the stench might cause him to vomit or to disturb his mind. Moreover, he should not go at once to where the corpse is, for the foul thing might be beset by wild beasts or non-humans who might harm him. In choosing the proper one to concentrate on, the corpse of a young and beautiful woman is not appropriate, for the sight of it might still arouse the passions, while for a nun, the corpse of a man is likewise inappropriate.

Through his concentration on the ten foul things, the candidate comes to the conclusion that not only the dead but also the living body is impure, ill-smelling, disgusting, and abominable. He sees the body as being "bound in skin and soaked in blood, covered with hide, overspread with masses of flesh, all overlaid with a thousand veins," [7] as being but an accumulation of bones, joints, tendons, skin, having pores that are constantly exuding impurities, a resort inhabited by worms, an abode of disease "where filth from the eyes oozes from the two eyes, filth from the ear from the earholes, mucus from the nose from the nose-cups, . . . excrements and water from the openings below." [8] Since the human body is but a bag of filth, why should one become attached to it? There is a story in one of the discourses that some young men took courtesans to sport with in the fields. The courtesans ran away, however, and as the young men went about looking for them, they came up to the Buddha sitting in concentration. They asked the Buddha whether or not he had seen some beautiful women pass by, whereupon the master replied that he had not, but upon further reflection, he admitted that just a few moments ago he had heard some skeletons rattling along the road.

After undergoing this discipline of concentration, the candidate will in due time attain to the different *jhanas*. This word is usually translated as *trance*, although it is not really a trance. A person who is in a trance does not know what he is doing, even though his faculties are functioning. It is really a hypnotic state, a state of insensibility to external surroundings. *Jhana* is not an insensible state, it merely involves the suspension of applied and sustained thought, so that what is left is a mind settled or hushed but in a state of lucid awareness, with preconceptions eradicated and ready for some flashes of the intuition. However, for want of a better English word, and since most of the literature on the subject use the word *trance*, we shall abide by the practice here.

Buddhist literature acknowledges the existence of two series of trances, the higher and the lower, the formless and those concerned with forms. When the mind is properly concentrated on the subject, it begins to empty its contents, and achieves the first of the lower trances. In this trance, the evil dispositions such as lust, hatred, sloth, pride, and doubt are removed, and a state of buoyant expectation and inward bliss sets in. The Buddhist distinguishes between these two by the following simile. A man traveling in the desert for a long day suddenly sees in the distance an oasis, the sight of which produces in him a feeling of buoyant expectation. After he arrives at the oasis and drinks the water, then the feeling that he experiences is that of inward bliss. In the first trance, there is calmness and serenity because there is absence of worldly desires. However there is still some activity of mind going on, consisting of reflection, directing the mind to one object and keeping it fixed and steady there, and investigation, or the continued exercise of the mind on the object. These two make up what we call discursive thinking, and they agitate the mind just as waves agitate the water.

From this first trance, the practitioner goes on into the second, which is characterized by the cessation of reflection and investigation, but with the state of buoyant expectation and inward bliss still present. The mind is still and detached, and from this state, it moves into the third trance, characterized by the cessation of buoyant expectation. In the fourth trance, even inward bliss vanishes, leaving behind a state of complete poise and equanimity, free from all roots of attachment.

With the attainment of the fourth trance, the practitioner has completed the four lower trances, but if he wishes to proceed further, he may strive to achieve the higher trances. These higher trances go beyond the perception and consciousness of forms, hence are known as the formless trances. Further practice in concentration enables the practitioner to reach the state where he pays no heed to distinction between objects, and reaches to the idea of infinity of space. Severed from all conception of objects, the mind now thinks only of space and sees everything as boundless space. This state is the first of the higher trances, but is the fifth if the preceding states are taken into consideration. From this stage, he passes on to the next, in which he reaches to the idea of the infinity of mind, and sees everything as unlimited consciousness. By passing beyond this sixth stage, the mind reaches up and concerns itself with the unreality of things, and is imbued with the idea that nothing exists. Rising above this realm of nothingness, he goes into the realm of neither perception nor non-perception. He has gotten rid of perceptions and so could not perceive ordinary things, but still it is said he is not absolutely without perception, for he retains a perception of extreme subtlety. Rising above this eighth stage, he goes into the realm of the extinction of perception and consciousness. Outwardly this is a state of coma, where motion, speech, thought, and consciousness are absent, a state that differs from death only in the fact that physical life and bodily warmth still remain. It is said that before entering this state, the practitioner must determine beforehand when he wishes to emerge from it.

Over the years numerous investigations have been carried out, some by reputable scientists, to determine whether or not the mind can really exercise such control over the physical body. The most famous experiment was that carried out at the end of the nineteenth century and concerned a famous yogin, or practitioner of yoga, named Haridas, who was buried alive and when disinterred after four months, was still alive. This particular experiment was carried out under the supervision of the Maharaja of Lahore, who had the body of the yogin sealed in a chest and buried in a grave. Above the grave was planted barley, while the place itself was enclosed with a wall and guarded by sentinels. Before burial the yogin shaved his face smooth, and the face remained the same four months after.

In the late 1950's, the pit experiment was investigated by a team of five research workers, including one European, at the Institute of Mental Health at Bangalore. A pit four feet by three feet by two and a half feet was dug. The Indian yogin, on which were attached numerous instruments to convey information on the electrical activity of the heart, the heart beat, and breathing motions, reclined in the pit, burnt incense, and then went into *samadhi* or concentration. The pit was then covered with a wooden plank one inch thick, on top of which was spread six inches of dirt. The experiment was repeated three times, with an interval of one month between the first and second, and two weeks between the second and third. In the first experiment, the subject was buried two hours, the second, nine hours, and the third, eight and a half hours. The results showed that electrical activity still went on in the brain even while the subject was buried and supposedly in a transic state. The heart beat was a little below normal, the lowest being forty per minute, but the rate of breathing showed a marked drop, from a normal of about sixteen per minute to the slow rate of one breath in a minute, and sometimes one breath in two minutes. It would appear that in such cases the yogin was able to slow up the life processes in the transic state, just as an animal would while hibernating during the winter.

In one of the Buddhist discourses, there is a passage which reads, "A brother who is concentrated knows a thing as it really is." [9] Thus the Buddha indicated the relationship between concentration and *panna*, wisdom or intuition, the third of the Buddhist disciplines, for to the Buddha, concentration is not to be an end in itself, but is to be a means to intuitive wisdom, or insight into things as they really are. To have insight into things as they really are means to hold to the right view of things, which to the Buddhists consists of three fundamental truths; all existence is suffering, all existence is transitory or impermanent, and there is no permanent self or soul.

The classic definition of suffering or misery is to be found in the very first sermon that the Buddha preached. "Now this, monks, is the noble truth of pain: birth is painful, old age is painful, sickness is painful, death is painful, sorrow, lamentation, dejection, and despair are painful. Contact with unpleasant things is painful, not getting what one wishes is painful." As to the cause of suffering, he said, "Now this, monks, is the noble truth of the cause of pain: the craving, which tends to rebirth, combined with pleasure and lust, finding pleasure here and there, namely the craving for passion, the craving for existence, the craving for non-existence." [10] To the Buddhists, therefore, this suffering which is universal is caused by craving, craving for existence, craving for repeated rebirth, craving for pleasure and power, all of which leads to acts that result in karma, and this karma in turn binds one to the cycle of rebirth. The Buddhist discipline is directed toward the destruction of this craving, so that there is no more craving for existence, sensual pleasures, or power, and consequently no more generation of karma.

The second fundamental truth is that impermanence is the inexorable law of all existence, and to the very end the Buddha stressed this truth in his last words to the community of monks, "subject to decay are all compound things." Existence to him is an eternal flux of becoming, without beginning or end. This idea of impermanence is very well expressed in the following passage, "In the ultimate sense, exceedingly short indeed is the life-moment of beings, lasting just once conscious process. Just as the chariot-wheel in rolling and standing, rolls and stands within the circumference of one rim, even so is the life of beings of the measure of one conscious moment. As soon as that consciousness ceases, the being is said to cease." [11]

If, as the Buddhists say, everything is a becoming, without beginning or end, then one would very naturally raise the question, just how did the universe originate? Although the Buddha discouraged speculation on the origins of the universe, there is a theory of evolution found in the Buddhist scriptures. In the limitless expanse of space, the Buddhists conceive of an infinite number of world systems coming into existence and passing away through beginningless and endless time. The process of evolving and devolving each of these world systems requires immense periods of time called *kalpas*, or aeons. Once the Buddha was asked how long a *kalpa* was, and he replied with the following simile. Suppose there were a mighty mountain crag, four leagues in dimensions all around, one solid mass of rock without any crack. Suppose also a man should come at the end of every century, and wipe that crag with a fine piece of cloth. That mighty mountain would be worn away and ended, sooner than would the aeon.

After the complete destruction of a world system at the end of the previous *kalpa*, then the evolution of a new world system began. The world at the beginning of evolution was in chaos, dark and covered with water, with no sun, moon, stars or constellations to be seen, so that there was no division of day and night, and no differentiation of male and female. After a long time, the earth began to appear on the surface of the water, like the scum on the surface of boiled rice. The beings living at the time of the passing away of one world system had been reborn in the world of radiance, self-luminous and able to traverse the air. Now at the evolution of the new world system, these beings became reborn on the newly appeared earth, and nourished themselves on the scum-like earth. As they found the earth to be pleasant tasting, a craving for it arose in them, and so they ate more of the tasty earth. This diet soon caused them to lose their ethereal bodies and their self-luminance, and in their place, they began to acquire solid bodies with definite shapes. With the disappearance of their radiance, the sun, moon, stars, and constellations appeared, day and night, the seasons and the years, became evident. As time went on, the first fungus growth such as mushrooms appeared, to be followed by creepers and rice, and when these were eaten by the beings, their bodies and forms became even more divergent, and the differences between male and female arose. With the emergence of the male and female, passions developed, and this gave rise to the whole chain of developments, hatreds, sexual morality, family, property, law, government, society, and social institutions. All these developments took place during the first period of evolution.

During the second period, which is a continuance of the evolving process, the world system maintained the progress started in the first. According to the Buddhists, we are now in the midst of this period, which will be followed sometime in the future by the third period, characterized by the beginning of the dissolution of the world system. At the end of the fourth period, the dissolution becomes complete, and what is left is only the ethereal, radiant world of Brahma. The time is ready for another cycle to begin its round, another *kalpa* to emerge with its process of evolution and devolution. This cycle is sometimes likened to the waves on the ocean, which are continuously rising and falling. Just as there are countless numbers of waves in the ocean rising and falling at different times and different places, so likewise there are countless numbers of world systems rising and falling, some evolving out of chaos, and others devolving into chaos.

Such a theory of evolution would, as one could see, fit in very well with the Buddhist doctrine of impermanence, for it is still fashioned in the scheme of a cycle, without beginning or end, just an eternal becoming. After its exposition in one discourse, there is no other reference to it in the sermons of the Buddha, and instead, the master often discouraged his disciples from speculating about the beginnings of life, saying that such speculations were fruitless and devoid of religious merits.

The third basic truth connected with *panna* or intuitive wisdom consists of *anatta,* or the doctrine that there is no permanent self or soul. It was already taught in the Upanishads that the individual self is the same as the universal self, and that as soon as one realizes this identity, he is liberated. Consequently, for followers of the Upanishads, the greatest object of attachment is this individual self, as evidenced by the following passage, "That self is dearer than a son, is dearer than wealth, is dearer than all else. One should reverence the self alone as dear. He who reverences the self alone as dear, what he holds dear, verily, is not perishable." [12] To the brahman, therefore, the individual self is his soul, which enters the material body at birth and leaves it at death. As it is immaterial and invisible, it remains the same amidst all the different states of existences that a living being undergoes, and its existence insures to each individual the fruits of his actions and thoughts, so that he may reap his rewards in immortality or punishment in hell.

The Buddha held that this belief in a permanent self or soul is one of the most deceitful delusions ever held by man, for it gives rise to attachment, attachment to egoism, egoism to cravings for pleasure and fame, which in turn led to suffering. In order to draw people away from this attachment to the self, the Buddha boldly denied its existence, hoping that by knocking down the main prop of the Upanishadic teachings, he would be able to gain a hearing for his ideas. He held that this false belief in a permanent self is due to an erroneous conception of a unity behind the elements that comprise an individual. He said that he had searched everywhere for this permanent self or soul, but found only a conglomeration of the five *skandhas* or aggregates, material body, feelings, perception, predispositions, and consciousness. At any one moment, according to him, we are but a temporary composition of the five aggregates, and as these change every moment, so does the composition. Therefore all that we are is but a continuous living entity which does not remain the same for any two consecutive moments, but which comes into being and disappears as soon as it arises. Why then should we attach so much importance to this transitory entity, in which there is no permanent self or soul? Once we accept this truth of the non-existence of a permanent self, when we see that what we call the self is nothing but a stream of perishing physical and psychical phenomena, then we destroy our selfish desires and self-interests, and instead of suffering from anxieties and disappointments, we will enjoy peace of mind and tranquillity.

If there is no permanent self or soul but only a temporary combination of the five aggregates, then what is it that suffers rebirth in the different states of existence, what is it that stores up karma and then expends it? Wouldn't the doctrine of nonself mean that there is no relation between a living being and his acts, for who is there to receive the fruits of acts done in the past and eventually enter nirvana? In answer to this problem, Buddhism furnishes the following answer. When a living being dies, the five aggregates that constitute the living being disintegrate, but because of the karma accrued in the past, there must be fulfillment, and so there is rebirth. The Buddhist belief in the regularity of the operation of karma is so strong that there can be no interference with its operation. The force of past karma causes a new being to come into existence, a new collection of the five aggregates, which inherits the fruits of the past karma and whose form is determined by those fruits. However, the Buddhists also explain that while this new complex which is reborn is not the same as the one just passed away, it is not different either, for a living being is not merely a combination of the five aggregates but is also a series of states, originating in dependence one upon the other, and continuing through endless numbers of existences. As one writer puts it, it is a continuity of an ever changing entity; there is continuity but there is no sameness, just as a flame is not the same nor a different flame.

Numerous similes are found in Buddhist literature to illustrate this idea. The favorite is the river of life. A river "maintains one constant form, one seeming entity, though not one single drop remains today of all the volume that composed the river yesterday." [13] A living being is like that river. Another favorite is that of the candle. If we light one candle with another, the transmitted flame is one and the same, for there is no interruption of the flame, but the two candles are not the same. Similarly there is continuity in the operation of karma, even though the two collections of aggregates are not the same. In further illustration of this point, the Buddha told the following story. A man bought some milk, and then said he would return the following day to get it. When he returned, the milk had turned into curd. The man said he had bought milk, not curd, but the milkman retorted it was milk yesterday, but curd today. In order to settle the dispute, the Buddha was consulted, and he decided in favor of the milkman, for, as he said, the curd sprang from the milk, it was in the same stream of development. To the Buddhist, therefore, the history of an individual does not begin at birth, but reaches back to countless rebirths in the past, and to the countless lives in the past that at one time or another had touched upon that individual stream.

The Buddhist doctrine of *anatta* or no-self may therefore be stated in the following terms. There is no self, no soul, there is only a living complex of mental and physical elements succeeding one another continuously, living on the fruits of its acts. Because of this, it can control itself, and can exert efforts to better itself, so that by the proper discipline, it is able to attain nirvana or deliverance. In nirvana, this living composite dissolves to be reborn no more, for there is no more karma to bring about a rebirth.

Why did the Buddha enunciate the theory of no-self? He denied the existence of the self as a permanent entity because he took his stand on the reality of moral consciousness and the efficacy of karma. If he had admitted the existence of an unchanging self, as the Upanishads did, it would have deprived the spiritual life as he taught it of all meaning, for the individual would not have been affected in spite of all his efforts for better or for worse. This would have led to inaction, which would have nullified all that the Buddha had taught about the efficacy of karma.

Some scholars have argued that the Buddha by his doctrine

of *anatta* merely denied that there was any permanent self in the physical and mental realms. To bolster their contention, they pointed to those passages in the discourses where the Buddha said he did not find any self or *atta* in the material body, or feelings, or perception, or dispositions, or consciousness. In other words, they believed that in these passages the Buddha was merely warning his followers that they should not consider as the self that which was not the self, and not the non-existence of any self whatever. The very fact that he spoke in the negative, of *anatta,* would imply that he had some notion of what the positive *atta* was. Such critics would go further and say that the attainment of nirvana would also imply the existence of a positive *atta* to enjoy the bliss of nirvana. However this may be, one would search the Pali suttas in vain for any positive statement by the Buddha concerning the existence of *atta.* When directly asked, the Buddha refused to answer affirmatively or negatively the question concerning the existence of the *atta,* taking the view that the truth concerning the matter is beyond words and thoughts.

Besides the fundamental truths of suffering, impermanence, and non-self, there is still another doctrine basic to Buddhism, and this is what is commonly called the law of causation, or dependent origination, formulated to present an explanation of the origin of suffering. It is likely that another consideration was involved also in the formulation, namely the pessimism of one of the heretical teachings at the time of the Buddha. This heretical group, called the Ajivikas, taught that there is no force of karma in operation, that a being is pure or depraved without cause, and that his fate is not dependent on his own or on others' actions. Such a teaching would deny that there are rewards or punishments for deeds performed, and would bring about the destruction of orderly existence and morality. Therefore the Buddha felt obliged to enunciate a law of causation to combat such pernicious teachings. His purpose was to show that there is a regular sequence of events, that events are not caused by the arbitrary will of a deity or are just disorder and confusion, but that each event arose as a sequence of a previous one. "I will teach you the doctrine; when this exists, that exists; with the arising of that, this arises; when this does not exist, this does not exist; with the cessation of that, this ceases." According to this doctrine, no phenomenon arises without a cause. Things and acts are not isolated but are connected with other things and acts in the universe. One act influences another and is in turn influenced by others.

As enunciated in the Buddhist scriptures, this is the way the formula is expressed. From ignorance as cause, dispositions arise. From dispositions as cause, consciousness arises. From consciousness as cause, then name and form, then six sense organs, contact, sensation, craving, grasping, becoming, birth, and finally old age, grief, death, lamentation, pain, and despair, twelve links in all.

Numerous attempts have been made to interpret this formula by modern scholars who all assumed that there is a logical connection between the members, and who devoted pages and pages to an attempt to find that connection. One considered the formula to be the evolution of a concrete entity from non-existence. Another believed that it was a cosmogonic myth describing the creation and destruction of the world as observed in human life. Still another contended that we should not look upon it as an explanation of the world, for the formula was merely intended to illustrate that events are linked one with another. The chief result of all the investigations is that so far there is no general agreement among the scholars. The problem is complicated by the fact that in some passages, certain links are missing, so that instead of twelve there are only nine or ten.

Instead of relying on what modern scholars of Buddhism have propounded, it might be more profitable to examine how the Buddhist commentators explained the formula, and how they attempted to weave all the elements into a logical sequence. This would present us with the point of view of the Buddhists themselves, and not the interpretations of non-believing scholars. These Buddhist commentators usually interpret the links in the formula as the different stages through which an individual passes during his existence in the world of change. Ordinary people are accustomed to think of time as running in a straight line from the past to the present to the future. The Buddhists, however, regard time as a cycle or circle, without beginning or end. Death is not the end of life, nor is birth the beginning. Time and again, the Buddha cautioned his followers not to fall into the bottomless pit of speculations about the origins of life, for such speculations would only lead to disputations which would not be conducive to the religious life. While this circle of life has no beginning, the Buddha felt that there must be a point of departure, and for his purposes he chose to start with ignorance for a very practical reason. This ignorance is not to be interpreted in the Upanishadic sense of ignorance of the transcendental truth, but in a more limited sense, as ignorance of the nature of the self and the phenomenal world. This ignorance sees happiness in misery and regards the unreal and transient as real and permanent. In the Buddhist scriptures, this ignorance is traced to the five hindrances, craving for existence, hatred, laziness, pride, and doubts, and is nourished by the sins of body, speech, and mind. Ignorance is considered as the beginning or root of the formula because it is the link that can be destroyed by the gaining of wisdom or insight, and when this first link is destroyed, then the whole formula collapses.

Ignorance leads to predispositions. These are the traces left in the mind by taking the wrong view of things. Ignorance generates acts, which leave behind impressions that determine future existences. These two, ignorance and predispositions, are the two causes of the past.

From predispositions arises consciousness. The appearance of consciousness marks the inception of the present life. The very fact of a fresh existence means that the individual has not rid himself of ignorance. Consciousness is said to correspond to the first moments in the conception of a child. Although the formula states that from consciousness arises name and form, the commentators hold that the transition from consciousness to name and form is immediate, that as soon as consciousness arises, the other four aggregates cluster around it to form the individual. Thus the scriptures say that if consciousness does not enter the womb, there would be no embryo; if it does not continue there, the embryo would die. With the formation of name and form, or the physical body, there arises the six senses, eyes, ears, tongue, nose, body, and mind. A more complex form is now assumed, and with the functioning of the six senses, contact arises. This stage is said to correspond to the first two years after birth. In a small baby, the sense organs reach a state of activity, but the sense of touch predominates, hence contact. With the operation of the six senses, sensations arise, pleasant and unpleasant, painful and indifferent. This stage is said to represent a child from three to five years old. His individuality is now recognized, and the status of the present life is formed.

These five stages, from consciousness to sensation, are often called the five effects of the past appearing in the present. The individual is formed, but he is not responsible for his formation, for the causes of the past had effected this formation. From now on, however, the individual assumes the responsibility for his own creation, and so we come to the three causes of the present.

From sensation arises craving. Each of the six senses generates its own kind of craving; the eyes crave to see beautiful sights, the ears crave to hear melodious sounds, and the body soft and fine objects. Craving is characterized by attachment to external objects, and this gives rise to the next stage, grasping; we grasp for the objects that we crave for and to which we feel an attachment. From grasping arises becoming, which is the link between the present and the future. Becoming is therefore treated as the act that produces future birth. The above three stages, craving, grasping, and becoming, are said to be the three causes of the present, for they constitute the three stages of adult activities. While the individual is enjoying the fruits of the past, he is also creating causes of the future, just as while the fruit is forming and ripening on the tree, the seed is also being formed, so that when the fruit is ripe and falls to the ground, the seed is ready to bring forth a new tree.

From becoming arises birth, the birth of a new stream of consciousness in the future. From birth comes old age and finally death. These last two are usually said to represent the future. When viewed from the three causes of the past, birth and death are the results, but when viewed in the light of the continuous circle of life, the future stages of birth and death contain in themselves causes for further birth. Thus every link is a cause when viewed from its effect, but when viewed from its antecedent it is an effect. In this manner, the Buddhist commentators sought to explain the formula as embracing the past, present, and future.

In order to give graphic representation of this formula, the Buddhist artist has often pictured it in the form of a wheel in which the rim is divided into twelve segments, one for each of the twelve links, with each segment containing a symbol. Ignorance is symbolized by a blind man with a stick; predispositions by a potter with the potter's wheel and pots; consciousness by a monkey climbing a tree with flowers; name and form by a ship with four passengers; the six senses by an empty house with many windows; contact by a man and woman embracing; sensation by a man with an arrow in his eye; craving by a woman offering a drink of water to a seated man; grasping by a man gathering fruit from a tree; becoming by a woman with child; birth by a woman giving birth; old age and death by a man carrying a corpse. The wheel has five spokes, representing the five states of existences, deities, men, animals, hungry ghosts, and denizens of hell. In the center of the wheel may be seen a dove representing lust, a snake representing hatred, and a pig representing delusion.

The traditional interpretation of the formula, as seen in the foregoing, has been that by the cessation of each member of the chain, one is freed from the entire chain and achieves enlightenment. Since this is a positive achievement, it has been argued by some that it should be possible with the cessation of each stage to attain some positive results that would lead progressively to illumination. Now it happens that such a formulation does exist in a sutta found in the collection of discourses entitled *Kindred Sayings*, 2.25-27 where the chain of causation is said to consist of 24 members. The first eleven members are exactly the same as the standard list, but the twelfth is not birth and death, but suffering or misery, which is but a different word for the same conditions. Dependent upon misery arises faith, which is the first member of the new series, to be followed by joy, rapture, serenity, happiness, concentration, knowledge, repulsion, absence of passion, literation, destruction of the cankers, and finally enlightenment. The unique feature of this new series is that the succession of stages is now stated in positive terms. This has given rise to what may be termed the positive school of thought concerning the meaning of the formula as opposed to the negative or traditional school of thought. The latter would contend that the formula is concerned mainly with the process of cessation, and by the cessation of all the elements in the chain, nirvana would be attained. Hence nirvana would be defined negatively, as a state that is not this and not that. The other or positive school would stress the positive factors that would lead progressively to nirvana, and would look upon nirvana as something dynamic rather than static. It is possible that during the early stages in the development of the doctrine, both interpretations of the chain of causation were held by the disciples, but that as time went on, with the ascendency of the conservative faction in the community of monks, the negative viewpoint won out, so that only one sutta presenting the positive interpretation of the formula is preserved in the Pali canon.

Thorough understanding of these fundamental doctrines of Buddhism leads to wisdom or intuitive insight, or the ability to see things as they really are. One of the by-products of this acquisition of wisdom is the attainment of the supernatural, or better still, supranormal faculties, which consist of the following:

(1) divine eyes, eyes which can see over long distances. Numerous examples of this faculty may be found in the canon, which present the Buddha as being able to watch over the welfare of his disciples from afar and to rescue them when he saw them in trouble.

(2) divine ears, the ability to hear sounds far away, or to hear and understand the language of birds and beasts. Time and again we find this virtue adumbrated in the biographies of famous monks.

(3) knowledge of the former existences not only of oneself but of others. The Buddha, for instance, was able to look backward hundreds of thousands of existences and tell exactly who or what he was at such and such a rebirth. It may be that the Bud-

dhist writers in their efforts to glorify the founder of their religion indulged in some fancy flights of the imagination, but it is fair to point out in their defense that modern psychologists have found out that under certain circumstances, especially under hypnosis, an individual would be able to recall events and incidents in early childhood which he never would have remembered under normal conditions. It would seem that the Buddhists were merely pushing back such memories not only to early childhood but to previous states of existences in line with their theory of repeated rebirths.

(4) knowledge of other people's thoughts.

(5) magic powers, such as the ability to fly through the air, walk over water, tunnel through mountains, etc. The ability to fly through the air was long considered one of the accomplishments of a sage, and the modern version of this is levitation. Ernest Wood in his book on *Yoga* (Penguin Books, 1959) p. 104 writes that levitation is a "universally accepted fact in India," and recalls one occasion when a yogi was levitated six feet above ground in an open field, while skeptics were permitted to move sticks in the space between. As for the ability to walk over water, there is a Buddhist story about a disciple of the Buddha who came to a river one evening and finding that the ferryman had gone for the night, entered into intense concentration and in that state successfully crossed the river. This story is often paralleled with the Biblical stories of similar feats. In recent years, many an American youngster reading the comic strips has marvelled at the feats of one Superman flying through the air or burrowing through the ground. It is possible that the creator of that Superman got his inspiration from the accounts of these magic powers which the Buddhist sage achieved.

The one who has attained perfection in the three-fold discipline achieves arhatship, or the state of one who is worthy of offerings. Although all monks strive to achieve this goal, not all of them can achieve it. For example, the cousin of the Buddha, Devadatta, was given the epithet "the incurable one" because he once drew the blood of the Buddha by throwing a rock at him.

It is also noted in the texts that matricides, patricides, arhanticides, and creators of schism in the order can never attain arhatship. These people are barred in the first place from joining the order of monks, and hence would never have the opportunity to progress toward arhatship.

The path to arhatship is marked by four stages described by stereotyped formulas. The first stage is that of the stream-winner, and the one who wins this state is no longer reborn in a state of woe. He has destroyed the three fetters (delusions concerning the self, doubt, and belief in the efficacy of ceremonies), he is bound for enlightenment, and will undergo seven more rebirths at the most before attaining arhatship. The second stage is that of the once-returner, one who will be reborn once more in this world because he has destroyed completely the three fetters and has reduced to a minimum passion, hatred, and delusion. One who has destroyed the five fetters (the above three plus ill-will and sensuality) will reach the third stage, that of the non-returner, for he will be reborn in one of the heavens, there to wane utterly, never to return to this world. This stage creates an awkward problem, for it contradicts the oft-repeated statement in the texts that arhatship is to be attained here and now in this world of human beings. It is probably because of this difficulty that Buddhist writers sometimes do not consider the different stages as operating progressively, but that it is possible to overleap one or two stages. Hence there are instances in the literature of stream-winners and even laymen winning the goal of arhatship, the fourth and final stage of spiritual progress.

From the standpoint of early Buddhism, arhatship involves high ethical and intellectual standards, brought to perfection by a long period of training in virtue, knowledge, and concentration, a training that might span over a number of rebirths. The arhat is always alert and adept at insight and knowledge, he has destroyed all cravings and desires, false views, and ignorance, he has reached a state of enlightenment and is no longer subject to the operation of karma. The idea behind the Buddhist quest for arhatship is that of becoming perfect. Herein lies a difference between Buddhism and the *Upanishads*. In Buddhism man can become perfect by his will and effort, whereas in the *Upanishads* man is already perfect and therefore there is no need to strive. In the canon, one comes again and again to the formulas describing the arhat: "Destroyed is rebirth, lived is the good life, done is what had to be done, and now there is no more of this state of things." "There arose in me the knowledge; unshakable for me is release of mind, this is my last rebirth, there is now no further becoming for me." The goal is achieved through training and character and not through family or caste connections; the lowest of the outcast as well as the highest brahman can achieve it.

In the Buddhist scriptures, the Buddha is often referred to as an arhat also, so that the term includes the founder of the religion. This very naturally raises the question, is there any difference between the attainments of the Buddha and the arhat? The traditions affirm that as far as enlightenment is concerned, there is no difference. However, since the Buddha is the revealer of the way while the arhat is merely the follower, the former is considered to be superior. This superiority is implied in the affirmation that the appearance of a Buddha is a rare occurrence, only one in a *kalpa* or aeon, while numerous arhats can live at the same time. Later traditions preserved in the Chinese translations state that the arhat is not the equal of the Buddha because the arhat does not gain insight without concentration, he cannot manifest his supranormal faculties at all times, and his body still contains insects and worms.

At what point does one become an arhat? If we look over the various versions of the arhat formula, we are struck by the unanimity of opinion on one point, that the final step in the attainment of arhatship occurs when the *asavas* are destroyed. The word *asava* means something that flows, and hence it is often interpreted as the impurities that flow into an individual to defile him. It has been translated as the cankers or intoxicants. The *asavas* in Buddhism are the desire for sensual pleasure, desire for continued existence, ignorance, and wrong views. With the destruction of the *asavas*, the individual no longer hankers for existence and pleasure, and harbors no more wrong views. This would suggest that the way to ascertain whether or not an individual has achieved arhatship is to question him to find out whether he really sees things as they are. The responsibility for determining this fact would seem to rest with the questioner, and not with the questioned. Moreover, since the Buddha and those who have already attained arhatship are omniscient, they can easily determine whether or not the individual has attained perfection.

In summary, the arhat is one who is no longer subject to rebirth, for he has destroyed completely all cravings that lead to karma. He achieves this goal by himself for himself through his own efforts. A cold, severe, stoical being, with indifference and detachment as his sources of strength and armor, he retains complete equanimity as he participates in human events, and is not affected by their success or failure. He never develops any sentiment toward anyone so as to be disturbed by the passing away of that one, nor does he allow his emotions to become involved in affection for others. To accomplish this, he prefers to live in solitude.

When the arhat passes away after his last existence, he enters into nirvana. The Buddha declared that nirvana is the very reason for the propagation of his religion. "As the great ocean has one taste, the taste of salt, even so, monks, does this dharma and discipline have one taste, the taste of freedom." [14]

The concept of nirvana may be clear to the Buddhists themselves, but the trouble is that the Buddhists never wrote in unambiguous language. The Buddhists may be satisfied with their descriptions of nirvana, but such descriptions are often unsatisfactory to others. The historians of thought have to work, not with concepts worked out by clear thinkers, but with ideas and notions recorded by men exhausted by weak diets, and hypnotized by the ecstatic trances, so that they did not make clear distinctions between facts and fancies. Then again, to the non-Buddhist, nirvana becomes an object of academic and intellectual interest, in spite of the Buddhist emphatic insistence that nirvana is not for the intellect to analyze and describe. For the Buddhist, it is a religious experience, whereas for the non-Buddhist, it is something to write about.

The word *nirvana* appears to have a two-fold meaning, that of becoming cold, as in the case of one who has cooled his passions, and that of blowing out, as in the extinguishing of a flame. In the very famous fire-sermon, the Buddha taught that the whole world was inflamed by the fires of greed, lust, hatred, and ignorance, and that only in nirvana were these flames quenched. In other discourses, the Buddha referred to two kinds of nirvana, nirvana with a residue and nirvana without a residue. The first appears to be the condition attained by the perfect living saint, where the five aggregates are still present, although the desires that bind him to existence are absent. This is the state of enlightenment attained by the sage here and now in this very life, and it is the nirvana attained by the Buddha when he was thirty-five years old. In the second type, there is a cessation of all existence, as in the case of the death of the Buddha at the age of eighty in Kusinara. Sometimes this condition is differentiated from the first by being designated as *parinirvana*. In *parinirvana*, all desires for existence are destroyed, all karma exhausted and there is no more cause for rebirth, and the Buddha or the perfect saint disappears from the world of impermanence.

Heated controversy has centered on the nature of this nirvana, or to be more exact, *parinirvana*. One school of thought has argued vehemently that it must be total annihilation, basing its arguments on the general principles of Buddhism and concrete statements in the canon. We have already mentioned in the foregoing the Buddhist analysis of the individual as a conglomeration of physical and psychical elements constantly changing every moment. In ordinary beings, this stream of life is not destroyed at death when the material body perishes, for because of karma and the desire for existence, a new organism is created, different in form from the preceding but still a continuation of the antecedent life process. Clearly there is no annihilation here. In the case of the perfect saint or the Buddha, however, all karma is exhausted and there is no more cause for further rebirth. The Buddha also taught that there is no possible existence outside the five aggregates, for he had destroyed the idea of a permanent self or soul. The following passages in the scriptures seem to confirm such a notion. "The Blessed One, passed away by that kind of passing away in which no root remains for the formation of another individual. The Blessed One has come to an end and it can not be pointed out of him that he is here or there."[15] "That bodily form of the Tathagata is abandoned, cut down at the root, made something that is not, made of a nature not to spring up again in future time."[16] Such ideas as these in the canon have therefore led a number of scholars to conclude that nirvana is total annihilation or eternal death.

We have seen that such a conception of the nature of nirvana is arrived at chiefly by logical analysis. Now logic is a dangerous tool, and often arrives at conclusions which are the direct opposite of some tenets cherished by a religion. When this happens, the conclusions are disregarded usually by followers of the religion. Such seems to have been the case with the concept of nirvana as total annihilation. The Buddhists do not accept such an interpretation, and they refer to a great deal of canonical evidence to show that the Buddha did his best to avoid such a conclusion. In the first place, if we say that nirvana is annihilation, that would be holding to one of the heretical views condemned by the Buddha. Secondly, in the canon, there are passages describing nirvana as the destruction of greed, lust, hatred, and ignorance. It is true that these are negative aspects, but this is not the whole story, for in other passages, nirvana is presented as a state full of confidence, tranquillity, freedom from fear, bliss, happiness, and purity, as steady and imperishable, and as eternal beatitude and timeless existence. It is a state in which false individuality disappears and true being remains, it is deep and enduring, and beyond the world of space and time. Because the Buddha considered it to be beyond the world of phenomenal experience, he felt obliged to resort to negative terms to describe it, as he felt that it was not possible to predicate this infinite transcendent state with our finite words.

This attitude of silence on the part of the Buddha is brought out most strikingly in his attitude toward a series of indeterminate questions. These questions are whether or not the soul is identical with the body, whether or not the world is eternal, or whether or not the saint exists after death. The last question is intimately connected with the nature of nirvana.

In the assembly of monks was one named Malunkya who wanted to know what the nature of nirvana was. He was displeased because the Buddha had not settled the question, and he threatened to leave the religious life if the master did not give a satisfactory answer. "If the Buddha does not know, . . ." he said, "the only upright thing for one who does not know or who has not that insight, is to say, 'I do not know.'" The Buddha however did not answer the question directly, nor did he say that he did not know. He first asked Malunkya, "Did I ever say to you, come, Malunkya, lead the religious life under me, and I will elucidate to you . . . ?" Malunkya of course answered that no such conditions were made. The Buddha then went on, "Anyone who should say, 'I will not lead the religious life under The Blessed One until The Blessed One shall elucidate to me . . . ,' that person would die, Malunkyaputta, before the Tathagatha had ever elucidated this to him." He then went on to say that man was poisoned by cravings and desires and suffering from the misery of repeated rebirths, and had to be saved at once. The situation was like that of a person who had been wounded by a poisoned arrow. His friends wanted to call a physician to attend to him but instead, he said that he would not have the arrow removed until he had found out what class the archer belonged to, what his name, clan, stature, complexion, etc. were. That man would die before learning all this. In the same way, the Buddha warned, individuals would die before he would elucidate these points. Moreover, he contended that knowledge of such metaphysical problems was totally extraneous to the discipline that destroys desires and cravings. Whether the dogma obtains or not, there still remains birth, old age, death, grief, and lamentation. Herein we see the Buddha's refusal to answer the indeterminate questions, "Because this profits not, nor has to do with the fundamentals of religion, nor tends to aversion, absence of passion, cessation, quiescence, the supernatural faculties, supreme wisdom, and Nirvana." [17]

From this, we can see that the Buddha took the position that nirvana or final deliverance is something that is not a matter of empirical observation, and so he refused to discuss this absolute and transcendental state with our limited and finite vocabulary. The Upanishads had already warned against applying categories of the phenomenal world to the ultimate reality, and the Buddha followed this Upanishadic tradition by remaining silent when questioned about the final goal. He only said it is profound, infinite, indescribable, hard to comprehend and beyond the sphere of reasoning. If one were to describe nirvana with words, one would then conceive of nirvana as finite, made of compound elements, and subject to human limitations. Therefore he did not wish to predicate anything of this nirvana which is beyond predication. Having destroyed the dogmatism of his predecessors, he did not want to substitute a dogma of his own, for he felt that such a procedure would only produce controversy that would hinder spiritual growth. Instead of being entangled by the fetters of the metaphysical jungle, he urged his followers to devote themselves to the practice of the religious life that would lead to deliverance. For his followers, it is not necessary to inquire about the nature of this deliverance; they know that the master was omniscient, that he had attained to the goal, and that they can safely follow him as the unparalleled caravan-leader. By following his example, and by practicing the discipline that he had specified, they too can experience personally the bliss of nirvana.

CHAPTER 4

Mahayana Buddhism

ANY RELIGION THAT PROPOSES to meet the religious needs
and aspirations of its followers will undergo constant changes to
accord with the changing times and circumstances. Buddhism is
no exception. As the religion developed in India, dissatisfaction
soon arose over what were considered to be shortcomings of the
Theravada tradition. As the Theravadins remained faithful to the
teachings of the Pali canon, they were criticized as being too
literal-minded and conservative, clinging to the letter rather than
to the spirit of the master's message. This literal-mindedness was
responsible for their failure to understand that the dharma of the
Buddha is simply a raft to carry one to the further shore of
enlightenment, and that once this enlightenment is attained, the
raft may be abandoned. The Theravada was also criticized as
being spiritually narrow and individualistic. This criticism was
directed against the Theravada ideal of the arhat, who practices
the religious life primarily for his own self-improvement and
salvation. This ferment of dissatisfaction gave rise to the second
aspect of Buddhism, called the Mahayana or the Great Vehicle.
To show their attitude of contempt and superiority over the
Theravada system, the Mahayana followers designated the latter
as Hinayana, or the Lesser Vehicle, since it offered salvation only
to the few. In our usage of the term Hinayana, however, no idea

61

of contempt is intended. On their part the Hinayana followers charge that the Mahayana is based on sutras which are not the words of the Buddha, but on works of later followers. To this charge the Mahayanists reply that the Buddha preached on two levels. To those who were not learned and ill-equipped to understand the message, he preached the simple Hinayana sutras, but to those who were wise and advanced in learning, he preached the profound and abstruse Mahayana sutras. These were transmitted by the elite disciples from generation to generation by word of mouth until they blossomed forth in the Mahayana sutras of the later age.

It is not clear just when this change took place, but it appears likely that it occurred during the two centuries immediately preceding the Christian era. Nor is it certain as to what extent external or non-Buddhist forces exerted in inspiring the change. For example, it is believed by many that the dissatisfaction with the narrow cold arhat ideal was engendered by the prevailing Indian notion of *bhakti,* or the passionate, emotional, and devotional attachment to a loving compassionate deity. Others contend that some aspects of Mahayana Buddhism, especially the belief in a western paradise presided over by a Buddha of boundless light and life, were borrowed from Zoroastrianism. Such problems are still unsolved because the historical annals and records giving information about events and personalities together with their dates are conspicuous by their absence in Indian literature.

Several important differences mark the Mahayana from the Theravada tradition. In the first place, the Mahayana regards the Buddha as an eternal being who is the embodiment of universal truth, while the Theravada looks upon the master as a human teacher. In the second place, the religious ideal of the Mahayana is not the arhat but the bodhisattva, a being destined for enlightenment and characterized as the epitome of compassion, love, and altruism. In the third place, the Mahayana stresses that enlightenment is attained, not by the strenuous discipline advocated by the Theravadins, but by living a life of faith and devotion to the Buddha, and love and compassion for all fellow men. Finally, the Mahayana teaches that all sentient beings possess the Buddha nature and hence are capable of being enlightened. This is in sharp contrast to the Theravada position that only the elite few can achieve enlightenment.

Concept of the Buddha

In a land where the tendency to deify is very strong, it is to the credit of the Hinayana that it has retained the human conception of the Buddha for so long. The formula that one finds most often in the Pali scriptures reads as follows: "The Blessed One is an arhat, a fully awakened one, endowed with knowledge and good conduct, happy, a knower of the world, unsurpassed leader able to control men, teacher of men and gods, the awakened, the blessed." The humanity of the Buddha is also expressed by a Theravada monk arguing against the encroachment of what he considered to be heretical views: "Was he not born at Lumbini, superenlightened under the Bodhi tree? Was not the Norm-wheel set rolling by him at Benares? . . . Did he not complete existence at Kusinara?" [18]

Soon after the passing of the master, a change began to set in. While some monks still retained the human conception of the Blessed One, others began to raise questions. Now that the Master was no longer present, to whom should they take refuge? In the beginning, the question was solved in a simple manner. The followers substituted for their master the dharma or the body of teachings which he left behind. The master was now considered to be, not a physical person, but a spiritual or moral person in whom the dharma was incarnated. Thus there arose two bodies, the body of the flesh and the body of the dharma or law. But now a further question arose, how could this body of form and flesh, tainted with illness, weakness, and impurities, realize the perfection of Buddhahood? To answer this question, a liberal wing in the community of monks called the Mahasanghikas or the Great Assembly, who broke away from the rest of the monks at a great council held in ca. 383 B.C., evolved some new and interesting views. This school regarded the Buddha as a supramundane, transcendental being. He possesses unlimited life and powers, is omnipresent, and exists in every direction of the world. He is not subject to fatigue, sleep, or dreams. All the sutras that he preaches are perfect and concerned with the truth. However, since he wants to follow the ways of man, he appears as a man and acts as a man. His feet are clean, but he washes them; his body is not touched by the rain and wind and sun, but he wears clothes. All the teachings of the Buddha are attributed to this apparitional body which the transcendental Buddha created for the instruction of mankind. Here we see the germs of ideas which were to evolve later into the fully developed Mahayana notions concerning the Buddha.

At the beginning of the Christian era, the transcendental nature of the Buddha became more and more pronounced. In such a scripture as the *Lotus Sutra,* one of the most important pieces of Mahayana literature, there is not much of the man left in the Buddha. He is now an exalted being, who has lived for countless ages in the past and will continue to live forever in the future. He calls himself the father of the world, he does not wander about to preach but just sits on top of a mountain, surrounded by a multitude of monks and nuns, Buddhas and bodhisattvas. The number of Buddhas are now too numerous to be counted, they are said to be as numerous as the sands of the Ganges, each one presiding over his own Buddha-world just as Sakyamuni is presiding over our world.

Inevitably the question arose, how could the Buddha Sakyamuni, within the short period of forty-five years of preaching, perform the innumerable deeds of a Buddha and convert bodhisattvas said to be carrying on their duties for millions of years? To this question the Buddha replies in the *Lotus Sutra* that he did not attain enlightenment only lately at Gaya. Instead, he had attained enlightenment incalculable ages ago, and had been preaching the law since that time. All the previous Buddhas and their achievement of nirvana are but his creations and are merely examples of his expedients for imparting the law. When he says that he was recently born and has just left the household life to attain enlightenment, it is his expedient aimed at appealing to a class of people who otherwise would not be convinced of the excellence of the law. From such passages, we see that the chief purpose of the *Lotus Sutra* is to reveal the Buddha as true and eternal, and that it is to save errant mankind that this eternal Buddha became incarnated as Sakyamuni, the son of Maya. Furthermore, he has done this countless times in the past and will continue to do so in the future. By this process, the *Lotus Sutra* makes it possible to account for the countless numbers of Buddhas, each one presiding over a Buddha-world. Sakyamuni is therefore just an appearance, created by the eternal Buddha who is neither born nor dies, but lives and works eternally.

As a result of this development, the historical Buddha recedes further and further into the background, for if there is an eternal Buddha, why bother about the historical one, who is after all an illusory being. The facts of the master's life are no longer of great importance; what matters are the metaphysical speculations about the eternal Buddha. Such speculations finally led to the formulation of the doctrine of the three bodies of the Buddha, the Body of Essence, the Body of Communal Enjoyment, and the Body of Transformation.

In this scheme of the triple body, which was fully formulated about the fourth century A.D., the Body of Essence refers to some permanent essence or truth that exists outside the human body. In nirvana only the human elements disappear but this permanent essence persists. The Body of Essence is the only real body of the Buddha; it is this body that unites and connects all the Buddhas of the past with those of the future. Though there are many Buddhas, there is only one Body of Essence. It is eternal and unknowable, but still the Mahayanists attempt to define it as far as language permits. They feel that this Body of Essence is mysteriously revealing itself in the moral consciousness of mankind. Groping around for words to describe this eternal and divine essence, they say it is immeasurable, beyond the functioning of the senses, ineffable, absolute, and devoid of all characteristics. This is how it is described in a Mahayana scripture: "It is not an individual entity, it is not a false existence, but it is universal and pure. It comes from nowhere, it goes to nowhere, it does not assert itself, nor is it subject to annihilation. It is forever serene and eternal. It is the one devoid of all determinations. This Body of Essence has no boundary, no quarters, but is embodied in all bodies. . . . There is no place in the universe where this body does not prevail. The universe becomes, but this body remains forever." [19] In this formulation of the eternal Body of Essence, we see an extension of the idea of the transcendental Buddha already held by the earlier Mahasanghika School.

When the Body of Essence is called upon to fulfill the spiritual needs of the bodhisattvas, it then appears in the second form, the Body of Communal Enjoyment. This is the body in which the Buddhas enjoy their full majesty, virtue, knowledge, and blessedness. It is the privilege of the bodhisattvas to perceive this body, which is a marvelous symphony of light and sound. Light emanates from every pore of his body, illuminating the entire universe. This body sits on Vulture Peak preaching the Mahayana scriptures to huge concourses of Buddhas and bodhisattvas.

Lastly, to explain the appearance of a Buddha like Sakyamuni among mankind, there is the Body of Transformation. The eternal Buddha creates a fictitious phantom of himself and causes this to appear among ignorant and wicked mankind in order to convert it. Sakyamuni was such a phantom; he took on all the characteristics of man, he followed the ways of the world, he lived, preached, and then entered into nirvana. The eternal Buddha has done this not once but countless times in the past and will continue to do so in the future. All these, however, are only illusions and appearances.

It must be emphasized that the three bodies do not constitute a homogeneous series. The Body of Communal Enjoyment is on the same plane as the Body of Transformation, it is still on the phenomenal plane though on a higher level. Both are illusory in relation to the absolute Body of Essence. The latter is not simply a more glorious body than the other two. It is on an entirely different plane, since it is the only real body of the Buddha, it is the cause of the other two, and is the whole inconceivable body of reality as such.

The bodhisattva

In order to establish some sort of connection between the realm of pain which is human and the realm of beatitude which is the Buddha, the figure of the bodhisattva or the being destined for enlightenment, was created by the Mahayana thinkers. This represents another important change ushered in by the Mahayana. It is likely that dissatisfaction with the passionless ascetic arhat of the Hinayana led to the emergence of the loving compassionate bodhisattva. Also during the centuries before the Christian era, the element of devotional attachment to a deity was developing in Hinduism, and this trend undoubtedly influenced Buddhism in the same direction. Some scholars have even gone so far as to suggest that the Zoroastrian amesaspentas, or the immortal beneficent ones, might have played a role also, since these are personified abstractions of truth, good thought, piety, immortality, and so forth.

According to the Mahayana, the already enlightened bodhisattva delays his entry into a final nirvana until he has saved all sentient beings in this world of misery. His main attributes are love, compassion, and altruism, for his vow is, "I must lead all beings to liberation, I will stay here till the end, even for the sake of one living soul." He is able to carry out his mission of universal salvation through a remarkable doctrine developed by the Mahayana: the transfer of merits. We will recall that the Hinayana arhat accumulates meritorious karma for his own salvation. Now the Mahayana bodhisattva, who has accumulated a huge stock of merits through interminable lives, is able and willing to transfer these merits to less fortunate creatures so that they too may enjoy the fruits of such merits.

The bodhisattva is usually presented as the personification of a particular trait of the Buddha, and as there are a number of such traits, so there are different bodhisattvas. The wisdom of the Buddha is personified by Manjusri, which means gentle glory or sweet splendor. This bodhisattva is declared to be the master of wisdom and knowledge, and his symbols are the book and the sword of knowledge which cuts through all doubts. The compassion of the Buddha is personified by Avalokitesvara, the Lord Who Looks Down, or the Lord of Compassionate Glances. He manifests himself everywhere in the world to save people from suffering, but he is specially on the lookout for those facing seven kinds of danger—sword, fetters, fire, water, demons, goblins, and enemy. To help him carry out his mission more efficiently, he is often endowed with a thousand eyes and a thousand arms. Anyone faced with these various kinds of dangers need only pray to him, and he will come to the assistance of the afflicted. If a woman desires a son, she should also pray to Avalokitesvara and in due time her wish will be fulfilled.

How does one become a bodhisattva? We are told in the Mahayana scriptures that three events mark the beginning of the bodhisattva's career. First, there is the production of the thought of enlightenment. This thought of enlightenment is said to be present in all of us, but it lies in a dormant state, and must be awakened by such acts as thinking about the Buddha, reflecting on the ills of material existence, and observing the deplorable states of sentient beings. Such reflections and observations would bring about the resolution to be enlightened, so that one would be able to help and save such creatures. This resolution is an heroic act on the part of the aspirant, for by so doing, he annuls the effects of past karma, frees himself from the evil modes of existences such as animal, hungry ghost, and denizen of hell, and becomes a member of the Buddha family.

Having made this resolution, the aspirant then appears before a Buddha to utter the earnest wish, which is a solemn vow of aspiration. This implies a strong will to carry out what one has set out to do. The aspirant may vow to distribute whatever merits he has accumulated to all sentient beings, to become thoroughly conversant with the good law, to preach untiringly the truth to all beings, or to leave nothing undone for the sake of the salvation of all living beings. Having declared his vow before a Buddha, the latter then prophesies the future success of the aspirant.

Once these three events, resolution, vow, and prophecy are completed, the aspirant embarks on his career, which will take him through countless lives before he can reach his goal, but reach it he will. This career is divided into ten stages, and in these ten stages the Mahayana thinkers are able to find a place for all the important teachings of the Buddha.

While progressing up the ten stages, the bodhisattva candidate also practices the ten perfections, which are positive virtues in contrast to the negative virtues expected of the Hinayana arhat. The more important of these perfections are liberality, virtuous conduct, energetic living, forbearance, skill in means, and wisdom. Liberality is taken to mean not only the gift of material goods and religious instructions, but also the sacrifice of body and the transfer of merits to less fortunate creatures so as to cancel out the demerits of the latter. Skill in means is defined by the Mahayana as the ability to choose the most effective means to bring about salvation and enlightenment to others. Individuals differ in capacity and attainments, and the means that will serve one individual may not prove effective for another. The bodhisattva knows just what to do in the case of each individual. For instance, the Buddha often compares himself to a physician, who prescribes different remedies for different persons, since the ills of individuals are not alike.

Having practiced the ten perfections and completed the ten stages, the candidate achieves enlightenment and is a full-fledged bodhisattva. Though qualified now to enter into nirvana, he delays that final step and dedicates his life to assist in the salvation of all sentient beings. Such a life of altruism, compassion, and love serves to explain why the bodhisattva ideal is so attractive and popular to the peoples of East Asia, and why it is considered to be so much nobler and richer than the arhat ideal of the Hinayana.

Faith and Devotion in Mahayana

In Hinayana Buddhism, the chief purpose of the strenuous religious discipline is the accumulation of meritorious karma which will lead to salvation and bring an end to the repeated round of rebirths. In Mahayana Buddhism, especially in the cult of Amitabha, the path to salvation lies not in the performance of good works but in a life of faith and devotion to the Buddha Amitabha. Amitabha, or Infinite Light, is the name of the presiding Buddha of the Western Paradise, which is described as being rich, fertile, comfortable, filled with deities and men but not with the evil modes of existences. It is adorned with fragrant trees and flowers, and decorated with the most beautiful jewels and gems. Rivers with scented waters give forth musical sounds, and are flanked on both sides with scented jewelled trees. Heavenly beings sporting in the water can cause it to become hot or cold as they wish. Everywhere one can hear the words of the Buddha, teaching love, compassion, sympathetic joy, patience, tolerance, equanimity, and so forth. Nowhere does one meet with anything unpleasant or painful. This is why the Western Paradise is also called the Pure Land.

This paradise was created by Amitabha out of his boundless love for all sentient beings. When he created it, he vowed that anyone who has faith in him as the savior will be reborn in that Pure Land. Faith and devotion, therefore, are the determining factors, not good works. In that Pure Land, Amitabha has as his faithful assistant the bodhisattva Avalokitesvara, who is described as being ever ready to come down to earth to lead the faithful and the devoted to salvation after their days on earth. All that the individual has to do to indicate his faith is to repeat the name of Amitabha, the formula being, namo Amitabha, or homage to Amitabha. This is indeed an easy and short cut path to salvation, and explains why the cult became so popular when it was established in China and Japan in later centuries.

This emphasis on faith and devotion represents an interesting development within Buddhism. Hinayana Buddhism teaches that only the doer can shape his destiny through his karma. The emphasis is on self-reliance and self-emancipation. The following passage in the Theravada canon exemplifies this spirit: "Be ye lamps unto yourselves, be ye a refuge unto yourselves." In the Amitabha cult, however, the emphasis is on the power of Amitabha to bring one to salvation.

This was another change which the Mahayana thinkers

wrought in the religion. They felt it is inconceivable that the Buddha, being the compassionate and loving figure that he is, would restrict the effects of his meritorious karma only to himself. Consequently they interpreted the salvation and enlightenment of the Buddha not as an isolated individual event but as a universal episode which all humanity should share. Such an interpretation led to the doctrine that meritorious karma which a Buddha or bodhisattva has accumulated is transferable to others. In the case of the Amitabha cult, those who have faith in and are devoted to Amitabha share in the merits and power of the Amitabha. The cult teaches that by himself, each sentient being is not able to win rebirth in the Western Paradise, but when he depends on the power of Amitabha, he will have no difficulty.

Strictly speaking, rebirth in the Western Paradise does not constitute the attainment of nirvana. The Western Paradise or the Pure Land is but one of the heavens in the Buddhist cosmology, and according to the teachings of the religion, rebirth in any one of the heavens is not eternal or permanent, but lasts only as long as karma permits it. As soon as such karma is exhausted, then the deity falls from his lofty status and becomes reborn in a lower state. However, in the Amitabha cult as practiced in China and Japan, it is believed that once a sentient being attains rebirth in the Western Paradise, he will remain there permanently, and as far as he is concerned, he has attained salvation in the sense that he is no longer subject to rebirth. There is no further striving to attain enlightenment or nirvana.

Nirvana

In Hinayana Buddhism, two planes of existence are conceived, the phenomenal, characterized by suffering and unrest brought about by cravings and desires, and the nirvanic, where karma ceases. The Hinayana adherent believes that he achieves nirvana when he is released and emancipated from the miseries of existence and repeated rebirths.

The Mahayana conception of nirvana is somewhat different. For an understanding of the Mahayana version, we must go back to the Hinayana theory of the elements of existence. According to the Hinayana, every being is a conglomeration of elements, just as a chariot is a combination of axle, wheel, rim, yoke, spokes, and so forth. The axle, wheel, rim, and spokes are the elements that compose the chariot and are considered as real and existing, but the chariot as the sum total of the parts is not considered as real. Likewise, the human individual is considered as the combination of the five aggregates, material body, perception, sensation, predispositions, and consciousness. These five aggregates are considered as real whereas the living being is not. Now the Mahayana comes forward with a very bold idea. Since these elements come into existence as a result of causes and conditions, they do not have an independent existence of their own, hence they are said to be void or empty. Take away the causes and conditions and the elements no longer exist. This is one of the daring and far-reaching doctrines taught by the Mahayana, that all the elements of existence are empty, void, and unreal. The Mahayana now goes one step further and teaches that not only all phenomenal elements but also nirvana is also void or empty, since nirvana is devoid of all discriminations, particularities, and definitions. One cannot predicate anything of this nirvana. Now if the phenomenal elements of existence and nirvana are both empty, then the phenomenal world and nirvana may be equated with one another. The Mahayana thus arrived at their second great thesis, the phenomenal world is nirvana, nirvana is the phenomenal world. The Hinayana follower suffers from a delusion when he talks about passing from the phenomenal plane of existence to nirvana. Since both are really the same, and since any discrimination between nirvana and the phenomenal plane is really a delusion, the Mahayana argues that in the ultimate sense there cannot be the abandonment of one and the attainment of the other. Whereas the Hinayana thinks of nirvana as the opposite of phenomenal existence, the Mahayana considers nirvana to be the cessation of all discriminations and dualisms and the realization that undifferentiated emptiness is the sole absolute truth. Nirvana is therefore that mental state in which one realizes that all things are really non-existent and that they are ultimately all the same. The moment an individual realizes this state of mind, he is enlightened and realizes the buddha-nature within himself. He eradicates from his own mind not only the concept of his own individuality but also the concept of substantiality of everything. He cannot distinguish himself from any other thing or even from the absolute, for he has merged into the absolute. Since the absolute or the buddha-nature is eternal, he also becomes eternal.

The Madhyamika School of Mahayana Buddhism

Such ideas concerning the non-dual nature of phenomenal existence and nirvana were first treated in a group of Mahayana scriptures known as the *Prajna* or Wisdom Sutras, which came into being about the beginning of the Christian era. They reached full development in the writings of Nagarjuna, who established the Madhyamika, or the School of the Middle Path.

Nagarjuna lived during the second century A.D. Although there is no doubt he is a historical person, very little is known about him, other than that he was of brahman parentage, and that he studied all the Hindu branches of knowledge before he was converted to Buddhism. The School of the Middle Path which he founded takes its position between the extremes of existence and non-existence, affirmation and negation, pleasure and pain. However, he also related this middle path to the Hinayanist doctrine of dependent origination, which he paraphrased by means of the eight-fold negation: "Nothing comes into being, nor does anything disappear. Nothing is eternal nor has anything an end. Nothing is identical or differentiated, nothing moves hither, nor moves anything thither." By means of this eight-fold negation, he seeks to explain the truth of emptiness or the unreality of all elements of existence. However, the word *sunya,* which is usually translated as empty, is also interpreted as relative. That is to say, a thing is *sunya* in that it can be identified only by mentioning its relation to something else, it becomes meaningless without these relations. A horse is a horse only in relation to a cow or a sheep. If there were only horses in the world and no cows or sheep or any other animal, then the term horse becomes meaningless. The School of the Middle Path accepts the truth that relations and dependence constitute the phenomenal world, but it also contends that one is unable to explain these relations intelligibly. In his writings, Nagarjuna proceeds to demonstrate by a merciless logic that all relationships are false and erroneous, and on the assumption that any contradiction is proof of error, he finds contradictions in every concept.

Nagarjuna takes whatever point of view that is necessary to contradict the system he is disputing. However, while contradicting and disputing other systems, he does not have any system of his own. He admits that any system is in danger of being criticized as contradictory and erroneous, but one is open to such attacks only if one has a system. If one has no system, then he cannot be attacked. Furthermore, Nagarjuna insists that when he denies a thesis of an opponent, it does not mean that he is holding the opposite view. To quote his own words, "They cannot deprive us of our liberty. Words possess a power to express something, but they are controlled by the intention of the speaker. Therefore the only result of our deduction is to repudiate the theory of the opponent. Our acceptance of the converse theory is not at all therewith implied." [20]

Let us see how Nagarjuna carries out his logical analysis. Take the concept of motion. Nagarjuna writes, "We are not passing a path that has already been passed, nor are we passing that which is yet to be passed. The existence of a path that has neither been passed, nor is yet to be passed is beyond comprehension." We may divide a path into two parts, the part already passed and the part not yet passed. There is no third possible. The first part is already passed, while the second is not yet passed. This makes the concept of passing an impossibility. If passing is impossible, then there can be no passer, no one who is doing the passing. If we are not passing that which is already passed, and not yet passing that which is not passed, then what are we passing? The answer must be, no path. Nagarjuna therefore concludes that the passer, the act of passing, and the path are all unreal, and the concept of motion is not understandable.

Another example is the relation between fire and fuel. If we say that fire is identical with fuel, that is not true. Fuel is that which is burnt. The agent that burns fuel is fire. If we make the identity of fuel and fire, then we are making the identity of agent and object, and this is impossible.

If we make the non-identity of fire and fuel, this is also impossible. If we say that fire and fuel are different, then we must say that there is something which burns outside of fuel. This is impossible since there can be no fire without fuel. If we say that fire is different from fuel, we would have to conclude that fire would not have to depend on fuel for burning, and that it would burn incessantly even if no fuel exists.

If we say that there is no fuel separated from fire, and no fire separated from fuel, then Nagarjuna would ask, which is the earlier condition? Some would say there is fuel first, then fire. Nagarjuna says this is impossible and false, for something that is not related to fire and does not burn is not fuel. Some would say the fire comes first, then fuel. This is also false, for it implies the absurdity of having fire without a cause. If we say that fire and fuel are mutually dependent, this is also false. If fire has not arisen, to talk about fuel would be like talking about the horns of a hare or the son of a barren woman. If fire has already arisen, it is already there and so there is no need to talk about the necessity of fuel. If we say that fire is contained in the fuel, that is false, for fire did not go to the fuel from another place. Nor is fire originally in the fuel, for if you are to chop up the fuel to look for fire there, you would not find it.

In this example of the relation between fire and fuel, one sees a good illustration of Nagarjuna's methodology of looking for contradictions in any statement and of his insistence on not being held responsible for any thesis or antithesis. By such merciless logic, Nagarjuna proves that the whole phenomenal world is empty or unreal because it is based on relations which cannot be explained satisfactorily.

Now if the net result of such an inquiry is to show only the futility of all views, then what room is there for the fundamental concepts of Buddhism as the Buddha, bodhisattva, nirvana, or causality? What room is there for any object of faith and devotion? Would not such a destructive system lead to negativism?

Nagarjuna and his school answer in the negative. They point out that genuine realization of the emptiness of the phenomenal world is at the same time a religious awakening, a direct intuition of the highest truth, and this spiritual intent gives the real meaning to the doctrine of emptiness. To Nagarjuna, the doctrine of emptiness is taught not as a theory but as a means to get rid of all theories, thus freeing one from the world around us. By getting rid of the ignorance that binds us to the phenomenal world through the realization that this world is empty and unreal, we achieve *prajna* or intuitive wisdom, that enables us to realize the absolute truth which is unconditioned, undeterminate, and beyond thought and word. Opposed to this absolute truth is what Nagarjuna calls relative truth, which consists of the products of man's reasoning and analysis. This relative truth enables man to see the universe and its manifold phenomena and to consider them as real.

Does acceptance of the doctrine of emptiness and the realization of *prajna* mean that we have to devaluate human experience and reject life altogether? The Madhyamika philosophers do not think so. They recognize that ordinary people live in the world of phenomena and relative truths where the laws of karma still operate. Such relative truths are important for practical life. The Buddha himself by virtue of his skill in means makes use of them freely in teaching others at different times at different levels. Moreover, Nagarjuna carefully points out that the absolute truth can only be realized by the removal of the relative truths. These relative truths therefore serve as the means or the ladder leading one to the goal or the absolute truth.

How is it possible for finite beings to have access to this absolute truth? The Madhyamika School teaches that the process is accomplished through an intermediary, the Buddha, who through his enlightenment under the bodhi tree experienced a direct intuition of this supreme absolute truth. Through this achievement, the Buddha is the personal embodiment of the absolute, and is able to teach and lead others to this highest truth.

It must be admitted that such a type of thinking as embodied in the Madhyamika system is not for the common man but for the religious thinker deeply immersed in the problems of his destiny and his salvation. It offers him a logical and systematic explanation for his detachment from the phenomenal world and leads him to a comprehension of the true nature of all things. Ignorance is removed and supreme wisdom or enlightenment is realized. The school thus appeals more to the intellect than to the emotions of its followers, and because of this, it did not command as wide an appeal as did the Amitabha cult in China and Japan.

Vijnanavadin or Idealistic School

The second great Mahayana school, the Idealistic, likewise shared in this tendency to cater to the mind rather than to the heart.

The Vijnanavadins take as their starting point the views of one of the Hinayana schools which admit the extra-mental existence of the outer world, but claim that we do not have a direct perception of it. We have only mental presentations through which we infer the existence of the external world. The Vijnanavadins or the Idealists now carry this idea one step further to its logical conclusion. They claim there is no need for an external world to account for our perceptions, they deny the existence of the outer world and enunciate the doctrine of mind only. To the followers of this school, the universe exists only in the mind of the perceiver. Drawing upon such experiences as that of the short-sighted monk who imagines that the spots in his almsbowl are flies, or upon the experiences of dreams, the school claims that an individual through meditation can create visions in his mind as vivid as those obtained through perception. Since such visions have no objective reality, the school concludes that it is not necessary to have external objects to account for perceptions.

The two individuals chiefly responsible for the establishment of this school were the brothers Asanga and Vasubandhu, who probably lived at the end of the fourth century A.D. Vasubandhu, the younger brother, was a famous Hinayana master before he was converted to Mahayana Buddhism, and his work the *Ab-*

hidharmakośa (*Treasury of the Higher Subtleties*) is still acknowledged as one of the most complete and authoritative expositions of Hinayana Buddhism. After his conversion by his older brother, he wrote the classical treatises on Vijnanavadin doctrines.

The main problem in Buddhism is the cessation of *tanha* or cravings, which if not controlled would increase and become the root of all miseries. For cravings to be effective there must be two things, subject and object, the self and the other. The Vijnanavadins seek to demonstrate that there is neither subject nor object, only the mind or consciousness. Their acceptance of the doctrine of *sunyata* or emptiness had already led them to hold to the non-substantiality of the self and the external elements. In such a situation, the Vijnanavadins conclude that there is no room for the cravings to arise, for there is no one who craves and nothing to crave for. By destroying the basis of craving, they seek to prepare the individual for the religious life leading to emancipation.

If everything is mind or consciousness only, then how does one account for the variety of ideas and impressions that exist in the mind? The Idealists say that they are left behind by previous ideas and impressions. They thus trace the activity of the mind to a beginningless past, to the existence of an eternal repository from which can be drawn every possible idea or image. This repository is called the *alaya-vijnana* or storehouse-consciousness, which is the storehouse of all the ideas and impressions experienced by mankind since the beginning of time. Everything in the universe may be found within it. It is common to all individuals, it is the ocean of consciousness out of which all ideas arise and to which all ideas return. During his waking moments the individual is conscious of but a small fragment of this repository but by meditation he becomes aware of its profundity and depth. Every thought or deed performed by mankind since the beginning leaves behind a kind of spiritual energy or seed which is deposited in the storehouse. Since this seed lingers on even after the thought or deed has ceased, it may be likened to memory in the widest sense.

One of the most vexing problems which the Vijnanavadins have to face is to explain why such external phenomena as mountains, lakes, rivers, trees, and so forth appear alike to everyone who sees them. To explain such a phenomenon, the school admits the existence of universal seeds that reside in the repository of all beings. Out of these universal seeds evolve the ideas of the mountains, lakes, and so forth, and since they are universal and common to all beings, the resulting appearance of mountains and lakes are alike in all beings. Out of this immediately arises another question, what about the differences in the bodies and sense organs of each individual? The school explains that these differences are evolved out of non-universal seeds, or private seeds which exist in the storehouse of that particular individual. Though the totality of phenomenal existence is one, still the facts of existence are manifested in limited individuals or streams of consciousness, who differ in karma and degrees of ignorance, thus giving rise to non-universal or individual seeds.

In arguing for the existence of this eternal universal *alaya* consciousness, we see the difference between the two Mahayana schools of thought. The Madhyamika says that only the truth of *sunyata* exists. The Vijnanavada asks the logical question, what is it that realizes this truth of *sunyata?* There must be something to realize it, and to the Vijnanavada, that something is the *alaya*-consciousness.

The same Asanga who founded the Vijnanavada School once wrote that the superiority of the Mahayana over the Hinayana lies in the following features:

(1) Comprehensiveness. The Mahayana does not confine itself to the teachings of just one Buddha, but embraces all the truths taught by all the Buddhas of all times.

(2) Universal love for all sentient beings and universal salvation. The Hinayana confines its salvation to the individual only, but the Mahayana teaches that all sentient beings possess the Buddha nature and hence are capable of attaining enlightenment. The Mahayana thus aims at universal salvation.

(3) Greatness in intellectual comprehension. The Mahayana not only teaches the non-substantiality of the self or soul but also the non-substantiality of all the elements of existence.

(4) Marvelous spiritual energy and activity of the bodhisattva. The Mahayana bodhisattva never tires of working for universal salvation, he manifests himself at all times and in all places to minister to the needs of all living beings. He also has inexhaustible resources at his command which he uses skillfully to cope with the needs of those he wants to save.

(5) Highter spiritual attainment. The Mahayana aims not at arhatship but at Buddhahood.

We shall let these words of Asanga serve as a fitting summary of this new aspect of Buddhism that was soon to transform it from an Indian to a world religion, bringing its message of salvation to the spiritually hungry masses of Asia.

Tantrism

In its inception, Mahayana Buddhism represented an attempt to cope with changing conditions and situations which the religion faced as it expanded beyond the confines of the Ganges into other parts of India, especially the northwest. In that area, the Buddhist missionaries during the two hundred years before Christ met with Greeks, Parthians, and Iranians, wandering nomads and hardy warriors, plainsmen and mountaineers. The religion that satisfied the religious yearnings of the Indians of the mild Ganges Valley did not suffice for these diversified peoples of differing temperaments and tastes and backgrounds. The changes which crept into the religion were in part inspired by a desire to win the support of a greater number of people.

In the course of time, Mahayana Buddhism also underwent some changes. For the purpose of implementing the cardinal Mahayana principle of universal salvation, the Mahayana preachers sought to reach as many people as possible, and to do this, they must make Buddhism acceptable to all classes. Since the uneducated and uncultured masses outnumbered all others, they offered the most inviting target. In its attempt to win these masses, Mahayana Buddhism accepted their religious intuitions and embraced their numerous deities and occult practices. The Mahayana teachers met the masses halfway and won them over by complying with their yearning for magic and sorcery. The new phase brought about by the blend of Mahayana Buddhism with the beliefs and practices of a primitive agricultural society is commonly called Tantric or Esoteric Buddhism. By the seventh century, it had become fully systematized in northeastern and northwestern India.

The chief difference between Tantrism and the other aspects of Buddhism is its emphasis on sacramental action. In order to attain redemption from ignorance and achieve salvation, the Tantras do not stress theoretical elaboration of such concepts as *prajna* or wisdom but place their emphasis on an esoteric consecration which consists of action of the body, speech, and mind. Since action is performed by the body, the body is not deprecated but is valued as the proper vehicle for salvation. The phenomenal world in which the body is involved is not therefore regarded as an impediment but as an aid to enlightenment. Moreover, since this action entails a variety of complicated ritual practices, this means that training in the Tantras must be carried out under the direction of a master or *guru*. Such practices are never fully committed to writing, and so it is dangerous to try to carry out such practices mainly by relying on the written texts. They are orally communicated by the master only to those who are initiated into the esoteric teachings, and this shield of secrecy between the sacred and the profane is responsible for much of the difficulty in presenting a comprehensive account of Tantric Buddhism.

The aim of the esoteric consecration is to bring about a transformation of the mind by significant sounds and movements. By sounds we mean the *mantras* or mystic syllables, and by movement we mean the *mudras* or movement of the hands, fingers, and body. The Tantric masters teach that every Buddha or bodhisattva is associated with a particular *mantra* or *mudra,* and by repeating the *mantra* and performing the *mudra* correctly, one can get in touch with the deity in question and partake of its transcendental powers.

A *mantra* consists of a string of syllables which have no meaning at all in many cases. To be effective, a *mantra* must be pronounced by an individual who has undergone the proper training and discipline and is familiar with its operation. When pronounced correctly, it can drive off evil spirits or thwart the operation of black magc by enemies. An interesting illustration of the power of these mystic syllables is found in a story where Ananda, the favorite disciple of the Buddha, was led to the house of an outcast girl who had fallen in love with him and induced her mother to cast a spell over him. The Buddha saw with his divine eyes what had happened to Ananda, and he uttered a *mantra* of greater power than that recited by the outcast woman, and was thus able to free Ananda. The most famous *mantra* is one uttered by every Tibetan, *om mani padme hum* (O the jewel in the lotus), and because utterance of this *mantra* can bring about a better rebirth, the Tibetans print it on banners, streamers, cylinders, prayer wheels, or barrels turned round by water. Cylinders with the formula are to be found on roadsides, and all that a traveler has to do is to turn the cylinder round in passing, and he will gain just as much merit as if he had recited the *mantra*. In some cases as when he is passing a barrel turned round by the water, he does not have to do anything, for the mere act of passing by the barrel with the *mantra* is considered to be meritorious. In efforts to produce rain, the Tantric master performs a most elaborate ritual and then utters the following *mantra:* "Om ghuru ghuru ghudu ghudu ghata ghata ghotaya ghotaya ka. O Lord of the nāgas (sea serpents) who causes the snakes to tremble, He-he Ru-tu Ka, those nāgas who have gone to the seven lower realms, drag them forth, drag them forth, rain, rain, thunder, thunder—Phuh phuh phuh phuh phuh phuh phuh phuh hūm hūm hūm phat svāhā." [21]

The use of *mantras* to bring about rain or to achieve good or evil results is an indication that the Tantric Buddhists now believe that miracles can supersede the operation of karma. It is now possible to avoid the effects of bad karma by merely uttering correctly the appropriate *mantra*. The Tantrists believe that even Buddhahood could be achieved through the miraculous power residing in the mystic syllables.

Going hand in hand with the *mantras* are the *mudras*, or ritual gestures of the body, hands, and fingers. The Tantrists believe that each deity has its own *mudra*, and this must be imitated correctly by the worshipper if the latter wishes to communicate with that particular deity. Ritual dancing is looked upon as gestures of the body and plays a role in the initiation ceremonies.

Initiation into the secrets of the Tantras is called *abhisheka,* or entry into the *mandala* or mystic circle. This initiation is conducted away from profane eyes and therefore it is impossible to have a complete picture of what goes on. Recourse to the written text does not help very much either, for descriptions of the ceremonies are couched in symbolical language which is unintelligible unless one has mastered the secret key which opens the door to its explanation. From what little we know, it appears that there are two types of initiation ceremonies, right-hand Tantric, and left-hand Tantric.

Right-hand Tantrism is concerned generally with the incantation of the mystic syllables, the ritual performance of the movements of the body, hands, and fingers, and the ceremonies and meditation in connection with the *mandala* or mystic circle. This mystic circle, which is so often depicted in Buddhist art, is considered to be the gathering place of the deities who are shown in their cosmic connections. It is usually painted on a piece of cloth or paper or even on the ground, with the deities presented in their visible forms or by letters of the Sanskrit alphabet. One of the most famous of such mystic circles is the Womb-element Circle (*Garbhadhatu-mandala*) which is divided into thirteen divisions containing four hundred and five deities. The central figure in this circle is Mahavairocana, the Great Brilliant One, considered by the Tantric Buddhists to be the highest being or the Absolute Buddha. The various Buddhas, bodhisattvas, and deities shown in the circle are but manifestations of this Supreme Buddha and the symbols of his multifarious activities. The aim of the circle is to provide a visible symbol aiding the practitioner to concentrate on the truth that the Supreme Buddha is always manifesting himself and always preaching. Sometimes a *mandala* is just a circle drawn on the ground to delimit it from its profane environment, and within it the initiation ceremonies of the neophyte are conducted. These ceremonies consist of the baptism by water, wearing of the diadem, placing the sacred band on the shoulder, touching with the bell and thunderbolt, swearing of the vows, taking a mystic name, and finally the receiving of the bell and thunderbolt from the master.

Left-hand Tantrism differs from its counterpart in its performance of sexo-yogic practices. Worship of the female element has been a feature of Indian cultic practices since ancient times. Left-hand Tantrism incorporated this feature into its practices and clothed it with an explanation that linked it with Mahayana theology. In Mahayana Buddhism, enlightenment is realized with the union of wisdom and compassion. Wisdom is interpreted as the realization of the non-existence of all phenomenal appearances, while compassion is the urge to carry out altruistic activities to save others. These terms are accepted by the Left-hand Tantras, but they now interpret wisdom to be female and compassion male. In order to achieve enlightenment, there must be a virgin who is the symbol of wisdom. Consequently one finds in Tantric iconography Buddhas and bodhisattvas locked in ecstatic embrace with their consorts. Such images are not considered vulgar; instead they are looked upon as appropriate symbols of the inseparability of wisdom and compassion, of the absolute and phenomenal.

The Left-hand Tantrists attempt to justify their actions on two grounds. They argue that the external world and all phenomena are mere illusions created by the mind. When the yogin enters the mystic circle for the yogic practices, his mind is so trained by meditation that he realizes perfectly the emptiness of all things. In this state of mind, there is no longer any duality between male and female, no distinction between morality and immorality, virtue and vice. He also argues that any action is to be judged by the motives behind it. This is a point which was already stressed by the Buddha in his explanation of karma. If the motive behind the sexo-yogic act is to attain salvation and enlightenment, then the act itself cannot be adjudged immoral. The intentions and the motives of the bodhisattva locked in embrace with his consort are noble and virtuous, and therefore whatever deeds he performs are also noble and virtuous.

Tantrism has often been condemned as a degeneration of Buddhism, and for a long time it was not considered an appropriate subject for serious investigation. Happily this attitude is changing now, and in recent years a number of studies have appeared, giving students a better idea of this aspect of Buddhism which played such a vital role in the religious life of the Tibetans down to recent times.

CHAPTER 5

The Sangha,
or Monastic Community

IN THE PREVIOUS CHAPTER, we have mentioned some of the practices in connection with the three-fold discipline, moral conduct, concentration, and intuitive wisdom, that must be pursued by the follower of the dhamma if he desired to achieve the goal preached by the Buddha. In order to provide a favorable climate for the actual pursuit of the path prescribed by the master, the institution of the monastic community, or the *sangha,* was established. In the community of monks, where the individual members no longer needed to worry about the cares and anxieties of family and society, it was felt that conditions would be favorable for the faithful to abide by the rules of discipline and the moral precepts laid down by the founder of the religion.

Before and during the time of the Buddha there were already in existence groups of religious mendicants, wandering around and living as recluses in the forests, or residing in a fixed hermitage. Ordinarily they had their heads and beards shaved, but some kept their tresses and beards long. They smeared their bodies with ashes, they wore clothing made from animal skins or from the bark and leaves of trees, or they wore no clothing at all. Such religious mendicants were called *samanas,* and the groups were called *sanghas,* which meant an assemblage. Each group was usually centered in a master or *guru,* who expounded the teachings to the followers and regulated their lives.

In the beginning, the followers of the Buddha followed these general practices. The Buddha was just another teacher, just another leader of a group of mendicants who followed him around. The early ideal of the Buddhist monks was thus an eremitical one, wandering around with no settled place of abode. This ideal was well expressed in the following passage, "So long as the monks shall delight in forest seats, so long they may be expected not to decline, but to prosper." It was also expressed in the refrain that is repeated again and again in one of the earliest pieces of Buddhist literature, the *Sutta-nipata,* "Let him wander alone like a rhinoceros." It was also exemplified by the practices that the monks were enjoined to follow, to live on alms alone, to wear clothes made from cloth taken from the rubbish heap, to sit and lie down at the foot of trees, and to take strong urine as medicine.

In this early stage, the admission of monks into the order was achieved by a simple ceremony, consisting mainly of the Buddha and the already ordained monks meeting together and the candidate requesting admission by uttering the following formula, "May we obtain departure from the household life and full ordination from the Blessed Buddha." The master then responded by saying, "Come, O monk, the dhamma has been well taught, practice the religious life that will make a complete end to suffering." With this response, the ordination was completed. According to this procedure, only the Buddha was qualified to grant ordination.

However, as the number of monks increased, and as they scattered to different areas to carry out their evangelical duties, it became increasingly difficult for them to gather as a body for the ordination ceremonies. Moreover it was also impractical for the Buddha to go to the different places where applicants for admission were to be found. Faced with these problems, the Buddha finally gave permission to monks living in different localities to perform the ordination ceremonies, with the one condition that there must be at least ten fully ordained monks present to confer the ordination before it could be valid. A distinction was also drawn between the departure from the household life and the full ordination as a monk.

The first procedure, going from the household to the houseless stage, was called *pabbajja*, and was not a formal affair. The individual merely uttered the formula of the three refuges, "I take refuge in the Buddha, I take refuge in the dhamma, I take refuge in the sangha." In order to qualify for this step, the candidate must be at least fifteen years of age, although numerous exceptions to this rule are mentioned in the scriptures. After he had uttered the formula, he shaved his head, put on the yellow robe, and resolved to abide by the ten cardinal precepts. He was now a novice or *sramanera*. For the full ordination, called *upasampada*, the candidate must be at least twenty years of age, preferably with a few years already spent as a novitiate, although this was not a condition. He was first examined as to whether he would be disqualified by any disease such as leprosy, consumption, or fits, or by any occupational impediments such as being in the royal service. Barred from admission also were thieves, jail breakers, debtors, slaves, scourged offenders, matricides, patricides, arhanticides, eunuchs, hermaphrodites, those who had violated a nun, those who had caused the Buddha to shed blood, those whose hands and feet had been severed, and those who had caused a schism in the order. If he was adjudged eligible, then he was presented by a senior monk, who asked the assembly of monks three times if they favored the admission of the applicant. If there was no dissent, the applicant was accepted. The newly admitted monk then chose a spiritual preceptor who must be a monk of ten years' standing, and began his period of spiritual tutelage under him.

Upon joining the order, the monk was permitted to keep the following articles as his personal possessions, three robes, one girdle, one almsbowl, one razor, one needle, and one water-strainer. If he had property, he might place it in the hands of his family for safekeeping. Departure from the household life did not mean that he had to renounce his property entirely, it meant that he was merely separated from it. The rupture from the world was merely the fruit of his ordination, and not a condition for it. Many examples might be found in Buddhist literature of monks who remained proprietor in absentia of property that they had not disposed of before ordination. For instance, when the Buddha returned to his village six years after his departure, his son Rahula went to reclaim his heritage from him. In the *Book of Discipline,* there is also the story of a monk who said upon leaving the order that he had a village which assured him of subsistence, fields and gardens which produced the products he needed and money and gold, which permitted him to live. As for the conditions among Chinese monks, numerous documents found in northwest China described the commercial activities of members of the *sangha,* such as lending money and property, and charging exorbitant interest rates.

Because monks owned property, there arose the problem of the disposal of such property after their death. Ordinarily, when a monk passed away, his personal belongings were given to those in the order who had taken care of him. However when the monk left important patrimony, then a distinction was made between heavy and light goods. Those belonging to the latter category, usually the personal effects of the deceased, were distributed to his personal attendants. The first category, which included such items as houses, fields, gardens, library, and monetary wealth, became the property of the *sangha* as a whole. A good example of this might be seen in the disposition of the property left behind by the Tantric master Amoghavajra in China, when his seals, translations, texts, and other religious objects were bequeathed to his disciples and pupils, and two cows, a chariot, fields and gardens, 87 ounces of gold, and 220½ ounces of silver, were left to the monastery he lived in. In China, however, it was possible for a monk to prevent his property from falling into the hands of the monastery by the simple device of going home when he knew that he was approaching death, for the practice there was that the layman in whose house a monk died could claim all the property of the deceased monk.

The eremitical ideal which was the characteristic of the early

Buddhist community soon modified by existing conditions in India. Instead of wandering about, the monks began to settle in fixed abodes during certain months of the year. This transition was brought about by the observance of the rainy season, which lasted throughout the entire summer. During this season, since it was too difficult for the monks to travel about and to take shelter under trees, it soon became the practice for them to remain in one spot and wait until the rains had ceased. This practice soon became a custom, and the custom gained sanctity through repeated usage. Out of this custom arose the institution known as the *avasa*, or colony, staked out for purposes of sojournment by a community of monks. The monks making up such a colony formed a complete community, with limits carefully defined and fixed, and within each colony, the monks lived a corporate communal life that found its formal expression in the observance of the fortnightly assembly or the *uposatha*.

When the monks settled down for the rainy season within the limits of the colony, the rich householders or the ruling princes in the vicinity soon realized that it provided them with a golden opportunity to acquire some religious merits by catering to the needs of the monks, and they soon initiated measures that changed the manner of living of the clerical community. Some of these rich patrons built houses for the monks to live in, and within these structures they furnished elaborate accommodations such as cells, cloisters, grounds for walking exercises, bathrooms, pavilions, storerooms, and so forth. Sometimes they would prepare food and invite the order to their homes to partake of the meal, thus relieving the monks of the necessity of begging for alms. In some instances, the ruling prince would endow a community with the proceeds from an entire village, thus assuring that community permanent support. During the lifetime of the Buddha, there was probably a struggle between the two ideals, the wandering and the settled life, for we find a group of monks advocating strict adherence to the more severe mendicant ideal of subsisting only on alms and dwelling only at the foot of trees. The problem was finally brought before the Buddha for adjudication, and his decision was that strict adherence to the severe mendicant ideal was to be left to the discretion of the individual monk. The strict adherents also advocated non-eating of meat and fish. This would imply that such a diet was not entirely taboo. The Buddha himself once declared that members of the clerical order could eat fish or meat as long as they did not see or hear the meat being prepared, or suspect that the meat was prepared primarily for them. As one can readily see, this left the door wide open for monks to indulge in the luxury of meat-eating.

With the institution of settled life, the dress of the clerics also changed, for instead of wearing clothes made from rags, they could now wear robes of cotton, wool, linen or even silk, presented to them at the end of the rainy season by faithful laymen.

As long as the monks wandered about begging for alms, there was no need for the storage of provisions. Moreover, one of the rules of discipline specified that all alms must be eaten in a single meal, and forbade the storage of food. However, when settled communities developed, it became necessary to have enough food in stock at all times to feed such a large group, not only of the resident monks but also of guests who might be stopping over. For the storage of food, clearly a storeroom was necessary, but this would be against the rule forbidding storage. In the beginning, the community of monks circumvented this rule by locating the storeroom just outside the limits of the colony, or by storing the provisions in the stables or houses of laymen living within the boundaries, but as time went on, such subterfuges were no longer resorted to, and storerooms became an integral part of the whole monastery. Any provision donated to the *sangha* could not be appropriated by any single monk. If a donor wanted to give alms to a particular monk, he must send it first to the *sangha,* with instructions that it was given with special reference to the designated individual. This communal ownership of all provisions was emphasized in one of the most important of the Pali discourses, the Sutta on the Great Decease, where a passage reads, "So long as the Brethren shall divide without partiality, and share in common with their upright companions, all such things as they receive in accordance with the just provisions of the order, down even to the mere contents of a begging bowl, so long may the Brethren be expected not to decline but to prosper." [22]

With the establishment of settled life, a division of labor also arose within a monastery, with members of the order being appointed as overseer of the storeroom, apportioner of rations, superintendent of buildings, keeper of financial records and so forth.

As Buddhism grew and spread, many communities of monks sprang up in different parts of the Ganges Valley. The main feature of these early Buddhist communities was the democratic nature of their internal polity, and in this respect, they differed from the existing mendicant orders of the time, which usually acknowledged one leader as the head of the *sangha* and empowered to establish the line of succession. Although the Buddha was the leader of the *sangha,* he steadfastly refused to initiate a line of succession when pressed by his disciples to name his successor; instead he declared that the dhamma and the rules of discipline which he had set forth would be sufficient to serve as the leader of the community of monks after his death. Within the *sangha,* whenever there was any *sangha* business to be transacted, a learned or virtuous monk was appointed president to preside over the meeting. At such meetings, every monk had the right to participate in the discussions and to vote. The quorum needed might vary in accordance with the nature of the business transacted, for the ordination of new monks, at least ten already ordained clerics had to be present, while twenty were required for the rehabilitation of a monk who had undergone penance for an expiable offense. The completeness of the quorum was considered one of the best safeguards against the deterioration of the *sangha.* As for the rules governing transactions of business, it was stipulated that a member not present at a meeting could not ratify an act later, but that if he wanted to vote, he could vote by proxy. To be acted upon, an item of business must be proclaimed three times, in the same manner of the three readings required of modern legislation. Silence on the part of the monks signified consent to the piece of legislation on hand. Should there be any difference of opinion concerning a *sangha* business, the matter was sometimes settled by a committee within the *sangha,* or by a referee from a neighboring community, or simply by a majority vote of the group.

Life within the community of monks was regulated carefully by a set of monastic rules, commonly referred to as the rules of discipline, or the *Vinaya* rules. Literally, the word *vinaya* means that which leads. These rules are usually regarded as an adjudication, a pronouncement on certain facts as they arose on a particular occasion. Therefore, in the *Book of Discipline* which contains the entire body of *Vinaya* rules, the Buddhist writers felt obliged to append a story giving the background of the rule, so that the facts on which the adjudication was based would be made known. These stories are often bewildering to the reader, for while some of them have a kernel of truth, others have no connection with the rules and are obviously later fabrications. However, apart from their connection with the promulgation of the rules of discipline, these stories possess some value of their own for the information which they contain about the social, moral, and intellectual atmosphere of the times.

As an example, let us repeat here the background story leading to the promulgation of the rule against the drinking of intoxicating liquor. A poisonous dragon living in the countryside had destroyed so much bird and animal life in the surrounding area by the poisonous gases it was exhaling that the inhabitants beseeched the Buddha to do something about the scourge. To accomplish the job of subduing the poisonous dragon, the Buddha called upon a monk named Sagata, who was considered foremost of all in the mastery of fire. When Sagata approached the abode of the dragon, the latter gave vent to its anger by causing rain, hail, swords, lances, spears, and other weapons to descend upon the monk, but these were all converted into various kinds of fragrant powders by the miraculous powers of the monk. When these weapons failed, the dragon then tried fire and smoke, but Sagata retaliated by causing his own body to appear like a flaming mass, searing even the abode of the dragon. The dragon was now frightened by this display of pyrotechnics and contemplated escape from his burning house, but all escape routes were blocked by flames, and only in the vicinity of Sagata was it quiet and cool. There was nothing for the dragon to 'do now but to seek refuge there. Sagata then insisted that the dragon take refuge in the Buddha and vow not to commit any more evil deeds, and this the dragon willingly consented to do.

For this deed of subduing and converting the poisonous dragon, the people in the affected area were exceedingly grateful to Sagata, and one of the resident brahmans invited the monk to take alms with him. When the latter consented, the brahman prepared excellent and wonderful foods, which the monk ate with relish. In his desire to assist the digestive process within Sagata after eating so much food, the brahman surreptitiously put some liquor into some broth which the monk drank. After finishing the meal, Sagata left, but on his way back to his quarters, he was overcome by the intoxicating liquor as well as by the heat of the sun and fell prostrate on the ground. When the Buddha with his divine eyes saw what had happened to Sagata, he created by magic a grass hut over the prostrate and intoxicated monk, lest some one should see him in that disgraceful condition. In front of the assembled monks, the Buddha then enunciated the rule against drinking intoxicating liquor.

The heart of the rules of discipline is the section called the *patimokkha* (bond, that which holds together), which consists of 227 rules in the present Pali canon, but which in the Chinese version consists of 250, and in the Tibetan, 253 rules. This *patimokkha* may be said to be a bare code of canon law consisting of an enumeration and classification of ecclesiastical offenses. After this code had been formulated, it was then recited during the fortnightly assembly of the monks, held on the days of the new and full moon.

The germs of this fortnightly assembly may be found in the early Vedic literature, when the days of the new and full moon were observed as sacred for sacrificial purposes. As a preliminary to this sacrifice, the sacrificer abstained from food and contact with women, and retired to a house where the ceremonies were held. This observance of the sacred days was carried over into Buddhism, where it became the embodiment of the corporate life of the community. Strict rules were laid down for the convening of this assembly. After the spot had been chosen formally, all the monks living in the particular colony were required to be present, as well as all monks who happened to be passing by and present at the time. No monk was permitted to leave the premise except on the most urgent *sangha* business.

With the recital of each rule in the *patimokkha*, there was a pause to allow for the confession of those monks who had violated that particular rule. It must be pointed out once again that this confession did not constitute removal of the demerits incurred by the commission of the offense, it merely meant that the monk resolved not to repeat the same offense. After the confession came the punishment, the nature of which was determined by the type of offense committed. By the infliction of disciplinary measures against the culprits, the *sangha* assumed jurisdiction over the conduct of its members, and it was this authority of the *sangha* that prevented the *patimokkha* code from degenerating into a dead letter.

In the present Pali canon, the 227 rules of the *patimokkha* consist of eight sections. Section One embraces the four great offenses, misconduct with women, theft, murder, and exaggeration of one's miraculous power, the commission of which entails expulsion from the order. The first three are generally recognized as being active in all civilized societies, while the prohibition of unchastity was already observed by practically all the religious groups before and during the time of the Buddha. It was of course based on the idea that restraints and self-control were necessary for winning the fruits of the religious life. The crime of stealing was considered grave especially in view of the fact that when he entered the order, the monk had vowed to regard everything he used as communal property. In the detailed discussion of this rule, there are some fine-drawn distinctions which correspond closely to the subtle points of modern law. For instance, if there is an object in the possession of another that is important and worth more than five units of value, and if there exists in a monk the intention to steal it, then the monk is guilty of wrong doing if he merely touches it, of a grave offense if he makes it quiver, and of defeat and expulsion from the order if he removes it to another place. This would indicate that there are three grades of punishment for stealing, defeat, grave offense, and wrong doing, with the last two drawing lighter punishment, merely temporary expulsion from the order or confession of the crime.

In the case of murder, the rule is very clear. Whenever a monk should intentionally deprive a human being of life, or praise the beauty of death, or incite one to bring about death, he is guilty of a crime that is punishable by expulsion from the order. There was an occasion when six monks were enamoured with the beautiful wife of a sick layman, and in order to hasten his departure from this life, they all pointed out to him that death was a more desirable state than life, for he would then be reborn in one of the heavens because of his good deeds, where all his sensual pleasures would be satiated. Attracted by this prospect, the ill layman ate and drank himself to death. When this incident was reported to the Buddha, he condemned the six monks to expulsion from the order, for he pointed out that even though they did not actually kill the layman, the intention was there.

It may seem strange that these three offenses, unchastity, theft, and murder should result in the same severe punishment, but it must be remembered that this was the case not only for the Sakyan monks but for all other recluses. The penalties therefore reflected the prevailing sentiment of Indian society at the time. It would be well to recall that up to very recent times, the crime of sheep-stealing in England and cattle-rustling in the western states of America resulted in hanging.

We come now to the fourth offense that resulted in expulsion, that of exaggerating one's miraculous power, or claiming the qualities or attributes of the superman. This offense must be viewed in a different light from the other three, and appeared to reflect some contrasting sense of values in the monastic community. Here was involved not merely a condemnation of lying or boasting, but a particular kind of boasting, the boast of having reached a stage of spiritual development attainable only after a long period of discipline. The fact that the Sakyan monks proclaimed that such a boasting was the most serious of offenses suggested that the monks themselves held in the highest esteem the stage of spiritual development they were striving after, and that one should never boast he had attained that stage when in fact he had not. Lying or boasting about worldly affairs entailed only confession for expiation, but boasting about the attainment of miraculous powers resulted in expulsion from the order.

SectionTwo consists of thirteen rules concerned with the monks' conduct toward women, toward each other, and toward the laity. Infraction of these rules resulted in temporary suspension from the order, and after the expiration of the punishment, the monk must appear before the *sangha* and ask for permission to rejoin it. The remaining sections are concerned with offenses that are not serious, such as lying, slandering, committing nuisances in public places, drinking liquor, and so forth, and expiation was obtained simply by confession.

It has been charged that the necessity to promulgate such rules governing the conduct of monks was evidence that members of the *sangha* did commit such crimes. Such a charge was stressed particularly by Chinese opponents of Buddhism, who claimed that the Indians were by nature addicted to such crimes as unchastity, stealing, and murder. Undoubtedly the Buddhist *sangha* did include such renegades, and we as historians of religion owe a debt of gratitude to these backsliders, for their misconduct resulted in this legacy of the *patimokkha* rules, which tell us so much about the early Buddhist *sangha*. However, the presence of these few wrong-doers should not blind us to the existence of a large number of pure and virtuous monks who were ashamed and complained about the misdeeds of their guilty brethren.

In the beginning, no women were admitted into the order in spite of the fervent efforts exerted to this end by Ananda and Mahapajapati, the stepmother of the Blessed One. However, when Ananda asked whether or not a woman could achieve the fruits of the religious life under the influence of the dhamma, the Buddha replied in the affirmative, whereupon the former pressed his point that if women were competent, then why exclude them from the order. Faced with this logic, the Buddha relented and gave his consent, but he specified eight points which women who entered the order must comply with.

(1) A nun, even a hundred years old, shall arise, salute, meet humbly and behave respectfully toward a monk, even though the latter was just ordained.

(2) A nun shall not reside in any place where no monks reside.

(3) Nuns shall follow the fortnightly assembly in accordance with the date set by monks.

(4) At the end of the rainy season, nuns shall invite criticisms in both congregations.

(5) If a nun is guilty of a serious offense, she shall undergo a half-month penance before both congregations.

(6) After a femals novice has practiced the rules of discipline for two years, she shall then seek ordination before both congregations.

(7) Nuns shall not revile or abuse a monk on any occasion.

(8) Nuns are not allowed to reprove a nun, but a monk may reprove a nun.

Furthermore, the Buddha is reported to have said if nuns were not admitted into the order, the good law would last a thousand years, but now that they were admitted, it would last only five hundred years. The whole tenor of these conditions would appear to indicate that the Sakyan sage was not happy over the admission of women into the order, and that even after they were admitted, did not consider them to be on the same plane of equality with the monks.

As the goals of the religious discipline in early Buddhism were arhatship and nirvana, both requiring a type of rigorous mental and spiritual training not compatible with the household life, laymen were not permitted to participate in the quest for them. It was felt that the household life, with its involvements of family, society, and occupation, and characterized by attachments to beloved ones, was not appropriate for the strenuous life to be practiced by one who sought the religious goals. However, although the Buddha addressed his message primarily to the members of the *sangha,* it was implied that there should be devoted laymen who would give alms to support the monks, so that the latter group could devote their entire attention to their monastic activities without having to worry about their material welfare. In the *Book of Discipline,* there is found another reason why the Buddha permitted lay disciples within the religion. It is said that criticisms arose against the Buddhists, that they were turning wives into widows, sons and daughters into orphans, and enticing young men from their homes, so that the normal life of the community was impaired. In response to this criticism, the Buddha made provisions for lay disciples who would be devoted to the religion but who would still live the household life and fulfill the functions in society.

While lay disciples were permitted within the religion, they were not expected to be proficient in the dhamma or to participate in the activities of the *sangha.* However, since the livelihood of the monks depended on the laity, amicable relations between the two groups had to be established. For instance, monks were prohibited from doing anything that would bring disrepute to a lay family, instead they were urged not to annoy or to vex the laity but to win its support.

Among the early lay disciples of the Buddha, two are worthy of mention because of the contributions which they made to the *sangha.* One was Anathapindada, a name which meant Giver of Alms to the Unprotected. The most generous patron of the *sangha* during his lifetime, it was said of him that in his home there was always enough food prepared to feed 500 monks at one sitting. By far his most magnificent gift to the *sangha* was the donation of funds to purchase the pleasure garden Jetavana in the city of Savatthi, which he turned over to the Buddha to be used as his permanent residence during the latter years of his life. The other layman was Jivaka, the physician of Bimbisara, king of Magadha, and also of the Buddha and the community of monks. Famous indeed are some of the surgical deeds attributed to him, such as trepanning (operation on the skull) and laparotomy (abdominal operation). His skill as a physician brought him more patients than he could treat, but he never neglected the *sangha,* consequently many sick people joined the order just to be treated by him. When he learned of this, he advised the Buddha to lay down the rule that people afflicted with certain diseases should not be permitted to become monks.

The formal procedure by which a person became a lay disciple of the Buddha was very simple. All he had to do was to utter the formula of the three refuges, "I take refuge in the Buddha, I take refuge in the dhamma, I take refuge in the *sangha*." Thus faith was the most important element, faith in the Buddha as the emancipator, the dhamma as the true path, and the *sangha* as the symbol of the doctrine. After formally becoming a lay disciple, he might even participate in the ceremony of the fortnightly assembly if he so desired, but before he was permitted to do so, he had to refrain from wearing ornaments and unguents, from going to entertainments, and from eating meats and contacts with women, and he had to observe the fast.

Now that lay disciples were admitted into the religion, it was necessary to provide a specific goal for them, since they were not permitted to aspire to arhatship and nirvāna. This goal was re-birth as a deity in one of the heavens, and in order to achieve this goal, the layman must first follow the five cardinal precepts, namely, to abstain from killing, stealing, adultery, lying, and intoxicating liquor. He must also practice faithfully charity to the *sangha*, control his anger, lead a life of compassion, respect his elders, and avoid the following professions, trading in weapons, trading in human beings, trading in flesh, trading in intoxicating spirits, and trading in poisons. He should not be proud of his birth, wealth, or class, and should seek the company of wise men.

Though lay disciples could only aspire to rebirth as a deity, still there were a number of instances mentioned in the canon of lay-men achieving the goal of arhatship. In such instances, the tradi-tion was that on the very day the householder attained to arhat-ship, he must take the yellow robe or he would die.

Since rebirth as a deity was now provided for, the Buddhists soon worked out a whole hierarchy of such deities, adapted mainly from the prevailing Indian religions and mythologies, and modified to suit the needs of the Buddhists. In Buddhism, such gods, instead of being masters of the known and unknown worlds and objects of worship, were endowed with moral nature, enjoying their lives and happiness because of past meritorious deeds, and freed from the ills that beset ordinary mortals. The deities were said to lead peaceful and happy lives, were handsome and luminous, tall and graceful, free from impurities, and could pass from one world into another without hindrance. Three main categories of such deities were created by the Buddhists, the deities of the world of sensual pleasures, the deities in the world of form, and the deities of the formless world. In the first and lowest category, there were six classes of deities who were all endowed with the six senses and who enjoyed them as mortals did, who married and took their pleasures with their wives, and who were often fond of the exhilarating effects of the soma juice. The second class, gods in the world of form, were those in whom the senses of taste, touch, and smell were absent. These were usually called the Brahma gods, who had achieved their state through meritorious karma, and who made periodic visits to earth to interest themselves in the affairs of man. Their status, however, was still below that of the arhat, for their knowledge was limited, and they were still subject to rebirth. There is a delightful story in the canon to illustrate this point. A monk was bothered by the question, where did the great elements, earth, water, fire, and air, go to upon the expiration of a saint, leaving no trace behind? He first went to the deities of the world of sensual pleasures, starting from the lowest, the four kings of the four cardinal directions, and put the question to them. They replied however that they did not know, and that there were other deities above them, more potent and wiser, who would know. So the monk went successively to each of the six classes of deities in the first category, then to the gods of the world of form, until he finally reached the highest deity in that category, the Great Brahma himself. When asked the question, the Great Brahma replied, "I, brother, am the Great Brahma, the Supreme, the Mighty, the All-seeing, the Ruler, the Lord of all, the Controller, the Creator, the Chief of all, appointing to each his place, . . . the Father of all that are and are to be." The monk replied, "I did not ask you friend, as to whether you are indeed all that you now say. But I ask you where the great elements. . . ." For the second and the third time, the Great Brahma gave the same answer. After the third time, however, Brahma took the monk by the arm and said, "These gods, the retinue of Brahma, hold me, brother, to be such that there is nothing that I cannot see, nothing that I have not understood, nothing I have not realized. Therefore I gave no answer in their presence. I do not know, brother, where these four great elements . . . cease, leaving no trace behind. Therefore you have done wrong, have acted ill, in that, ignoring the Exalted One, you have undertaken this long search, among others, for an answer to the question. Go you now, return to the Exalted One, ask him the question, and accept the answer according as he shall make reply." [23]

Finally in the third and highest class, in the gods of the formless world, only consciousness remains. These are the gods who have practiced the four formless trances.

Rebirth as such gods living in these heavens was the reward held out by Buddhism to the faithful lay disciples. Since the laymen on which the order depended for its sustenance were generally worshippers of the multifarious gods in the Indian pantheon, the Buddhists found it necessary to incorporate such gods into their own system in order to satisfy the needs of the laity. By incorporating such gods as Indra and Brahma into the religion, Buddhism made it possible for the newly enlisted layman to feel that after all he was not joining an alien system, but one in which he could feel at home. As for the religion itself, once these gods were incorporated, Buddhism no longer remained a system of monastic discipline, but became transformed into a religion of heavens and hells. Again, by making deities as Indra and Brahma inferior to the arhat and Buddha, Buddhism succeeded in impressing upon the new converts the authority and the elevated position of its own masters and teachers, who were even more powerful and wise than those who were formerly powerful and wise.

The composition of the Buddhist community, monks, nuns, male and female novices, laymen, and laywomen, has remained unchanged in Theravadin countries since its inauguration in the early days of Buddhism. Even the procedure of entry into the order of monks has followed faithfully the steps specified in the *Vinaya*. The following is a description of the *pabbajja* (leaving the household life to become a novice) and the *upasampada* (full or final ordination) ceremonies as observed in Ceylon.

In order to carry out the ceremonies, there must be at least ten fully ordained monks present, presided over by one who is of ten years' standing. The candidate who is to undergo the *pabbajja* ceremony appears in the dress of a layman but carrying the monkish robes with him in his arms. He is accompanied by his spiritual preceptor. After paying his respects to the presiding officer, the candidate then kneels and asks three times for admission into the order as a novice. He repeats this threefold petition three times, thus making nine times in all. The presiding officer then takes over the monkish robes from the candidate. The latter then asks the presiding officer to give him the robes, so that he may work for the destruction of sorrow and attain nirvana. After this request has been made three times, the presiding officer returns the robes to the candidate, reciting at the same time the formula concerning the perishable nature of all parts of the body, hair, nails, skin, teeth, and so forth. The candidate then arises and retires to take off his layman's dress and put on the monkish robes. While putting on the robes, he resolves that he will wear them merely as protection against the elements and insects and not for ornament. Now attired in his robes, he takes his stand again beside his spiritual preceptor and asks the presiding officer to give him the three refuges and the ten precepts. The officer recites the three refuges and the ten precepts, and the candidate repeats them after him. With the recital of the above, the candidate arises and the ceremony is completed.

The novice now receives instruction in the rules of discipline and the dhamma under his spiritual preceptor, and in return serves him as a personal attendant. When the novice is duly qualified, he presents himself in the company of his preceptor to the assembly of monks for the full ordination. He asks the presiding officer for permission and support to become a monk, and when this is given, the novice retreats to the foot of the assembly to have his almsbowl strapped on to his back. He is then escorted to the head of the assembly in front of the presiding officer, where he is now examined by his teacher and another monk. First he is asked his name, then whether or not he has his robes and almsbowl. He replies in the affirmative, then he retires to a corner of the assembly. His tutors now join him to instruct and examine him. Before putting their questions to him they exhort him not to conceal anything and not to hesitate in giving his answers. They then inquire whether or not he is afflicted with leprosy, boils, itch, consumption, or epilepsy. If he answers that he is free from such diseases, they then proceed to ask him whether or not he is a free man, free from debts, exempt from military service, and has parental permission. When the tutors are satisfied on all points, they go forward to the presiding officer and report to him that they have examined the candidate and found him acceptable, and that it is now time for the assembly of monks to accept him. They beckon the candidate to come forward. The latter does so, and in the company of his preceptors he asks the assembly for ordination. He makes the request three times. Before the assembled monks, his preceptors now put to him the same questions that they did a moment ago. After the proper answers have been given, one of the preceptors then reports to the assembly that the candidate has been instructed and examined, and found free from any disqualifications. The preceptor thereupon requests the assembly to approve the ordination of the candidate. This request is repeated three times. Those who approve are asked to be silent, while those who oppose are asked to speak out. If the assembly remains silent after all three requests, the candidate is considered to have received the full ordination and is now a full fledged monk.

After the ceremony, the newly ordained monk is addressed by one of the senior monks. He is exhorted to wear robes made of rags, not to commit sexual intercourse, not to steal, not to destroy life, and not to claim more than human perfection. With these exhortations over, the meeting disbands.[24]

For the newly ordained monk, life is now bound up intimately with the procedures in the monastery where he resides. For the monasteries in Theravadin countries such as Ceylon, Burma, and Thailand, such procedures are fairly uniform. We shall therefore let the following description of life in a Thai monastery serve as an example of monastic life in those regions.

At 4 A.M. the monks are awakened by the ringing of a bell. After performing their morning ablutions, they put on the three robes, light candles on an altar where the Buddha image is placed, kneel down and bow three times before the altar. They then change from a kneeling to a sideways sitting position, in which posture they repeat the formula of the three refuges and then chant some popular sutras. With the chanting over, they change to a cross-legged position and meditate for a few moments, after which they leave their residence and walk around the monastery for their morning exercises. They usually walk in pairs, one confessing to the other all infractions of the rules of discipline which he might have committed after his last confession. All these activities are completed before sunrise. When they are completed, the monks return to their residence hall for a rest.

After sunrise, the monks put on their robes and take their almsbowls to go out for the morning rounds for alms. By about 7:30 A.M. they are back in the monastery ready to eat their breakfast. With breakfast completed, the monks and novices assemble at 8:15 in the sanctuary for the morning chanting ceremony. The monks are seated according to seniority, with the older ones in front and the younger ones and novices in the rear. They are then led by the head of the monastery in chanting the formula of the three-fold refuges and in reciting some well-known sutras. Such chanting is in Pali, even though the monks and novices may be ignorant of the language. At about 9:00 A.M., the head of the monastery gives instructions in the rules of discipline and the dhamma to the newly ordained monks for about half an hour. After this instruction, the latter would then repair to the residence of their preceptors to perform the duties incumbent upon a personal attendant. Between 11:00 and 11:30 the monks take their main meal for the day, and all eating must be finished before the noonday. Then follows the period of rest, and after that the monks may spend their time reading the scriptures. At 6:00 P.M. another meeting is held in the sanctuary. Here again the monks have to wear the three robes, and at the meeting they often group in pairs to confess to each other any infractions committed since the morning confession. This done, the entire assembly joins in the chanting of sutras. This service usually lasts about forty-five minutes. In the evening the newly ordained monks have to attend another instructional session on the dhamma, the rules of discipline, and the life of the Buddha. After this session they may visit older monks for further instruction or they may retire to their residence to prepare their lessons. Then just before retiring at about 10:00 P.M. the monks bow before the Buddha image, chant a few scriptural passages, or meditate for a few moments.

All the monks living within the monastery must attend the fortnightly assembly. At the beginning of the ceremony, all the monks chant the formula of the threefold refuges. When this is completed, one specially trained monk ascends the pulpit to recite the 227 *patimokkha* rules. The entire recitation usually takes about 45 minutes, and at the end of the recitation, the rest of the monks chant in union an exclamation of approval.[25]

One will notice here in this recitation of the *patimokkha* a slight deviation from the custom in early Buddhism. Originally, the 227 rules would be read one by one, and after each rule, an opportunity was given to the monks to confess any infraction of that particular rule. As carried out in the Thai monastery, there is no such confession; instead the confession is usually made by one monk to another.

Though the fundamental nature and purpose of the *sangha* remained the same, there arose variations in composition and practice as Buddhism migrated to different areas. In Theravadin countries, as we have seen, the *sangha* consisted of six categories, monks and nuns, novices of both sexes, laymen and laywomen. As the *sangha* was constituted in China when the religion was popular during the middle ages, it consisted of eight groups, the above six plus two new groups which for want of a better term we shall call male and female postulants or probationers. In Tibetan monasteries there is likewise a group of probationers called *dge-bsnyen* (pronounced *ges-nyens*) whose status is lower than that of the novice. It was felt by the Chinese that a candidate should not become a novice immediately but should undergo a period of training lasting about a year. As a probationer, he had to follow the five cardinal precepts but he did not have to shave his head, nor was he exempt from the customary tax and labor services. After one year of study, the probationer was eligible to take an examination to determine whether or not he was qualified to become a novice. The examination usually consisted of reciting a certain number of leaves from a popular sutra; a male probationer at some periods had to recite 150 leaves and a female 100 leaves.

In India and in Theravadin countries, entry into the order in the past was customarily an individual affair, dependent upon the wishes of the family or the individual. In China, however, for many periods during her history, entry into the order and the ordination of monks were matters subject to the regulation of the state. The central government from time to time limited the number of people who could join the *sangha*, and it also supervised the examinations held to determine whether or not a candidate was qualified to enter the order. If the candidate were successful in passing the examination, he was given an ordination certificate by a governmental bureau and only then could he come up for the ordination ceremony before the assembly of monks.

Besides the examination system, ordination in China could also be obtained by two other methods, by the favor of the emperor and by the purchase of the ordination certificates. On certain occasions such as the imperial birthday or imperial visitation to a newly established temple, the abbot of a certain temple would submit a list of qualified probationers to the local government officials with a petition asking for their ordination. If the government officials approved, the ordination ceremony was carried out, and this was known as ordination through the favor of the emperor. With reference to the second method, purchase of the ordination certificates, the government during certain periods of financial stringency offered such certificates for sale to the public, and those who bought the certificates could then go through the ordination ceremony. This was indeed an easy way to join the *sangha*, for all that was necessary was the required amount of money to purchase the certificate; no knowledge of the religion was required.

During periods when the central government was strong in China, the civil authorities not only interfered with the ordination of monks but also supervised the administration of the *sangha*. In the central government was a bureau charged with control over the census of monks and the ordination of the clergy. Under some dynasties there were offices organized to oversee the affairs of the *sangha*, headed by a chief of monks appointed by the emperor. By virtue of this appointment, the chief of monks became a member of the imperial bureaucracy, and acknowledged the supremacy of the civil authorities over the religious. During the T'ang Dynasty (seventh to tenth centuries), when Buddhism was enjoying its apogee in China, an office designated as the Commissioner of Religion was created in the capital, whose duties were concerned with activities that earn merits, such as erecting statues of the Buddha, constructing temples and monasteries, and so forth. The holders of this post were not monks but powerful eunuchs. In the provinces there were monk administrators appointed by the government and exercising jurisdiction over the local monasteries and temples, but these were usually under the supervision of the local civil officials. Monks had to render homage to the emperor just as any other Chinese subject did, even though this was against the Buddhist injunction that a member of the order should not reverence a householder. On different occasions, the government also took drastic steps to reduce the number of monks in the *sangha* by purging it of undesirable elements and forcing the purged monks to return to the laity.

In one of the Buddhist schools in China, the Ch'an or Zen School, the rule that monks should live on alms was disregarded, and in accordance with the slogan that one who did not do a day's work should not eat, the members of this school cultivated fields or gardens to earn their daily bread. Likewise, the most popular of the Buddhist schools in Japan, the Shin School, permits its priests to marry and have families.

In general, we may say that Mahayana Buddhism broadened the basis of the *sangha*. In Hinayana Buddhism, the Buddha preached mainly to the monks, but in the Mahayana sutras, the Buddha preached to a multitude of listeners, Buddhas and bodhisattvas, gods and demons, laymen and spirits. As long as the bodhisattva has taken his vows, he need not join the *sangha* at all. Moreover, since monks and laymen are potential Buddhas in accordance with the basic Mahayana doctrine, there is no need to assert the superiority of the monk over the layman. Consequently there is not much point in giving up the householder's life for that of the monastery. It is this broader interpretation of the *sangha* that is probably responsible for the relaxing of rules governing the conduct of monks in China and Japan.

This then is the Buddhist *sangha* that is looked upon as the embodiment of the dhamma. Its purpose is two-fold, to provide the best possible conditions for the spiritual advancement of its members, and to proclaim the dhamma to mankind. Whereas in the dhamma there arose a later division between the Hinayana or Lesser Vehicle and the Mahayana or Greater Vehicle, in the monastic community there is no such division, there is only one universal *sangha*. Consequently, even in the Mahayana schools that developed in Tibet and China, the rules of discipline which governed the conduct of monks and nuns are the same as those followed by the Hinayana schools. With minor exceptions, therefore, the *patimokkha* rules recited by the Tibetan and Chinese monks during the fortnightly assembly are similar to those recited by the Theravadin monks in Ceylon and Burma. From the very beginning, the Buddhist monks recognized but one universal brotherhood, and later on, when different schools arose within the religion because of conflicting interpretations of the dhamma, monks who belonged to dissimilar groups still lived and practiced the religious life within the same monastery. Ample evidence of this might be found in the records left behind by Chinese monks who journeyed to India when the religion was still powerful in the latter land. The experience of these Chinese monks in India, and of the Japanese monks in China during the T'ang dynasty also illustrated the universality of the *sangha,* for even though these monks were traveling in strange lands far away from home, they had no difficulty in finding lodging as well as suitable places to carry on their studies of the dhamma. Even today, when so many differences divide the peoples of Asia, this vow of taking refuge in the Buddha still serves as one of the links holding the children of the Sakyan sage together in common brotherhood. The Master himself, if he were to possess any consciousness in nirvana, would indeed be happy that the monastic community he established some 2500 years ago is still so vigorous in so many lands.

CHAPTER 6

The Spread of
Theravada Buddhism

DURING THE FIRST TWO centuries of its existence, Buddhism was confined mainly to the Ganges Valley in eastern India. In the middle of the third century B.C., it burst out of its confinement for new regions to convert, southward across the sea to Ceylon, and northwestward in to Gandhara and Kashmir in northwestern India. The primary impetus to this expansion was furnished by the religious zeal of one of the greatest monarchs in Indian history, King Asoka, who ruled from ca. 274-236 B.C.

King Asoka and Buddhism

All that we know about King Asoka is derived from two main sources, the Buddhist legends concerning him and the lithic records bearing the edicts of the monarch and scattered throughout his vast empire. The difference in the image of Asoka presented by these two sources is indeed remarkable. The Buddhist legends present Asoka as being an active supporter of the Buddhist order of monks, whereas the edicts indicate that he was primarily interested in the religion of the laity. The legends speak of a council convened by him to settle doctrinal differences in

111

the religion, but the edicts make no mention of such a council. If we follow the legends, Asoka was a tyrant who killed his brothers in order to seize the throne, while the edicts inform us that his brothers were still living during his reign. Since the lithic records bear the stamp of authenticity and reliability, we shall draw upon them mainly for the information about Asoka and his activities.

During the early years of Asoka's reign, before he was converted to Buddhism, he must have ruled as any other king of India, indulging in the pleasures of hunting and permitting merry-making by feasting and drinking. In the ninth year of his reign, he sent an expedition to conquer a tiny enclave of Kalinga on the eastern coast of India, which still remained independent up to that time. The horrors engendered by the expedition, which involved the killing of some 100,000 people, filled him with such remorse that he became converted to Buddhism. Henceforth he indulged in no more warfare and devoted the rest of his life to the protection and the propagation of the Buddha's teaching. It was about this time also that he embarked on his practice of inscribing his rescripts on rocks and pillars, for he felt that rocks are durable and offer the best medium for the spread of his message to posterity.

After Asoka's conversion, he decided that his mission was to work for the welfare and happiness of all his subjects. In one edict, he said, "All men are my children, and just as I desire for my children that they may obtain every kind of welfare and happiness both in this world and the next, so do I desire for all men." [26] To fulfill this aim, he had wells dug alongside the well-traveled roads to provide water for travelers and animals, made provisions for the medical care of all living beings, propagated useful plants for their medicinal values, issued regulations restricting the slaughter of animals for food, denounced the excesses of profitless ceremonies in public and private life, and substituted edifying spectacles and pious conferences in place of hunting and holiday excursions. Here indeed is the unique feature of Asoka's reign; for the first time in Indian history a monarch has embarked on a program of social welfare for the benefit of his subjects. Undoubtedly his espousal of Buddhism, a religion of infinite love and compassion for all sentient beings, led him in this direction.

Asoka was not merely contented to enunciate his aims, he also arranged for their implementation. To this end he appointed a special staff of ministers called Chief Commissioners for the Religion for the administration of the program. They were also called upon to work for better relations between members of the different castes, to give assistance to the aged and decrepit, to promote harmony among followers of the various religious sects, to distribute the gifts given by the royal house to religious groups, to promote charitable activities, and to redress misfortunes and wrongs. These commissioners were to circulate over the entire country to carry out their mission of promoting and spreading the teachings of the Buddha.

To manifest his zeal for the religion, Asoka embarked on a pious tour of the sacred sites connected with Buddhism. He visited the birthplace of the Blessed One, and took advantage of the occasion to set up a pillar to commemorate the spot. The inscription on this pillar reads as follows: "By his Sacred and Gracious Majesty the King, consecrated 20 years, coming in person, was worshipped this spot, inasmuch as here was born the Buddha Sakyamuni. A stone bearing a figure was caused to be constructed and a pillar of stone also set up, to show that the Blessed One was born here." [27]

From the contents of the lithic records, what is the nature of the Buddhist religion advocated by Asoka? As seen in the numerous edicts which he issued, the following virtues were repeatedly stressed; goodness, freedom from depravity, compassion, liberality, truthfulness, purity, gentleness, and tolerance. Translated into action, they resulted in non-killing of animals, non-injury to living things, obedience to parents and elders, reverence to teachers, liberality toward friends and acquaintances, and tolerance toward other creeds. Let us take one example, non-killing of animals. At the beginning of his reign, animals were slaughtered for the table and sacrifice, but after his conversion this was reduced to two peacocks and one antelope. From the thirteenth year on, all killing of animals for the royal table was stopped. At the same time he prohibited animal sacrifice in the capital and abolished the royal hunt for pleasure. Later on, an elaborate code for restricting slaughter and mutilation of animals was imposed on all classes. For instance, castration of bulls and rams, and the caponing of cocks became unlawful. All this was to indicate his high regard for the sanctity of life as taught by Buddhism. The spirit of liberality was taken to mean almsgiving to all creeds and faiths. As a personal example, he donated huge sums of money to carve out cave dwellings for the naked ascetics or to restore temples for the brahmans. To his fellow men, however, he felt his greatest gift was the gift of the Buddha's teachings, and it was for the purpose of spreading this gift to as many as possible that he appointed the Commissioners of the Religion. As for religious toleration, he developed this idea fully in one of his inscriptions, in which he exhorted his people to hearken to the teachings of other creeds. He felt that the effects of this would be that although the people would see that the creeds differ from one another in many details, still they would agree on important points. Thus the attention of the people would be drawn to the areas of agreement that would be considered the essentials of all religions. He also felt that by listening to the teachings of another group, one would become learned, possessed of much knowledge, and would be able to evolve his own religious system in a satisfactory manner. Furthermore, knowledge of other creeds would produce restraint in criticizing others, and this would help to promote the sense of unity among the various creeds.

The nature of Asoka's Buddhism may also be determined by an edict in which he recommended seven scriptural texts to be learned and memorized by all monks and laymen. The contents of these texts give us a clue as to what kind of Buddhism appealed to Asoka. What interested him was not the external elements of the religion, the rituals, ceremonies, regulations, and so forth, but the inner growth, self-realization, and cultivation of the religious life. Simple clothing, plain food, humble dwelling, delight in meditation, these are the things that a Buddhist should be content with. In his every day conduct, he should scrutinize carefully every act of body, mind, and speech.

What is the goal for which the religion is to be practiced? Interestingly, Asoka held that the fruit for practicing the religious life was not arhatship or nirvana, but rebirth in one of the Buddhist heavens, which he said was attainable by the accumulation of merits through the performance of deeds for the welfare of mankind.

It is this simple nature of the goal and the teachings which Asoka stressed that have puzzled many students of Buddhism, and have even led some people to suggest that the monarch was not a Buddhist at all, but only a true Indian monarch teaching the ideas common to all Indian creeds and performing the duties prescribed for Indian kings. To support this contention, such people point to the fact that nowhere in the lithic records is there any mention of such fundamental Buddhist teachings as the four truths, the eight-fold path, dependent origination, nirvana, and so forth. Such a conclusion is not justified by the evidence, however. In one edict, Asoka declares his faith in the Three Jewels, Buddha, dhamma, and *sangha*, and in another, he speaks of being a faithful layman for over two years, and then living in a monastic community and working actively for over a year. Additional evidence that Asoka was a Buddhist may be seen in his pious tour to the sacred spots of Buddhism, and in his attachment to the Buddhist symbols such as the elephant (signifying the conception of the Buddha), the horse (signifying the great renunciation), and the wheel (signifying the propagation of the doctrine), which were used prominently on the Asokan pillars. If he were a Buddhist, then why did he not mention the fundamental doctrines usually associated with Buddhism? The most plausible explanation appears to be by the time of Asoka, Buddhism had already developed into a religion at two levels, the monastic order for the monks, and the laity for those who wanted to be followers of the Buddha but did not wish to become monks. Asoka for the greater portion of his life was a devout Buddhist layman, and he was merely emphasizing those aspects of Buddhism which were acceptable and applicable to the laymen. For those in the monastic order, the main teach-inks would be the four noble truths, the eight-fold path, and nirvana, but for the layman, the stress was on those virtues which could be practiced in ordinary daily lives, with rebirth in heaven as the goal.

As a result of Asoka's conversion and promotion of Buddhism, the moral tone of his empire was undoubtedly improved. There was a greater respect for life. His emphasis on tolerance resulted in a greater cosmopolitanism and humanitarianism among the Indians. Much more important for the Buddhist historian was his role in extending the sphere of the religion not only to other parts of India but also to the outside world. In one rock edict, it is said that Asoka dispatched missionaries to countries in the Mediterranean region, Syria, Cyrene, Macedon, Egypt, and Epirus. Some doubts have been cast on the authenticity of these missions to the Hellenistic world, on the ground that not one bit of information has been found in the Greek records concerning such missionary efforts from India. However, the missions are not as implausible as it may seem. Asoka did have extensive diplomatic relations with some of the Greek kings. Greek envoys from the Seleucid Kingdom in the Mesopotamian region and from Ptolemy of Egypt were stationed in the Asokan capital. Along with the diplomatic agents which Asoka sent to the distant Hellenistic countries, it is very possible that propagators of the religion were also dispatched to minister to the needs of the members of the embassy but also to preach to the local people if the occasion should arise.

Of much more importance to the spread of Buddhism was the dispatch of Buddhist missionaries not to the distant Mediterranean region but to the areas adjacent to India. It was during the reign of Asoka that such missionaries introduced the religion to northwest India, south India, and Ceylon. The conversion of Ceylon is attributed to Asoka's own son and daughter, Mahinda and Sanghamitta. From northwest India the religion was then carried into central Asia and eventually to the civilized countries of the Far East, China, Korea, and Japan, and from south India

and Ceylon, it was transmitted to the countries of southeast
Asia, Burma, Thailand and Cambodia.

Ceylon

According to the chronicles of Ceylon, Tissa, king of Ceylon,
sent a mission to King Asoka soliciting his friendship. In response to this, Asoka not only sent some presents but also seized
the opportunity to put in a favorable word about Buddhism and
recommended that the Ceylonese adopt the religion. Without
even waiting for a reply from the Ceylonese about his recom-
mendation, he sent his son Mahinda as a missionary to Ceylon.
Mahinda was soon joined by his sister Sanghamitta and the two
working together succeeded in converting the king and the court
ladies to Buddhism. Sanghamitta took along with her to Ceylon
a branch of the bodhi tree, and the tree in Anuradhapura now
venerated by the Ceylonese is regarded as the outgrowth of that
branch.

After its introduction into Ceylon in the middle of the third
century B.C., the history of the religion was one of growth and
development until the fifth century A.D. in a country that was
rich and at peace. This prosperity of the religion was reflected
in the magnificence of the temples and the splendor of the festivals celebrated throughout the island. The Chinese traveler Fa-
hsien, who was in Ceylon during the early years of the fifth
century, furnishes vivid testimony of the flourishing and prosperous state of Buddhism. For instance, he writes that there
were sixty thousand monks in the land, that the king always prepared a supply of food sufficient to feed about five thousand
monks at any time, and that whenever a monk wanted to be
fed, all he needed to do was to go to the proper place with his
almsbowl and take as much as he pleased.

From the sixth to the eleventh centuries, the religion suffered
a period of decline as a result of internal political dissensions
and external invasions by the Tamils from south India. After a
temporary revival of the religion between the twelfth and fourteenth centuries, Buddhism again succumbed to a period of eclipse

brought about first by the further invasions of the Tamils, and then after that by the domination of European powers, Portugal (ca. 1540-1658), Holland (1658-1795), and finally England (after 1795). The Portuguese attempted to convert the Ceylonese to Catholicism, and to this end pursed a policy of ruthless destruction of monasteries and libraries, pillage of temple treasures, and execution of any monk found wearing the yellow robe. After the Portuguese had been expelled, there were no more than five fully ordained monks in the entire island. Monks from Burma had to be invited to go to Ceylon to restore the order and to reinstate and validate the ordination ceremonies.

The Dutch pursued a different policy from that of the Portuguese. Instead of trying to convert the Ceylonese, they showed little concern for the religious and educational welfare of the people, as they were more interested in trade and profits. The Ceylonese, however, in an attempt to be on good terms with the Dutch, sought conversion to Protestant Christianity in large numbers, and this tendency affected the fortunes of the Buddha *sangha* adversely. Such conversions to Christianity in order to acquire civil status and honors continued under the British, with the result that there was a large number of so called government Christians. By far the greatest danger to Buddhism under the British was the horde of Christian missionaries who poured into the island with the proclamation of religious liberty by the British. The schools which these Christian missionaries established sought to demonstrate to the Ceylonese "the subtle errors of their idolatry, to expose the absurdities of their religion, and to bring home to them the civilizing influences of Christian life." [28]

In order to preserve their traditional Buddhist heritage against the onslaughts of the Christian missionaries, the Buddhists in Ceylon launched their counteroffensive during the latter half of the nineteenth century. The movement was first led by a gifted young Ceylonese monk named Mohottivatte Gunananda, who was clever enough to study the Christian scriptures and the rationalist writings of the west critical of Christianity. Armed with these anti-Christian arguments, Gunananda went from village to village preaching against the missionaries and advocating a return to Buddhism. Possessed of tremendous energy and a powerful attractive personality, he attracted thousands of listeners wherever he went. Emboldened by this success, he challenged the Christian missionaries to a debate on the relative merits of the two religions. The challenge was accepted and a series of debates were held in 1866, 1871, and 1873. Alone, Gunananda defended his faith against some of the foremost Christian missionaries of the time. These debates aroused intense interest among the Buddhists and to them their champion was the victor in the debates.

In far away America an American named Henry S. Olcott read about the debates and with his curiosity aroused, he journeyed to Ceylon to study Buddhism. Convinced that Buddhism was one of the most sublime religions created by man, he formed a Buddhist Theosophical Society in Ceylon in 1880 for the purpose of establishing schools throughout Ceylon to offer instruction in Buddhism. The program sponsored by this society contributed further to the awakening of interest in Buddhism among the Ceylonese.

There was still a third individual, Dharmapala, who was instrumental in reforming and reviving the religion. Stirred by the activities of Gunananda, Dharmapala yearned to do something for his fellow Ceylonese. To this end he took the vows of a monk, but he chose to live in the world instead of in the monastery, for he believed that only by so doing could he preach the dhamma to his people. For the purpose of achieving his program, he organized the Mahabodhi Society in 1891, the aims of which were:

(1) to make known and disseminate the sublime teachings of the Buddha to all the world.
(2) to help the cause of Buddhist religious education in Ceylon.
(3) to train young men of unblemished character to carry abroad the message of Buddhism.
(4) to revive Buddhism in India by establishing colleges and monasteries at such places as Benares and Calcutta.

He urged his fellow Ceylonese to do the things worthwhile doing, for to him Buddhism is not a passive religion but is one characterized by activity such as alertness against lust, passions, anger, and pride. He criticized the Ceylonese monks who lived lives of idleness and aloofness in the monasteries, and charged that they were not exemplifying the spirit of the Buddha who exhorted his disciples to go forth to preach for the good and welfare of the many.

Through the activities of these individuals and the societies which they formed, Buddhism regained its position of supremacy in Ceylon. According to the census of 1953 there were over five million Buddhists as against one million five hundred thousand Hindus, seven hundred thousand Christians, and five hundred fifty thousand Moslems.

From the very beginning of its history in Ceylon, Buddhism was the state religion of the island kingdom, and only a Buddhist could become the ruling king. To the Ceylonese, Buddhism exerted a protective influence over the island, repelling the inroads of foreign encroachments. The king was regarded as the secular head of the Buddhist organization. One of the Ceylonese kings during the tenth century declared that it was his duty to protect and defend the almsbowl and the robe of the Buddha. The term *parinibbuta,* used to denote the death of the Buddha, was sometimes applied to the death of the king. Whenever the doctrine became tainted or corrupt, the king initiated a movement to purify it, and likewise, it was his responsibility to settle disputes that might arise within the monastic community. However, if his decisions were contrary to the wishes of the monks, the latter sometimes disregarded them.

From an early date the Buddhist monks took advantage of the fact that Buddhism was the state religion to meddle in politics. Often they manipulated behind the scenes to have their favorite candidate chosen as ruler even though he was not the rightful heir to the throne. So powerful did the monastic order become during some periods that it claimed to be the organ expressing the will of the people, and that its approval was necessary for the coronation of a king. Mindful of the influence of the order, the king courted the favor of the monks and sometimes held the coronation services in the Buddhist temples.

The Buddhist temples shared in the favored status enjoyed by the clerical order. Temple property was considered inviolate and theft or destruction of such property was punishable by death. Temples were usually supported by the state through taxes and fines. The relics brought to Ceylon, such as the almsbowl, tooth, and hair of the Buddha, and the bodhi tree transplanted in Ceylon from a branch taken from the sacred tree at Bodhgaya, were also considered as state property.

The long history of involvement by Buddhists in the affairs of state serves to explain why, even after the monarchy has been abolished, the monks are still deeply engaged in political activities, forming political parties, and disseminating political propaganda. In 1956, when Ceylon achieved independence from England, a Buddhist party came into existence, and in conjunction with two other parties formed a coalition government that chose S.W.R.D. Bandaranaike as premier, and advocated a neutralist policy in international politics and a Sinhalese nationalist Buddhism at home. In May 1959, a split occurred within the coalition, and the premier, steering a complicated course to maintain power, alienated some of his Buddhist followers. A fanatic Buddhist monk, angered by the premier's attempt to work out some sort of compromise with the hated Tamils, assassinated him on Sept. 25, 1959. The monk was executed in 1962, but just before execution he was baptized as a Christian so that he, in his own words, could ask for the forgiveness which Buddhism could not give him.

Undoubtedly the most famous Buddhist relic in Ceylon is the tooth of the Blessed One kept in Kandy. Buddhist traditions say that after the cremation of the Buddha seven pieces of relics, including four teeth, were recovered from the ashes and not included in the distribution of relics among the eight contending cities. The later history of the four teeth makes fascinating reading, with fact and fiction intertwined inextricably, and national interests being added to stoke up the fires of controversy. According to the Chinese traditions, for instance, one of the four teeth was taken to one of the heavens, another to the kingdom of the sea serpents under the ocean, another went to Ceylon, and the fourth found its way to China. This was said to have been recovered in China, and is now on display in Peking. It was loaned to the Burmese for exhibition in 1955, and to the Ceylonese in 1961. All over the Far East, however, there are temples which claim to have one of these sacred teeth, and if one were to add up the number of such claimants, the sum would be many times four, in fact, many times the number of teeth in a human being.

According to Ceylonese traditions concerning their famous relic tooth, it was recovered from the funeral pyre and given to the king of Kalinga on the east coast of India, who enshrined it in a temple at Dantapura. Sometime during the fourth century, when an attack on Dantapura was imminent, the tooth was taken to Ceylon, where it was received with profuse honors by the Ceylonese king and deposited in a temple within the capital. Once every year it would be taken out and paraded through the streets. According to the Chinese traveler Fa-hsien, who witnessed the parade in ca. 413, a man mounted on a lavishly decorated elephant rode about the city proclaiming that the procession would take place ten days hence. On the appointed day, the main street in the capital was swept clean and smooth, and strewn with an abundance of flowers. On both sides of the street were pictorial representations of the five hundred previous rebirths of the Buddha. For ninety days the celebrations continued, with monks and laymen participating in the ceremonies of venerating the relic.

From the time of its arrival in Ceylon, the tooth was regarded as a symbol of good omen for the country. Whenever the court moved the capital from one place to another, the tooth was always moved also, and often housed in a palace more magnificent than that occupied by the ruler. It was always kept under close guard after an attempted theft was made by a Chinese monk in the seventh century. This Chinese was at first welcomed and treated well by the Ceylonese, but one day he was apprehended with the sacred tooth in his possession. After this, the most elaborate precautions were taken to ensure that no such incident would be repeated.

The later history of the tooth in Ceylon is filled with intriguing complications. Early in the fourteenth century it was carried away by the Tamil invaders, and no sooner was it recovered than the Portuguese were said to have pounded it to pieces in their campaign to obliterate Buddhism in Ceylon. However, the action of the Portuguese did not destroy the tooth, instead two rival claimants to the Ceylonese kingship asserted that they possessed the genuine one, while that destroyed by the Portuguese was a fake. In 1592 the tooth preserved in Kandy was accepted as the genuine specimen.

Closely associated with the history of Buddhism in Ceylon are two monasteries, the Mahavihara and the Abhayagiri, both located in the ancient capital of Anuradhapura. The former was founded by King Tissa upon the advice of Mahinda, and for many centuries after its establishment it was the acknowledged center of Theravada learning. Numerous scholars from various Buddhist countries flocked to this center, the most famous being Buddhaghosa (fifth century A.D.) who familiarized himself with the whole of the Theravada tradition and wrote his authoritative commentaries there.

Approximately two hundred years after its establishment a dispute arose within the ranks of the monks living in the Mahavihara over a very minor question of whether or not monks could visit lay families. The majority of the monks voted against the practice and expelled those who had made such visits. Thus we see from the very beginning that the attitude of the Mahavihara monks was one of conservatism and strict orthodoxy. The expelled monks met by themselves to form a new monastery called the Abhayagiri, which rapidly grew in importance, wealth, and stature that it soon rivaled the Mahavihara. At the time Fa-hsien was in Ceylon during the early years of the fifth century, there were three thousand monks in the Mahavihara and five thousand in the Abhayagiri. The later history of these two institutions was marked by intense rivalry between them, and whenever one won the ruler over to its cause, then it plundered and looted the buildings and property of the other.

With the invasion and the capture of the capital Anuradhapura by the Tamils in the tenth century, the devastation wrought on the two monasteries was complete. The center of Ceylonese Buddhism for over a thousand years was systematically destroyed by the invaders, and in that once great religious, intellectual, and social citadel of Buddhism there was no ordination of monks for five years. After the Ceylonese had succeeded in driving out the invaders in 1071, one of the first tasks to which the Ceylonese addressed themselves was the reconstruction and reestablishment of the Mahavihara, so that it was soon restored to leadership once more. From that time on, in spite of the ups and downs of the religion in the island, the Mahavihara has retained its dominant position as the center of Theravada scholarship. It owes this position to the fact that the first missionary to Ceylon, Mahinda was associated with its establishment. Since Mahinda had been ordained as a Buddhist monk in India and then introduced the ordination ceremonies to the Mahavihara, the Ceylonese monks believe that the Mahavihara alone has preserved the legitimate line of apostolic succession, and that the ordination ceremonies were valid only when conferred by the Mahavihara monks.

Burma

Tradition has it that Buddhism was introduced into Burma during the reign of Asoka. This tradition is based on the identification of Burma with a land called Suvannabhumi, or the Golden Land, but this identification is by no means reliable. It is only in the fifth century A.D. that we are on firm grounds concerning the presence of Buddhism in Burma. In 1926 a number of gold plates bearing Pali inscriptions were discovered in the country, and on these gold plates we find the well-known Buddhist formula, "The dhamma of which the origin and cause has been preached by the Buddha, their cessation had also been spoken by the Great Sage." A number of passages from the Buddhist canon were also quoted. This epigraphic evidence, all dating back to the fifth century, and some Buddhist sculpture also datable to the same period, point to the presence of a flourishing Buddhist community in South or Lower Burma, and that the followers belonged to the Theravada tradition. Further evidence of the existence of Buddhists in Burma was furnished by the Chinese traveler I-tsing during the latter part of the seventh century.

The Theravada community prospered in Lower Burma until the middle of the eleventh century, when an invasion from Upper Burma suddenly disturbed the peace of the region and resulted in the absorption of Lower Burma by Upper Burma. For the background of this invasion, it is necessary to shift our attention to Upper Burma. In this region another form of Buddhism had been in vogue, Mahayana in tendency and belonging very likely to the Tantric tradition. The followers of this brand of Buddhism were called Aris, and they were described in the local chronicles as a sect which had rejected the teachings of the master, believed that one could escape the effects of karma by reciting magic formulas, and made a practice of sending virgins to priests before marriage. In the area were found also numerous figures of the Mahayana bodhisattvas, Avalokitesvara, Maitreya, and Manjusri. On the walls of some temples, pictures of deities in embrace with their consorts were also painted, another indication of the Tantric nature of the Buddhism practiced.

When Upper Burma set out to invade Lower Burma during the eleventh century, there were these two brands, Tantric Buddhism in the north and Theravada Buddhism in the south. The invasion itself was rooted in a religious issue, with a prominent role played by a Theravada monk, Shin Arahan.

Shin Arahan was a well-known cleric in Lower Burma before he went north to preach to the king of Upper Burma, Anawrahta. After hearing the exposition of the Theravada doctrine, the king was convinced of its superiority over the Ari teachings and embraced it. Now he decided to propagate his newly acquired teachings throughout the entire kingdom. He was unable to do so, however, for lack of Buddhist texts. Shin Arahan informed him that in Lower Burma there was an abundance of such texts and suggested that he ask the king of Lower Burma for some of them. The latter was intent on keeping the scriptures to himself and refused the request. Angered by this refusal, Anawrahta invaded Lower Burma, seized the capital and the king, and carried away some thirty sets of the canon. With the Theravada canon now in his possession, Anawrahta introduced an intensive campaign to spread Theravada teachings over the opposition of the Aris.

The conquest of Lower by Upper Burma marks a significant event in Burmese history, for it signified the union of the two regions under one ruler, and the beginning of authentic Burmese history. Shin Arahan was made chief of the religion by Anawrahta and the fame of Burma as a center of Theravada Buddhism began. Under the patronage of the dynasty inaugurated by Anawrahta, Buddhism followers began building the thousands of temples in Pagan, the capital, of which the most famous is the Ananda Temple, a masterpiece of Burmese architecture. These temples were supported by generous donations of villages, land, animals, and even slaves from the people.

During the reign of the Anawrahta dynasty, there arose within the Burmese community a controversy over the apostolic succession. The older Burmese school of Theravada Buddhism claimed that it had received the direct transmission of the law from India through missionaries sent out by King Asoka, and consequently it claimed to be the only community authorized to validate the ordination ceremonies. Another group of Burmese monks who had been to Ceylon and received ordination there claimed that they were the authorized body, since they were in the direct line of transmission from Mahinda. The controversy lasted for nearly three hundred years until a king named Dhammaceti settled it in favor of the Ceylonese tradition. This king believed that the Mahavihara was the only center of Theravada Buddhism which had remained pure and unsullied throughout the centuries.

This link with the Mahavihara tradition firmly established

the tone of Burmese Buddhism. As we have seen, the Mahavi-hara stands for orthodoxy, purity of life and conduct, and monastic consolidation. The Burmese Buddhists are thoroughly committed to this conservatism. Consequently the Burmese are less concerned with metaphysical speculations and more with a strict adherence to the rules of discipline. All the major movements of reform, and all the controversies within the community, were connected in one way or another with the rules of discipline. The Burmese accepted the Theravada tradition without question and adhered strictly to the letter of the teachings. As for the rules of discipline, there were occasional instances of laxity in observance, but movements for reform always arose immediately to restore purity in the monastic community, and such movements invariably had the support of the ruling house. Since its introduction into Burma, Buddhist monasticism has changed very little, and we can safely say that of all the Theravada countries in southeast Asia, Burma is the country where Theravada Buddhism is preserved in its purest form.

As the dominant force in Burma, Buddhism has wielded a tremendous role in Burmese history. In the first place, it exerted a great civilizing force, for it converted a rude uncivilized people to a highly cultured one sharing in the general stream of Buddhist culture and producing some of the most authoritative interpretations of Buddhism. Secondly, the religion has acted as a catalytic force knitting together the different ethnic groups into one united nation. In the third place, the religion has helped to spread education. It was the Buddhist monk who taught the art of reading and writing and who conducted schools in the Buddhist temples. Until recent times, every Burmese boy had to spend a certain period of time in the monastery as a novice, and no one was considered mature unless he had done so. More than anything else, this program of education has been responsible for the tremendous influence which the religion wields over Burmese society. The Burmese strive to live up to the moral standards emphasized by the religion, they are peaceful and honest, they are kind to each other and to strangers. Cruelty to animals is abhorred, and little acts of kindness are often met with.

Finally the religion has provided pageantry, color, and variety to the daily lives of the Burmese. The numerous Buddhist festivals throughout the year, all centered in the temple, furnish an opportunity to the people to express themselves in music and dances, thus providing for an element of gaiety and fun.

The leadership of Burma among Theravada countries was demonstrated clearly by her convening the Sixth Great Council of Buddhism which was held in Rangoon for two years and which ended on the twenty-fifth hundredth anniversary of the Buddha's nirvana (May 1956). In calling this council, the Burmese issued an invitation to the Buddhists all over the world to cooperate in the task of devising some measures for the spiritual and moral well-being of mankind as would remove all traces of greed, hatred, and delusion, which they claim are the root of all violence and destruction in the world. The government of Burma also hoped that the Council would establish a great Buddhist university to serve as the seat of Buddhist learning which would spread the wisdom, truth, and righteousness of Buddhism to the rest of the world. The main task of the council, however, was to reexamine and collate the texts found in the different Theravada countries with the idea of translating them eventually into such modern languages as Burmese, Hindi, and English.

Thailand

Even before the Thai state was founded, the region now occupied by the country was already exposed to Buddhist influence emanating from Lower Burma before the seventh century. In the eleventh century, after King Anawrahta had adopted Theravada Buddhism, he invaded and conquered northern Thailand and introduced his newly acquired religion to the conquered region. Thus, when the Thai people, who are of Mongol stock, settled in what is now Thailand during the twelfth and thirteenth centuries after having been driven out of the Chinese southwestern province of Yunnan, they entered a region already strongly influenced by Buddhism. They adopted the already established religion, and when they formed the Thai kingdom in 1238, they accepted it as their state religion.

With the rise of the Sokhotai kingdom in the thirteenth century, Buddhism began to flourish, especially in the capital of Ayuthia, which was filled with beautiful edifices and images dedicated to the Buddha. About 1360, the king dispatched a mission to Ceylon with a request that a senior Ceylonese monk be dispatched to Thailand to preside over and validate the ordination ceremony. When this was done, the Thai monks also claimed that they could trace a direct line of descent to Mahinda, and by so doing, acknowledged the authority of the Mahavihara tradition.

Though the Thai kingdom upheld Buddhism as the state religion, they embarked on a number of occasions on adventures which were contrary to the spirit of Buddhism. Taking advantage of the military weakness of neighboring Burma and Cambodia, Thai forces repeatedly invaded those two countries during the thirteenth and fourteenth centuries, and went so far as to destroy the magnificent Cambodian city of Angkor Wat. The day of reckoning finally came, however. The initial invasion by Burmese troops occurred in the sixteenth century, but not much damage was done on this occasion. In 1766-1767, the Burmese again invaded Thailand, and this time, the victorious Burmese army behaved like any other marauding force, for after the troops had captured Ayuthia, they systematically destroyed the temples of their own faith, hacked the beautiful images of the Buddha to bits, and carried off whatever gold they could obtain after melting the Buddha images. So completely destroyed was the capital that when the Thai people recovered it in 1782, they decided to forsake it and built a new capital in Bangkok, the present capital.

At present, Theravada Buddhism is still the state religion of Thailand. In 1959, there were 21,380 Buddhist temples and about 250,000 monks and novices, the highest number in any country in Southeast Asia. The king must be a Buddhist, and he is the highest authority in all matters pertaining to the order. During his early youth it is customary for the king to spend a certain length of time in a monastery, and this personal experience binds him closely to the religion. Formerly all young men in the country also spent a few months studying in the temples, and though this practice is still followed, it is not as widespread as before.

The Thai monks on the whole enjoy a good reputation among the people. They live pure, moral lives and are faithful to the rules of discipline. They are also diligent in their efforts to improve their educational level. Before ordination, they must attain a certain level of proficiency in the canon, and after ordination they are still encouraged to study further in order to qualify for the higher examinations. In recent years, when a law was passed requiring military service of all young Thai, there was a sudden influx of young men into the monasteries, whereupon the civil authorities passed another law specifying that a monk cannot escape military service unless he has passed the first of nine established grades of examination. This first examination is not a simple affair, for it involved four different tests on successive days concerning the doctrines of the religion, the rules of proper living, the life of the Buddha, and the rules of discipline.

Before Thailand established a modern system of education, the Buddhist monasteries provided the instruction to boys living in the vicinity of the institution. When the system was first established, the monasteries and temples were pressed into service as classrooms and the monks as teachers. Religious education is still provided for in all the schools, with textbooks on Buddhist ethics and doctrines being used for all grades.

Cambodia

While the present form of Buddhism in Cambodia is Theravada, this was not so for a long time, for the earliest influences in that region were Hinduism and Mahayana Buddhism. Monuments found in Cambodia dating from the first to the seventh centuries show strong Hindu influences, and the kings of this period bore Sanskrit names. From 800 to 1400 Cambodia was the most powerful kingdom in Indo-China, and it was then that the Cambodians created those masterpieces of art and architecture in Angkor Wat. The temples and monuments in this fabulous city were mostly dedicated to Hindu and Mahayana deities.

After the fourteenth century, a change began to take place. The neighboring kingdom of Thai was established in the thirteenth century and began to exert some influence over the religious history of Cambodia. As early as the end of the thirteenth century, the Chinese traveler Chou Ta-kuan visited Cambodia and reported Hinayana was gradually replacing the Mahayana aspect. The invasions and conquest of the country by the Thai hastened the process, for the Cambodians began to borrow heavily from the victorious Thai. After the capture of Angkor Wat by the Thai, the Cambodians abandoned it to their enemies, and when the Thai armies left, the jungle took over. From the fourteenth to the nineteenth centuries the jungle did not reveal its secret of the glory of Angkor Wat. In the middle of the nineteenth century a French botanist in search of exotic plants accidentally stumbled over the ruins and saw to his amazement the remains of the magnificent architecture and sculpture which the Cambodians had created during the peak of their history. Since that time the slow tedious task of reclaiming the imposing Buddhist edifices, images, galleries, chapels, and cloisters from the tenacles of the jungles has proceeded apace, and now one is able to visit the ruins and admire the legacy of the Cambodians when they were at the peak of their power.

Today, the Cambodians themselves claim that their country is about 99% Theravada Buddhist, with some 2800 monasteries and 82,000 monks and novices. The religion enjoys the enthusiastic support of the royal family, which has contributed generously to the establishment of Buddhist schools and libraries throughout the kingdom.

Vietnam

Geographically, Vietnam should be included in southeast Asia, but as far as Buddhism is concerned, it is more closely identified with Chinese Mahayana Buddhism than with the Theravada tradition. Strictly speaking, therefore, this short discussion of Buddhism in Vietnam should be included in the chapter on Buddhism in China, but for the sake of geography, it was finally decided to insert the discussion in this chapter, even though Vietnamese Buddhism is not Theravada Buddhism.

As early as the first century A.D., Buddhism was introduced into Vietnam via the sea route. By the end of the second century there was already a flourishing Buddhist community, whose presence is attested by a Chinese convert living in the area. He wrote that the Buddhist monks shaved their heads, wore the saffron-colored robes, ate once a day, and guarded their senses.

Down to about 1000 A.D., Vietnam was under the domination of China, and even after the country achieved her independence, she still looked admiringly at the culture and institutions of her huge neighbor. Chinese cultural influence was the leading factor in Vietnamese life. Of the Vietnamese, the Buddhist monks were the only large group who studied assiduously Chinese language and literature, mainly for the purpose of gaining access to the voluminous mass of Chinese translations of the Buddhist canon. Consequently the leaders of the country were drawn mainly from the ranks of the educated Buddhist monks, who were familiar with the Chinese language and consequently acquainted with the whole body of Chinese learning.

During this period of Chinese cultural domination, the Ch'an School of Chinese Buddhism was introduced into the country, and three branches of the school developed and flourished. This Ch'an School has remained dominant down to the present, although in recent years the Pure Land School has made some headway in winning followers.

Today it is estimated that about seventy-five percent of the Vietnamese are Buddhists.

Java

Buddhism is no longer practiced in Java, but there was a period in the previous history of the island when the Mahayana

Buddhism commanded the respect and attention of the ruling dynasty and the common people. It was under the Sailendra Dynasty, which ruled from the seventh to the ninth centuries, that Mahayana Buddhism was the dominant religion of the Javanese, and as visible evidence of their faith, the Sailendra kings built that masterpiece of Buddhist art and architecture, the Borobudur, which still stands today as one of the artistic wonders of Asia.

Decline of Buddhism in India

Even as Buddhism was making its way into the countries of southeast Asia, it was slowly fading away in its homeland. With the passing of the Madhyamika and Vijnanavada masters of the seventh century, the religion was gradually being submerged under the overwhelming force of Hinduism in India. In a way, this process was hastened by the Buddhists themselves. During the previous centuries, Mahayana Buddhism incorporated many of the Hindu deities into its pantheon in an attempt to gain adherents among the populace. This accommodation with Hinduism resulted in many Hindus looking upon Buddhism as just another sect of Hinduism, and the Buddha was regarded as just another of the numerous incarnations of Vishnu, the protector and sustainer of the world. With the invasion of the Moslems in the eleventh century, the final blows were administered to the religion. The Moslems initially invaded and overran northwest India in 1001, and on this occasion they destroyed the Buddhist temples, libraries and manuscripts, and iconography in that area. In 1193, they captured Magadha, the heartland of Buddhism in India, and with the destruction of Buddhist institutions in that area, Buddhism as a religious and intellectual force disappeared in India.

CHAPTER 7

Buddhism in China

EVER SINCE THEY ESTABLISHED their civilizations in their respective areas, India and China, the population giants of Asia, have enjoyed millenniums of peace in their relations with each other until the border warfare of 1962. Separated by the towering Himalayas, the Abode of Snow, the two countries walked their individual paths, developing contrasting ideals of life and modes of living. The Chinese philosophers were intensely interested in the problems of this mundane life, how to improve human relations, how to make their social institutions stable, how to create a just and enduring political system. Their world was very much limited by what they experienced in the present life. Chinese society was characterized by a remarkable degree of social mobility. By ability and by conquest a bandit could become the founder of a new dynasty and the head of the imperial family, while by education a son of the soil could rise to become the prime minister of the land. The Chinese thinkers insisted that all able bodied men and women should marry and beget children, and that they should engage in some sort of work which would produce goods for others to use and to enjoy. This life is something good and is to be lived to the utmost. In contrast the Indian philosophers were concerned primarily with problems of the mind and spirit, such as the nature of the supreme impersonal creator of the universe, the wisdom uniting man with that creator, the quest for supreme wisdom that is beyond duality, and so forth. In their fanciful and mystical speculations, they peopled the universe with countless word systems, they extended the life-duration of an individual through successive rebirths, and they created heavens and hells that the earth-bound Chinese never dreamt about. Society was stratified into the four castes and the outcasts. Life was characterized by misery and suffering and the purpose of life was to escape from it. Celibacy and mendicancy were proclaimed as the highest ideals of life. Between these two great civilizations so different from one another, the sublime religion of love and compassion and the oneness of mankind taught by the Buddha served as a bridge for well-nigh a thousand years.

The impetus responsible for the initial thrust of Buddhism that was finally to result in the introduction of the religion to China is the same as that which pushed the religion to south India and Ceylon, namely the missionary activities during the reign of Asoka. These missionary activities resulted in the propagation of the religion in Gandhara and Kashmir in northwest India. During the first centuries before and after Christ, that region was under the sway of a strong Kushan dynasty started by a race of people known as the Scythians of Indo-European origin. Of the Kushan kings who ruled over this vast empire, the most famous was King Kanishka, who lived during the first or the second century after Christ, and whose conversion to Buddhism is attested by both epigraphic and numismatic evidences. Using the bases established in Gandhara and Kashmir, Buddhist missionaries began spreading out to propagate their religion in various central Asiatic kingdoms, and it was only a matter of time before they would reach the populous Chinese empire in the east.

A traveler who wished to make the overland route to China from India at that time usually started from northwest India. His travels would take him to Afghanistan, then across the Hindukush Mountains, to the Pamirs Plateau before stopping at Kashgar. At this point he rested while deciding which route to take from then on. He could travel on the northern route which skirted the northern fringes of the Takla-makan Desert, or the southern route which followed the southern edge of the desert. The two routes converged on Tunhuang, a Chinese outpost on the Chinese northwest frontier. Besides the central Asiatic highway, there were two other land routes, though these were seldom used. One passed through Assam through Upper Burma into Yunnan in southwest China, while the other took one through Nepal and Tibet to western China. It was also possible to travel by the sea route, which followed closely the coastline around the Malay Peninsula to south China.

It is likely that by the first century before Christ commercial travelers were already making the hazardous journey across the sands of central Asia to the populous Chinese Empire in the east. In the wake of these commercial travelers some Buddhist monks followed. Eventually one or a few of them arrived in China to become the pioneers in a movement of cultural interchange and transformation that is without parallel in human history.

It is not known definitely just when the religion was first introduced into China. One of the most widely circulated versions, which the Buddhists themselves generally hold to be historical, was that the Indian religion was introduced as the aftermath of a dream which Emperor Ming (ruled 58-75 A.D.) of the Han dynasty had. However, there is evidence that a Buddhist community already existed in east China even before the dream took place. Moreover, as early as 2 B.C., an oral transmission of the Buddha's teaching was said to have made by a Scythian to a Chinese. We would be safe in saying that by the first century A.D. Buddhism had already appeared on the Chinese scene.

China at that time was ruled by the great Han dynasty which had been in power since 206 B.C. The ideology which the Han emperors upheld was Confucianism, a system of political and ethical teachings embodied in a corpus of classics left behind by ancient Chinese sages and arranged in a systematic order by Confucius, who lived in the sixth century B.C. According to this system, the ruler was the Son of Heaven who ruled in accordance with the mandate of heaven. This mandate required that he rule for the welfare of the people under him, so that the people would enjoy peace, prosperity, order, and justice. If he failed to rule for the welfare of the people, he was said to have lost the heavenly mandate, and the people were justified to rise up against him and install another ruler in his place. To assist the ruler in his administration, a body of officials was chosen who were proficient in the Confucian classics. These scholar-officials were the experts on the norms of proper conduct which every one in society had to follow. As long as each member of society performed the functions that pertained to his status, orderly, stable, and harmonious government would prevail. Confucius once said that when the ruling prince ruled, the ministers ministered, the fathers behaved as fathers should, and sons conducted themselves as sons should, then orderly government would prevail. It was the duty of the ruler and the officials to rule and to lead, and that of the common people to follow and obey. By word and by deed, the ruling class should indicate to the masses what to believe and how to behave.

When Buddhism appeared in China, this Confucianism was the dominant ideology, and in order to make some headway among the Chinese, the new religion allied itself with another native system, Taoism. During the Han dynasty, Taoism had already developed its two aspects, Taoism as a philosophy and Taoism as a religion of salvation. As a philosophy, Taoism is concerned with the metaphysical *tao* or the natural law of the universe. This *tao* brings all things into existence and governs their every action. The aim of the Taoist philosopher is to achieve union with this *tao,* and since the *tao* is said to be eternal, everlasting, and unchanging, the individual achieving unity with it also achieves eternity. Taoism as a religion on the other hand was concerned with achieving immortality of this material body. To achieve this end, the Taoist abstained from eating meat and cereals, practiced meditation, controlled the breath, and absorbed the essence of the cinnabar, a mercuric sulphide.

This alliance between Buddhism and religious Taoism was facilitated by certain external similarities between the two. For instance both systems worshipped without sacrifices, practiced meditation, and indulged in respiratory exercises. The Buddhists taught that one could attain rebirth in one of the numerous heavens, just as the Taoists claimed that one could be reborn as an immortal in the Eastern Seas. For the Buddhists, this alliance represented an important advantage, for it enabled them to avoid some of the prejudice which the Chinese harbored against a foreign system. Still, the religion was able to maintain only a precarious foothold on Chinese soil, there were only three known Buddhist communities in all of Han China, monks few, and converts even fewer.

With the downfall of the Han dynasty in A.D. 220, the outlook for Buddhism changed. China now entered a period of disunity that lasted until 589, when the whole country was reunited under the Sui dynasty. During those three centuries there existed two Chinas, one in the north comprising roughly the basin of the Yellow River, and one in the south consisting of the area drained by the Yangtze River. The area in the north was overrun and governed by non-Chinese tribes, while the south was governed by a succession of short-lived and weak Chinese dynasties.

The non-Chinese rulers in the north, generally Turkic or Tibetan in origin, were free from the pressures of the Confucian classics and ideology, and encouraged their subjects, both Chinese and non-Chinese, to embrace and promote Buddhism. The Chinese rulers in south China, while professing to be supporters of the traditional way of life, were sometimes struck by moments of doubt as to whether the Confucian ideology was a sufficient force to unite the country and to recover the north from the barbarian tribes. They had seen the strong centralized Han empire built on Confucian principles crumble to fragments, and they wondered whether some other way of life, such as that which Buddhism offered, might not offer some answer to their doubts. In this mood, some of the Chinese scholars and aristocracy in the south began to take an interest in Buddhist teachings and to consort with Buddhist monks. Thus during these three centuries when Confucianism was weakened and no strong central government existed, the intellectual and religious climate in China was favorable for the growth of Buddhism.

The development of the religion in the two regions followed different trends. The type of Buddhism developed in the south has often been designated as gentry Buddhism. It emphasized

Buddhist and Chinese learning, philosophical speculations, literary activities, and friendly contacts between learned monks and the literati in Chinese society. The monastic community generally asserted its independent status and claimed exemption from civil authority. It was able to insist on these features because the short-lived imperial houses in the area were generally weak. In the north, the monastic community was under the control of the state and very often was an instrument to carry out state policy. The prominent monks were those who were skilled in political and military counsel and in prognostication concerning the shape of future events, and because they possessed such skills, they were often appointed as advisers to the rulers. Instead of wisdom and learning which the Buddhists in the south valued, faith was emphasized in the north. Let us look at these developments more closely.

Buddhism in South China

The barbarian inroads into north China during the third and fourth centuries led to an exodus of literati and scholar-officials from that area to the region south of the Yangtze, where they assisted in the establishment and administration of the Chinese dynasties. However, as these dynasties were weak and the area which they controlled were small, the scholars and literati who normally served in the civil bureaucracy now found that such opportunities were limited. In this situation, many of them turned away from practical problems and mundane events to find solace in poetry, wine, and the speculations of philosophical Taoism. Probably the unstable troublesome times under which they lived also influenced their decision to take such a step. To them the Taoist doctrine of naturalness or spontaneity offered the consolation and solace which they sought. In human activities, they believed that the individual should be free to act and talk as he pleased, free from the restraint of Confucian conventions. The interest in naturalness also led them to contemplate the mystery that is behind all mysteries, the ultimate principle behind the phenomenal world. As they speculated on the regularity of the seasons and the orderliness of the animal and vegetable worlds, on the rising and setting of the sun and moon without fail, and on the blooming of flowers and trees which bloom in due time without anyone doing anything about it, they concluded that there must be some absolute principle responsible for this universal harmony. The principle they finally conceived was *wu* or non-being. "Though Heaven and Earth, in their greatness, are richly endowed with the myriad things; though their thunder moves and their winds circulate; though through their revolving operations the myriad transformations come to be—yet it is the silent and supreme non-being that is their origin." [29] The one who is completely identified with this non-being is the sage. As a sage, he forgets all distinctions between the self and others, life and death, right and wrong, and by forgetting such distinctions he becomes one with the universe and lives as long as the universe exists.

While the scholars and the literati were engaged in such Taoist speculations in south China, the learned Buddhist monks in the same area were concentrating on a body of Mahayana Buddhist literature known as the Prajna or Wisdom sutras. One could argue plausibly that this interest on the part of the Buddhists was in part stimulated by the prevailing intellectual atmosphere of the time among the Chinese scholars. The main doctrine taught in the Prajna sutras was that of emptiness. The Hinayana Buddhists in accordance with their doctrine of dependent origination say that a thing comes into existence depending upon a previous cause or condition and disappears with the cessation of that cause or condition. The Prajna sutras now teach that because a thing comes into existence depending upon something else, that thing is empty or void, since it does not possess its own self-nature and does not exist on its own right. Thus emptiness or *sunyata* is the highest truth of all. To attain to this highest truth is to realize *prajna* or wisdom.

During the third and fourth centuries, interest in these Prajna sutras was supreme among the learned Buddhist monks in the south, at the same time that the Taoist concept of non-being was the main topic of speculation among the literary circles. When the two groups came face to face with each other and started their dialogue, they found startling similarities in their ideas. The Taoist philosophers held that all things have non-being as their origin, while the Buddhists believed that all things are by nature empty. For the Buddhists, emptiness is the highest truth, while for the Taoist, non-being is the ultimate principle. The Taoist sage is identified with non-being just as the Buddha is the one who has realized the highest truth of emptiness. Both the Taoist sage and the Buddha were considered to be eternal and beyond all distinctions. Once these affinities were discovered, very naturally increased contacts between the two groups resulted, with each group taking greater and deeper interest in the literature and thinking of the other group. This Buddhist-Taoist dialogue is of the greatest importance in the history of Buddhism in China, for it meant that Buddhist monks for the first time could intermingle freely and establish friendly relations with the famous literary men and scholars who were the elite of Chinese society. It also meant that for the first time Buddhist scriptures became proper objects of study by the native scholars, and this redounded to the benefit and spread of Buddhism. Concrete evidence of this benefit may be seen in the fact that some members of the most powerful aristocratic families in south China joined the Buddhist community as monks, while others supported the religion as pious and devoted laymen.

The rising popularity and prestige of the Buddhist community of monks soon gave rise to an interesting problem during the fourth century in south China, that of the relation between the community and the head of state. In India the community of monks was considered to be an autonomous body governed by its own monastic law, but when this concept of the order was introduced to China, where the emperor was considered to be supreme, there was bound to be some difficulty. During the fourth century the problem arose as to whether or not a monk should render homage to the ruler. In spite of the position taken by the Confucian officials that monks should prostrate before the emperor just as any other subject, the Buddhists held successfully to their thesis that monks had left society and had no concern with worldly affairs, and therefore should not be called upon to abide by the ordinary rules of society.

The steady growth and popularity of the religion also led to stronger opposition from the traditionalists in Chinese society. The arguments advanced by the opposition against Buddhism may be grouped under four general headings, nationalistic, intellectual, economic, and political.

The nationalistic position is best stated in a tract entitled *Treatise on the Barbarians and Chinese*. Here the author argued that Buddhism is a foreign religion suitable for the barbarians but not for the Chinese. Such customs of the Buddhist monks in cutting off their hair, wearing their robes loose, and cremating the bodies of the deceased, were not practices for the Chinese to follow. He also charged that the Indians were by nature evil and coarse and that the Buddha had to proclaim the five cardinal precepts to restrain them. Therefore, while Buddhism was suitable for the Indians, it was not for the Chinese, who were by nature good and gentle and needed no monastic rules to restrain them.

The intellectual arguments against Buddhism were advanced by a Confucianist named Fan Chen, who lived during the fifth and sixth centuries. He centered his criticism mainly on the Buddhist doctrine of karma and the indestructibility of the soul. The Confucian viewpoint denied the operation of the karmic process, and insisted that the fate of kingdoms and men was controlled by a heavenly mandate concerning which man could do very little or nothing. A predecessor of Fan once wrote that when a man is born, his nature is already determined, and that all the deeds that he performed in his life would not make him good or evil. For instance, he argued, some people perform evil deeds all their lives, yet are not punished, while others who have acted humanely and righteously have lost their lives. Other Confucians argued that since man can attain divine intelligence and has natural endowments, he should not be compared with animals and fishes, and consequently no evil karma is incurred when he kills animals and fishes for food.

The second doctrine, the indestructibility of the soul, was a peculiar Chinese Buddhist concept. After Buddhism was intro-

duced, the Chinese had difficulty understanding the fundamental
doctrine of no-soul or no-self (*anatta*). They could not comprehend the idea of successive rebirths without some abiding spirit
or soul that connects the different rebirths, and to resolve their
difficulty, they created the concept of an entity called *shen*, spirit
or soul, that transmigrated from one life to the next. The Buddhists
insisted that this idea of an indestructible soul is not so strange
after all, for it is found in the native Chinese writings as well.
For instance, they pointed out that in Chinese practices, when a
person dies, someone goes up on the roof to call back the soul of
the departed one, as if to indicate that though the material body
has died, the soul still remains alive to heed the call. They also
referred to passages in Taoist writings saying in effect that when
the body dissolves, the soul does not change, and with the unchanging soul availing itself of the changing body, transformations
go on endlessly. The Confucian viewpoint was that Buddhism is
wrong in teaching that souls live on through endless rebirths, for
it held that such matters as life after death is beyond our sight and
hearing and therefore cannot be discussed profitably.

The Confucianist Fan Chen was undoubtedly aroused to his
attack against Buddhism by the prevailing pro-Buddhist sentiment
of his times. He wrote that people were exhausting their fortunes
in trying to flatter the monks and the Buddha, abandoning their
dear and beloved ones, and terminating their line of descendants.
He felt that if he could disprove the fundamental Buddhist tenets
of karma and the indestructibility of the soul, he would have
struck a telling blow against the religion.

To this end, Fan argued that birth and death, prosperity and
poverty, follow a natural sequence and are determined by factors
beyond the control of man. He compared human lives to flowers
blooming from the same tree. Some flowers are blown by the wind
to fall on rugs and mats; these represent the elite in society. Others
are stopped by a fence and fall on the manure pile; these become
the humble and the lowly. As for his stand against the indestructible soul, he contended that the body is the same as the soul, and
that one exists only as the other exists. The body is the substance
of the soul, while the soul is the functioning of the body. The

two cannot be separated from one another. To clinch his argument, he resorted to a clever analogy. He wrote that the soul is to substance what keenness is to the knife; the body is to functioning what the knife is to keenness. Take away keenness and there is no knife; take away the knife and there is no keenness. He had never heard of a knife disappearing and the keenness still remaining, so he asked, how could the body dissolve and the soul still remain?

The most severe attack against Buddhism was leveled by an individual named Hsun Chi who lived during the early sixth century. In scathing and biting words, he charged that Buddhism was responsible for all the turmoil and disorder during the period of disunity by its rupture of the normal relations between father and son, husband and wife, and prince and minister. He also claimed that Buddhism was ill-omened, for it shortened the duration of all those dynasties which espoused it. However the brunt of his attack was economic and political. Economically, the religion was draining the resources of the land, for though the monks did not cultivate the land nor did the nuns weave, they still ate food and wore clothing; in a word they were parasites on society. Moreover by their celibate lives, they were depriving the country of much needed manpower to fill the imperial armies and to perform the labor services. Politically, he charged the Buddhist religion with sedition, and adduced the following counts to substantiate his indictments; (1) the Buddhists were building monasteries and temples to imitate the imperial palaces; (2) they were translating seditious works; (3) they were usurping the imperial prerogative of imposing fines and punishment by saying they could save people from hell; (4) they were setting up another calendar in opposition to that of the dynasty by their days of fasting and festivals; (5) by describing the peace and happiness of the Buddhist heavens, they were indirectly criticizing the dynasty for not maintaining peace and prosperity on earth; and (6) they were imitating the imperial insignias with their banners and pennants.

Bitter and forceful though these attacks were, it must be pointed out that they remained on the level of verbal warfare. It is conceivable that the Confucian virtue of moderation served as a restraining influence on any attempt to resort to force to settle the differences of opinion, plus the fact that now the foreign religion was enjoying the support of some of the great families of the land.

Buddhism in North China

In north China, the religion faced an entirely different set of conditions. We have already pointed out that the rulers in that area were non-Chinese, and as they were not inhibited by the native Confucian conservatism against accepting a foreign religion, many of them embraced Buddhism and supported it. The very fact that Buddhism was a foreign and not a Chinese religion favored it in the eyes of these non-Chinese rulers and peoples.

Unlike south China which was ruled by one Chinese dynasty, north China during the fourth century was the arena of contention by a number of non-Chinese tribes vying for supremacy. During a period when such struggles for political and military paramountcy were so common, those individuals who possessed such skills as the ability to forecast the outcome of expeditions and battles, the loyalty of allies and subordinates, or the fate of kingdoms, were especially desirable and valuable. In north China at the time there were a number of Buddhist monks who possessed such talents, and these offered their services to the rulers to become their military and diplomatic advisers. Such services had very little to do with the propagation of the religion directly, but indirectly they were beneficial, for in return for the counsel given them, the rulers often became converted to Buddhism.

The best example of such a type of Buddhist monk serving in north China is that of Fo-t'u-teng, a cleric of central Asiatic origin who arrived in the north during the early years of the fourth century. Realizing that the unsettled conditions in the north were not conducive to his missionary activities, he proceeded to gain the confidence of the barbarian ruler of a minor kingdom by his display of magic, such as using spirits as his messenger, drawing water from a dried up well with toothpicks, or growing lotus flowers out of a bowl of water. Once having gained the confidence of the ruler, he served as his adviser for more than twenty years, assisting him in military and political strategy. In this fashion, he initiated the policy of monks participating in the affairs of state. He also exercised some civilizing influence on the conduct of the barbarian rulers.

Other non-Chinese rulers in the north manifested their support of the religion by sponsoring state supported translation bureaus and housing them within the imperial precincts. It was under the auspices of one such translation bureau that the most famous of the Buddhist translators, Kumarajiva, carried out his prodigious activities. With the assistance of a thousand monks in the bureau, this worthy cleric was able, during the brief span of just about a decade during the early fifth century, to render into Chinese the fundamental texts of both Hinayana and Mahayana Buddhism.

By far the most important of the non-Chinese dynasties in the north was the Northern Wei, which gradually absorbed all the petty kingdoms in the area, so that by 440 it controlled an empire embracing all of north China. This dynasty is of peculiar interest to us because it carried out the first large scale persecution of Buddhism in China, and because it was responsible for those magnificent and imposing rock sculptures at Yun-kang and Lung-men in north China.

The persecution of Buddhism started in 446. It was inspired largely by the machinations of two individuals, one a Taoist and the other a Confucianist, who had the same objective in mind though they were working for different purposes. The Taoist wanted to establish a holy empire on earth under the auspices of Taoism, with himself designated as the grand Taoist pope. The Confucianist wanted to establish an ideal Confucian state to sinicize the barbarian Northern Wei people. Such a Confucian state would consist of the feudal society idealized by Confucius, where the literati would hold all the powers of state while the masses of people would remain ignorant but loyal. Because Buddhism was the religion of the barbarians, and because it advocated the equality and unity of all classes, withdrawal from society, and celibacy, it was to be violently opposed. Under the influence of these two persons, the Northern Wei emperor was slowly brought about to the position of favoring the suppression of Buddhism. In the third month of 446, the emperor issued the fateful decree in which he ordered that all the temples, sutras, stupas, and paintings were to be destroyed, and all the monks to be executed. How many members of the monastic community were actually executed will never be known, but it is certain that the decree was not fully carried out, for as soon as the emperor and the two instigators passed away from the scene a few years later, Buddhist monks emerged to revive the religion.

The creation of the artistic masterpieces in Yun-kang was closely connected with this persecution of 446. The person chiefly responsible for conceiving and carrying out the project was T'an-yao, who became Chief of Monks in the Northern Wei Empire during the period 460-464. This office of Chief of Monks was established by the Northern Wei dynasty to exercise administrative control over the monastic community in north China. The office was filled by a monk chosen by the emperor. Scattered throughout the realm were Regional Chiefs of Monks appointed by the Chief of Monks in the capital and subject to his supervision. Such a chain of control enabled the emperor through his appointment of the Chief of Monks to maintain close supervision over the entire Buddhist community in the land. It also provided the means by which a forceful and enterprising Chief of Monks could take advantage of the power and prestige of the central government to promote the activities of the Buddhist church. T'an-yao was just such an individual.

As T'an-yao reminisced over the persecution of Buddhism and its revival, he conceived of a bold project which would connect the fortunes of the religion with the interests of the ruling dynasty, the sculpturing of images of the Buddhas and bodhisattvas out of the rocky walls of the Yun-kang grottoes. Such a project would serve a two-fold purpose. For one thing, it would not only be a manifestation of the support given by the imperial house to the religion, but also an expression of repentance for the suppression of Buddhism in 446. For another, it would be a memorial commemorating the restoration of the religion. These lasting images chiseled out of the hard rocks were to serve as enduring symbols of the permanence of the dharma and to inspire future rulers to exert themselves for the protection of the law. After having seen how easily destroyed were the images of the Buddha made of wood, clay, or metal, T'an-yao felt that only symbols created out of stone would be saved from destruction. His project was approved by the ruling authorities, and by combining official support with the talents and techniques of the monastic community, the imposing array of caves and images at Yun-kang was created.

The most noteworthy objects at Yun-kang are the five gigantic figures of the Buddha, with the tallest standing about seventy feet in height. These five Buddhas were regarded by the Northern Wei people as the representatives of the first five emperors of the dynasty, in accordance with an idea formulated by the Buddhists that the rulers were the present-day manifestations of the Tathagatas. It is very likely that these figures were modeled after the imposing Buddha images at Bamiyan in Afghanistan. Next in importance are the caves in which the entire Buddha legend is depicted on the walls. Here one finds scenes portraying the birth of the Buddha, his athletic training at youth, his luxurious mode of living in the palace, his encounter with the four signs, his departure from the palace, his period of asceticism in the forest, and finally his enlightenment.

The Northern Wei court and the Buddhist community continued their joint efforts of rock sculpture at Lung-men near Loyang during the closing years of their dynasty, roughly from 495 to 530. On this new site, great or small images were again chiseled out by the Northern Wei artisans, or caves dug into the hard rocks, with their walls filled with countless niches and each one occupied by a Buddha. Sakyamuni and Maitreya were the most popular deities worshipped by the Northern Wei people, judging by the preponderance of images dedicated to them. The most imposing and magnificent of the caves was the one sponsored by the imperial family. In this cave are seen images of the emperors and empresses advancing to render homage to the Buddha and the bodhisattvas.

Attached to the images in Yun-kang and Lung-men are numerous inscriptions that furnish valuable information about the donors and their motives for sponsoring the artistic enterprise. We learn that all elements of Northern Wei society, the imperial family, the nobility, monks and nuns, and the common people contributed to the project. Very often the common people would band together to form a religious society and pool their resources in order to raise the necessary funds for carving an image. The inscriptions also tell us that the motives behind the creation of the images were: (1) to attain enlightenment; (2) to achieve rebirth in the Pure Land of Amitabha; (3) to express gratitude to the Buddha for the fulfillment of certain wishes, such as recovery from illness, completion of a certain enterprise, and so forth; (4) to realize material benefits such as prosperity, longevity, power, influence, or prestige.

Much more valuable, however, is the information furnished about the state of the religion under the Northern Wei. First and most important, we know through the inscriptions that the brand of Buddhism accepted and practiced by the Northern Wei people was Mahayana Buddhism. The stress was on such Mahayana virtues as compassion, charity, and altruism. Again and again, the donors, whether they were nobles or commoners, made the earnest wish that salvation be obtained by all living creatures. Such sentiments clearly indicated that the Mahayana emphasis on universal salvation was already widely pervasive. In the second place, close and cordial relations existed between the religion and the state. The inscriptions frequently mentioned prayers for the well-being and longevity of the ruling house, and tranquillity and prosperity for the realm. This close relationship was concretely illustrated by imperial sponsorship of one of the caves in Lung-men, which depicted the ruling house paying its respects to the Buddha. In the third place, the inscriptions show that Buddhism in China was becoming more sinicized. The frequent references to filial piety indicate that a subtle change had taken place in the religion after its introduction and spread among the Chinese. This filial piety was expressed by the wish of the donors that their ancestors might be reborn in the Pure Land and live there without blemish. Instead of renouncing all family and social ties, we now find monks and nuns praying for the well-being of their departed ancestors. Fourthly, the religion as practiced by the people was characterized chiefly by faith and devotion, devotion to the numerous deities of Mahayana pantheon and faith that the Buddha through his love and compassion will bring about universal salvation. Only this deep and sustaining faith could have inspired the creation of the statues and images in Yun-kang and Lung-men in such prodigious numbers and on such a gigantic scale. This was in contrast to the situation in south China, where the main emphasis was not so much on living the religious life faithfully and devotedly as on learned discussions concerning the abstruse Mahayana doctrines. Finally, we can truly say that during the Northern Wei dynasty, Buddhism captured and held the attention of large numbers of the common people. It is only a religion with a broad base of popular support that could have initiated and executed successfully the Yun-kang and Lung-men sculpture. This is indicated by the many religious societies organized by the common people for the express purpose of carving the statues out of the hard rock. It is also reflected in the tremendous increase in the number of monks (two million) and temples (thirty thousand) by the end of the dynasty.

Because Buddhism enjoyed such a wide base of support, the emperor of the Sui dynasty who finally reunited north and south China in 589 under his rule decided that the religion could be utilized as an ideology to knit the Chinese and non-Chinese of the entire country closer together. After so many centuries of division and disunity, he felt that some symbolic act was needed to call attention to the fact that the country was unified not only politically but also ideologically. This act was the enshrinement of the relics of the Buddha. Thirty relics were carefully packed in jars, and in 601 he dispatched thirty monks with these relics to various prefectural centers. Stupas to contain the relics were then constructed in those centers, and on the fifteenth day of the tenth month, 601, all the relics were simultaneously enshrined in the stupas. The day was declared to be a national holiday, with all government offices closed so that officials and people could witness the ceremonies. At the same time, the emperor held an elaborate ceremony in his palace. This symbolic act was repeated two more times, for in 602 fifty-one more relics were enshrined in stupas, and in 604 thirty more relics. By distributing the relics to various prefectural centers, the emperor hoped that all the people in the empire would have an opportunity to accumulate meritorious karma by worshipping them. The stupas in which the relics were enshrined were the concrete symbols of imperial support of Buddhism, and the ceremony of simultaneous enshrinement, with officials and commoners and the clerical community participating, was to convey the idea that the entire empire was united in support of the religion.

The tremendous growth of the religion in its external aspects was also accompanied by similar developments internally. At the beginning of the Period of Disunity, there was only a bare handful of translations of the sacred scriptures, and these were piecemeal, insignificant, and poorly done. In time, however, more and more foreign monks arrived in China, bringing with them the sutras in ever increasing volume. As these foreign monks made more converts, they could draw on a greater pool of linguistic talent to assist them in their translations, and this resulted in a more accurate and readable body of literature. In the beginning, such translations were usually individual affairs, with the foreign monk collaborating with his Chinese assistant. When lengthier translations had to be made, such individual operations did not suffice, and the translation bureaus came into being. Such bureaus usually enjoyed imperial support and comprised a large number of monks who divided their labors. A typical translation bureau would consist of a chief of translation who presided over the bureau, a reciter of the Sanskrit text, a translator of the text, verifier of the meaning of the text, scribe who copied down the translation, a checker who compared the written Chinese text with the original text, an editorial reviser, and a proof reader.

As the Chinese converts learned more about their religion, some of them decided that they should undertake the hazardous journey to India. A number of motives were behind such a decision. Some made the journey to search for the sacred scriptures which they could bring back to China. Some went to study under famous Indian masters to resolve problems in the doctrine which they had encountered in China. A few went to visit the holy sites of Buddhism; Lumbini Grove where the Buddha was born; Gaya where the Buddha attained enlightenment; Benares where he first preached the law; Kusinara where he died. Others journeyed to India to seek for Indian teachers and invite them to China. In a number of instances, these Chinese pilgrims remained in India for a number of years, perfecting their knowledge of Buddhism and mastering the Indian language. After their return to China, they spent the rest of their lives translating the sutras which they brought back with them. Equipped as they were with a knowledge of both Chinese and the Indian languages, these returned Chinese pilgrims rendered meritorious service in the propagation of Buddhist literature.

These Chinese pilgrims made one other contribution not connected with Buddhism that was of immense value to later historians and archeologists. Fortunately for later historians, Chinese pilgrims were traveling in India during periods when important events were taking place, and these Chinese took careful notes of what they saw and heard. The travel records which they wrote after their return to China have served to illumine many episodes of Indian history for historians and archeologists.

From the record left behind by the first of the Chinese pilgrims to go to India and return, Fa-hsien, who made the trip in 399-414, we can live through the fears, hardships, and dangers that he experienced. While crossing the desert, he wrote, "In the desert were numerous evil spirits and scorching winds, causing death to anyone who would meet them. Above there were no bird, while on the ground there were no animals. One looked as far as one could in all directions for a path to cross, but there was none to choose. Only the dried bones of the dead served as indications." In these days of rapid and mass transportation, it is indeed difficult to imagine the problems and challenges which these few lonely pilgrims faced while trudging across the trackless wastes of the central Asiatic desert or clawing up the untrodden slopes of snow-covered mountains. Only their faith in the saving grace of the Buddha and their devotion to their religion could have inspired them onward in their quest for the holy land of Buddhism.

Buddhism under the T'ang

Through the translation activities of these intrepid Chinese pilgrims and the foreign monks, nearly the whole corpus of Buddhist sutras was made available to the Chinese. Fed and nurtured by the contents of these sacred scriptures, the religion finally came of age in China during the seventh and eighth centuries. There were the years when the T'ang dynasty was in power, governing an empire that embraced the whole of China proper and portions of central Asia. The strong emperors of this dynasty pursued a policy of religious toleration, giving all foreign religions, such as Nestorian Christianity, Islam, Manichaeism, Zoroastrianism, as well as Buddhism equal opportunity to develop. Since Buddhism was already so widespread, it very naturally profited from this situation and rose to unprecedented heights under the friendly patronage of the rulers. Its source of strength lay mainly in its ability to serve all classes of Chinese society, the imperial household, the nobility, the great and wealthy families, and the common people. This service was rendered in a number of different ways. For the imperial household, the Buddhist organization served as a sort of spiritual arm of the government, whose duty it was to protect and promote the spiritual welfare of the empire. The Buddhist monks were to take the proper measures to insure that the protective influences of the Buddhist deities were extended to the person of the emperor and his family, and that no spiritual mishap might happen to the administration. Such measures included the celebration of imperial birthdays and commemorative ceremonies in honor of deceased emperors in Buddhist temples. Likewise, state temples were established throughout the empire, where the maintenance of the monks was undertaken by the central government. For the nobility and the wealthy families, the religion offered them an opportunity to display their gems and their finery to the public during the numerous Buddhist festivals held throughout the year. More important was the economic advantage which the Buddhist temples often offered to these families. As land owned by temples were tax-exempt, wealthy families often resorted to a device which enabled them to give the appearance of donating land to the temple, whereas in reality they still retained ownership of the property. Such a device was the establishment of a Buddhist institution known as a merit cloister, usually on the private burial grounds of the family. Once the cloister was established, land was donated to it, and this land became tax-exempt. However, since the cloister was established by the family in the first place, the family regarded the cloister and the land assigned to it still as private property. For the common people, the Buddhist festivals provided entertainment and diversion to the throngs in the cities and villages, while the spacious grounds of the Buddhist temples with their trees and flowers served as a sort of pleasure garden. Through the plays, story-telling, and religious lectures sponsored by the temples, these common people would derive their knowledge concerning the rudiments of the religion.

Besides their purely religious functions, the Buddhist temples during the T'ang dynasty took on a host of secular activities, economic, commercial, and charitable. Already mentioned was the land owned by the Buddhist temples. In fact, they were among the great land-owners of the empire. Such land was acquired by outright genuine donations from the imperial household and the great families of the realm and by purchase.

The temples were also the recipients of contributions from the devoted followers of the religion. Very often such contributions far exceeded the needs of the monastic community living in the temples, and gradually accumulated to form a sizable surplus. Also, the income in the form of produce from the land owned by the temple or monastery was often more than sufficient to feed and clothe the monks, and again there was a surplus. Now, monastic law does not permit the sale of such surplus goods for the private benefit of the monks, but if the income derived from the sale was used for the furtherance of the religion, then the sale was allowable. In order to dispose of the surplus, the Buddhist organization established a peculiar institution known as the Inexhaustible Treasury, which proceeded to use the surplus as its capital to carry on commercial transactions. Loans were made to people, grains to peasants and goods to traders and merchants, with sizable interest being charged in all instances. The treasuries soon broadened their activities to include the pawn brokerage and banking operations. It must be pointed out, however, that the motive behind these commercial activities was religious. The goods or land were donated in the first place for the accumulation of meritorious karma, and the disposal of the surplus goods was also for the purpose of furthering the dharma.

During the T'ang dynasty, the Buddhist institutions also engaged in such industrial enterprises as operating water-powered mills and oil presses. The water-powered mills, often donated to the temples, were utilized by the farmers to husk and to grind their grains upon paying a small charge, while the oil presses were used to make the oil so urgently needed. In addition, the temples also operated bathhouses and hostels. Bathhouses were specially desirable in north China where water was not so easily procurable as in south China. Hostels performed a vital function for merchants on the road, for military and civil officials traveling to assume new posts, and for the students who went to the cities to take the civil service examinations.

With the Buddhist temples engaging in such lucrative industrial and commercial enterprises, and with T'ang society being so affluent that it continued to heap donations to the religion, it comes as no surprise that these temples and monasteries became the repositories of immense wealth and art. Some of the Buddhist temples of the period were described as architectural masterpieces, rivaling the imperial palaces in magnificence and grandeur, while their sizes were so great that thousands of monks could reside in some of them. On the walls and pillars within them were the paintings and decorations of the renowned artists of the age, while on the altars gilded images of the Buddhas and bodhisattvas, and the ritual objects made of gold, silver, jade, and bronze, dazzled the eyes of the multitudes who saw them on festival days. Inevitably the concentration of such wealth within the walls of the temples and monasteries aroused the ire of the Confucian moralists, who felt that such wealth should not remain idle but should be put to productive use for the welfare of the country. The Confucianists also complained that the imperial treasury suffered from the loss of revenue brought about by the large number of tax-exempt clergy and the extensive tax-exempt land owned by the Buddhist church.

These economic considerations against Buddhism were reinforced during the early years of the ninth century by an ideological struggle between the Taoists and Buddhists, and some Taoist priests were urging the emperor to take strong repressive measures against Buddhism. Factional strife within the imperial court also fanned the anti-Buddhist sentiments, with the scholar-bureaucrats allied with the emperor on one side opposed to Buddhism, and the eunuchs on the other favoring it. These considerations finally led to the suppression of 845, undoubtedly the most widespread of its kind in China. According to the imperial edict summing up the effects of the suppression, more than 4,600 monasteries and 40,000 temples and shrines were destroyed, over 260,000 monks and nuns were returned to the laity, all temple lands confiscated, and all images made of gold, silver, jade, and bronze turned over to the government. Because this suppression dealt a crippling blow to the Buddhist community in China, it is one of the significant events in Chinese history, for it marked the end of the apogee and the beginning of the decline of the religion in China.

Before the religion declined, it stimulated Chinese thought by the establishment of a number of Buddhist schools. To these different Buddhist schools in China we shall now turn.

Buddhist Schools in China

In our previous discussion we have already mentioned the two important schools which developed in Mahayana Buddhism in India, the School of the Middle Path and the Idealist School. The doctrines of the former school were introduced to the Chinese through the translations of Kumarajiva during the first decade of the fifth century. Because its emphasis was upon intricate metaphysical speculations, the school did not make much impression upon the mass of Chinese Buddhists, but it did command the attention of a few learned monks, and during the sixth and seventh centuries, the basic texts of the school were popular within a group of intellectually inclined monks led by Chi-tsang (549-623). As for the Idealist School, its basic texts were first translated into Chinese by the Indian monk Paramartha during the sixth century, but the important individuals connected with the establishment and the promotion of the school were the famous Chinese pilgrim Hsuan-tsang and his disciple Kuei-chi, both of whom lived during the seventh century.

Hsuan-tsang during his early youth had studied the doctrines of the Idealist School, but he found so many problems which puzzled him that he decided to go to the source of Buddhism to find the answers there. With this objective in mind, he left China in 629 and made his way across central Asia to India, where he spent about fifteen years visiting the sacred spots of his religion and studying Sanskrit and Buddhist thought in the famous Buddhist university at Nalanda. Upon his return to China in 645 he devoted the rest of his life translating the considerable amount of literature which he brought back. Though his translations embraced the whole range of Mahayana sutras, his main interest was on the teachings of the Idealist School. As a school, it commanded limited following among the Chinese, probably because its hair-splitting analysis of the mind and consciousness was not attractive to the practical-minded Chinese.

These were Indian schools of Buddhism introduced to the Chinese. Other schools which developed in China were products of the Chinese mind, and represented the Chinese response to the Indian religion. To that extent, these schools are no longer Indian systems introduced to China but are schools of Chinese Buddhism. In many cases, they are the products of Chinese monks studying the Buddhist sutras and singling out one text as containing the epitome of the Buddha's teachings. The first of such schools that we shall discuss is the Sect of the Three Stages, which developed in the sixth century.

Sect of the Three Stages

In the *Lotus Sutra,* it is stated that there are three stages in the duration of the Master's teachings: (1) the period of the true law; (2) the period of the counterfeit law, when the true law is superseded by something which resembles it; (3) period of the decline of the law, when the teaching is in disrepute and about to disappear. Heated debates were carried out regarding the span of the first two periods, and in China the most prevalent view was that the true law would last five hundred years, and the counterfeit law one thousand years. The Chinese Buddhists of the sixth century also believed that they were living at the beginning of the third period, basing this belief on the state of confusion, degeneration, corruption, and strife rampant in Chinese society at the middle of the century.

This chronology of the Chinese, that fifteen hundred years elapsed between the nirvana of the Buddha and the middle of the sixth century, requires some explanation. If we accept the usual date that the Buddha passed away in 480 B.C., one thousand five hundred years after that would be about 1000 A.D. However, the Chinese at the time did not accept this date; instead they generally dated the nirvana at 949 B.C. The reason for this unusual date is to be found in the polemics between the Buddhists and their critics during the Period of Disunity. Among other things these critics had charged that Buddhism was ill-omened and had shortened the duration of dynasties. To answer this charge, the Buddhists fabricated accounts which purported to show that Buddhism was introduced into China during the Chou dynasty (1100-250 B.C.) shortly after the nirvana of the Buddha in 949 B.C. This dynasty was the longest in Chinese history, and provided just the point which the Buddhists needed to rebut their critics.

During the period of the decline of the law, the adherents of the Sect of the Three Stages contended that people were ignorant of the true law, could not distinguish right from wrong, disobeyed all the rules of discipline, and believed in heresies. To correct the evils of the age, the sect advocated a sort of pantheism in which all the Buddhas were to be worshipped equally. All people, regardless of their station in life, were regarded as possessing the Buddha-nature and hence were worthy to be honored and respected as future Buddhas. Almsgiving and altruistic activities were encouraged by the sect, strict adherence to the rules of discipline was required, and austerities were looked upon with favor.

Opposition to the Sect of the Three Stages soon arose from among the ranks of other Buddhist groups, who objected to its claim that it possessed the sole formula to salvation during the period of decline. Its view that in this period, no government existed which was worthy of respect by the people was unacceptable and obnoxious to the reigning dynasty, and it was no surprise therefore to find the T'ang emperors condemning the sect as heretical and inimical to the interests of the state.

Pure Land School

The strongest rival to the Sect of the Three Stages in claiming the attention of the common people was the Pure Land School. This school also accepted the theory of the three periods and that the sixth century was the beginning of the decay of the law. However, the school taught that the remedy for the evils of the age was to take refuge in Amitabha, the presiding Buddha of the Pure Land. When the rival Sect of the Three Stages was suppressed by the throne, the Pure Land School had the field all to itself and it soon developed into one of the most popular schools of Buddhism in China.

To Tao-ch'o (562-645) and Shan-tao (613-681), the two leaders who were mainly responsible for establishing the school on a firm basis, the most important prerequisite was faith in Amitabha. No matter how depraved or sinful an individual may be, he will be saved by the limitless grace of that Buddha. By keeping his thoughts constantly preoccupied with Amitabha, by repeating endlessly the formula, homage to Amitabha, the sinner will be purified, and when he dies, he will be reborn in the Pure Land of Amitabha. Beans were used by the faithful to record the number of times they repeated the formula; one monk recited the formula a million times during a seven-day period, while another nun counted enough beans to fill eighty bushels.

The popularity of the Pure Land School was also promoted by paintings on temple walls depicting the Western Paradise. In fact, this was one of the most common themes painted by the artists of the age, and a number of such paintings dating back to the eighth and ninth centuries have been preserved. As the multitudes visited the temples and saw these paintings illustrating the joys and blessings of the Pure Land, it is not surprising that their minds turned more and more to the teachings of this school, especially since the means to achieve rebirth in that paradise was so simple and easy.

T'ien-t'ai School

The founder of this school was Chih-i (538-597), who systematized and brought to final completion its basic doctrines. As Chih-i lived on Mt. T'ien-t'ai in what is now Chekiang, the school is called the T'ien-t'ai School. In the doctrines and methods followed by this school we may see an example of the Chinese genius for compromise at work.

By the time Chih-i appeared on the scene, a tremendous mass of Buddhist sutras had already been translated into Chinese. As the Chinese read this enormous volume, they were puzzled by the division of the Hinayana and the Mahayana, and they asked how it was possible for one individual to preach so many sutras teaching so many diverse ideas, and how the contradictions and doctrinal differences were to be explained. Other monks before Chih-i had already broached the idea of classifying the sutras according to chronological periods, but it remained for Chih-i to work out the classification in full details.

According to Chih-i, all the sutras of the Buddha may be classified into five periods of teaching. Immediately after enlightenment, the Buddha preached the *Avatamsakasutra* (*Garland Sutra*) an idealist text of profound depth and meaning. However, the audience appeared as if deaf and dumb and did not understand what he was preaching. This convinced the master that the people were not yet ready for his profound message and that he had to shift his emphasis. This is the first or the Avatamsaka period, which lasted three weeks, since that was the span of time he took to preach the entire *Avatamsakasutra*.

During the second period, which lasted twelve years, he preached the Hinayana scriptures which contained such doctrines as the four truths, the eight-fold path, and dependent origination. By preaching these doctrines which beings of lower capacity could understand, the Buddha hoped that he could elevate his audience spiritually and intellectually to advance to the third stage.

In the third stage, the Buddha told his audience that the Hinayana scriptures do not contain the full and final truths, but that there are higher truths which must be realized to gain deliverance. During this third period, which lasted eight years, the Buddha taught the elementary Mahayana sutras that were mainly concerned with pointing out the inferiority of the Hinayana as compared to the Mahayana. The Hinayana ideal of the arhat was criticized as still being subject to pride and self-satisfaction, and not as complete an ideal as the bodhisattva, who was mainly interested in saving others.

After this third period, the Buddha felt that the audience was ready for the advanced Mahayana sutras, and so in the fourth, he spent twenty-two years teaching the Prajna or Wisdom sutras. Now he taught the nature of the highest or absolute truth, which he said is free from attributes, undefinable, unconditional, and therefore empty or void. All the distinctions that we see in the phenomenal world are the products of our illusions and have no objective reality.

In this fourth period, the Buddha taught the non-existence of contrasts; in the fifth and last period, which took up the final eight years of the master's life, he emphasized the absolute identity of the contrasts. All the vehicles or paths leading to salvation are united in the one path or vehicle as taught in the *Lotus Sutra,* which is considered to be the epitome of the Buddha's teachings.

This T'ien-t'ai classification represents the Chinese attempt to establish a unifying principle bringing together all the divergent forms of Buddhism. It included all the Buddhist scriptures, and considered them as being gradually revealed by the master as he found his audience becoming more advanced spiritually and intellectually. It did not deny the validity of the Hinayana, nor did it see any antagonism between the Hinayana and the Mahayana. It looked upon the former as containing only the lower or relative truths, which must be mastered if one were to advance to the higher truths of the Mahayana sutras.

In the realm of doctrine, the T'ien-t'ai spirit of compromise may be seen in its formulation of the three-fold truth of emptiness, temporariness, and the middle. All things have no independent existence of their own for they are dependent upon causes and conditions for their existence. This is called the truth of emptiness. In formulating this truth, Chih-i was but following the concept of emptiness as expounded by Nagarjuna and the Prajna sutras. The concept of emptiness does not mean nothingness or non-existence, however, for though a thing is empty, it does enjoy temporary existence as a phenomenon in the world of change. This is the truth of temporariness, which establishes the temporary existence of phenomena so that they can be grasped by the senses. The synthesis of emptiness and temporariness, or, to put it in another way, the fact that a thing is empty and temporary at the same time, is called the middle truth. This middle is not something between the two but contains and surpasses the other two.

Chih-i formulated this three-fold truth to emphasize the idea of totality and mutual identification; phenomena and the absolute are identical. As the T'ien-t'ai masters put it, all the Buddhas may be present in one grain of sand, or one thought is the three thousand worlds. Expressed in terms of the religious life, this means that phenomenal life is not denied but is affirmed as part of the absolute. Thus the everyday life of the layman is part of the life of the Buddha; samsara is nirvana.

The identification of phenomena with the absolute is further seen in the T'ien-t'ai doctrine of the absolute mind. This absolute mind is said to contain the two natures, pure and impure. Out of the pure nature rise the attributes of the Buddhas, and out of the impure nature rise the myriad things in the phenomenal world. The T'ien-t'ai masters analyze this pure mind in terms of the

Chinese concepts of substance and function. In its substance, the absolute is one and undifferentiated, but in its functioning, it is diverse and particular. Despite this diversity, all phenomena are integrated in the absolute mind. When people persist in viewing things in the world as being different from one another, they are subject to illusions which must be destroyed by the cultivation of concentration and insight. By concentration we realize that all phenomenal things have no self-nature and do not enjoy real existence; they appear to be real because of our illusions. By insight we realize that although the myriad things in the world do not have real existence, still they are created by the mind, they enjoy temporary existence, and they perform some vital functions. They are likened to dreams or to the magic man created by the magicians; such seem to exist though in reality they do not.

The T'ien-t'ai tenets have been regarded as being among the finest products of the Buddhist philosophical development in China. In the synthesis as worked out by the school, there is no longer the dichotomy between Hinayana and Mahayana, between the absolute and the phenomenal; everything is integrated in the absolute mind.

Hua-yen School

Besides the T'ien-t'ai school, there was another school in China that appealed to the intellect; this was the Hua-yen School. The basic scripture of this school is the *Avatamsaka* or *Garland Sutra,* which was supposed to have been preached by the Buddha immediately after his enlightenment. This was a purely Chinese school, for no predecessor had existed in India. Such being the case, the main problem stressed was the age-old problem of substance and function, absolute and phenomenon. Basing itself on the contents of the *Garland Sutra,* the school established two fundamental principles, that the absolute and phenomenon are interfused with each other, and that all phenomena are mutually related one with another. According to the first principle, every thing or event in the phenomenal world is a manifestation of the absolute completely and perfectly. The Hua-yen slogan to express this is, one in all, all in one. Translated into religious terms, the Buddha-nature is in all of us, all of us possess the Buddha-nature. Since every phenomenon is a manifestation of the absolute, it follows that each individual phenomenon is related to every other phenomenon. To illustrate this principle of interrelationship, one of the Chinese masters of the Hua-yen School resorted to a clever stratagem. He arranged ten mirrors, eight at the eight points of the compass, one above, and one below. A Buddha figure was then placed in the center, lighted up by a torch. When this was done, it was seen that not only was the Buddha image reflected in the ten mirrors, but the image in each mirror was also reflected in all the other mirrors, and the reflection was multiplied without end. Applied to the world of living beings, this means that since every one possesses the Buddha-nature, each one is related to all other beings. The unity and universality of all life is thus affirmed.

The Ch'an or Zen School

The Chinese word *ch'an* is a transliteration of the Sanskrit *dhyana*, which means meditation aimed at controlling the mind and focusing it on one point. Such meditation exercises had always been practiced in India, but invariably in conjunction with the other aspects of the Buddhist discipline, such as following the moral precepts, studying and reciting the sacred scriptures, and worshipping the images. While the Ch'an School in China still retained the emphasis on meditation, it broke away from traditional Buddhist practices and attitudes by its iconoclastic attitude toward the Buddhas and bodhisattvas, and its disregard for literature and rituals. Meditation for this school means a kind of intuitive method of spiritual training aimed at the discovery of the mind or Buddha-nature within us that transcends individual differences and is the fundamental unity beneath all existence. Since this Buddha-nature is inconceivable in thought and inexpressible in words, the Ch'an masters often resorted to negation or to silence to express it. It can only be realized intuitively, directly, and instantly. In order to realize it, the mind must be tranquil and free from conscious thought. Conscious thought brings out the distinction between subject and object and gives rise to attachment to external objects. Such examples of conscious efforts as reciting the sutras, worshipping the images of the Buddha, and performing the rituals are really of no value as far as the realization of the Buddha-nature within us is concerned, and therefore should be discarded or disregarded. Such disregard is expressed in pungent and striking language. For instance, one master wrote that one should kill the Buddhas or the bodhisattvas if one should meet them, while another called such venerated figures as Sakyamuni and Manjusri as dung-heap coolies. The purpose of such strong language is to jar the mind of the follower and to destroy his dependence upon traditional concepts and practices, so that his mind may be free to realize the Buddha-nature or the highest reality naturally, directly, and spontaneously.

Since the Buddha-nature is in all sentient beings and not just in an elite few, its realization is not conditioned upon entry into the monastic community; one can remain in lay life and still practice the spiritual training that leads to the goal. For instance, the Ch'an master Hui-neng, who was the sixth patriarch of the school, was still a lowly menial in the monastery when his spiritual eye saw the truth. Many did join the *sangha* because the quiet meditative life in the monastery was more conducive for the spiritual training that the Ch'an follower practiced. Such training usually consists of the direct method of instruction between master and pupil, with the master prescribing a case or a problem, a riddle or a conundrum, for the pupil to ruminate over. Very often there is no intellectual solution to the problem, an example of which is, what is the sound of one hand clapping? As long as the student tries to analyze the problem logically and conceptually, he is far from the path to truth, and for his efforts he is rewarded often with a kick, a blow, or a shout. When he realizes that logic and reason are stumbling blocks, and that he must rely on other resources, he has achieved a notable advance. Sometimes the student feels he is not getting anywhere in one monastery under one master, so he takes to the road to find another master. As he travels about, he meets with all kinds of people and experiences. Such experiences accumulate to make him a wiser man, and one day, without any advance notice, a shaft of light descends upon him to dispel all his doubts and solve his problems. He has experienced what the Ch'an calls the awakening or enlightenment. He has realized the Buddha-nature within himself and he is now aware only of the unity of all existence. All differences are merged and he is one with the universe. The Ch'an masters point out, however, that this does not involve the acquisition of something new, but is only the realization of something always within us; it is our own ignorance that prevented us from realizing it.

Of the different schools of Buddhism which developed in China, the Pure Land and the Ch'an Schools managed to survive the persecution of 845 and remain active during the succeeding centuries. The Pure Land School with its easy method leading to salvation continued to prove extremely attractive to the masses of Chinese. The Ch'an School was able to survive for two reasons. Its non-dependence on the externals of the religions, such as the images of the Buddha and the body of sacred literature, enabled it to carry on even after the destruction of such externals. In the second place, the Ch'an School was not branded as being parasites on society, for the monks of the school were required to work in some productive labor every day. Its slogan was, one day no work, one day no food.

Contributions to Chinese Culture

It is often said that Buddhism was the great civilizing influence in Asia. Wherever it went, it introduced not only the fine arts and literature to uncivilized peoples, but it also provided the ideology to unify diverse ethnic groups within a country and to divert the attention of the people from the arts of war to the arts of peace. When the religion was introduced into China, it collided with a civilization that was already well-advanced. Understandably the influence upon the Chinese and Chinese culture could not be as great as that exerted on the Ceylonese and the Burmese. Still, the influence was not minor, and in the remaining pages we shall try to point out such contributions.

In Chinese thought there arose during the Sung dynasty an

intellectual movement known as Neo-Confucianism which was designed to draw the attention of the educated Chinese away from Buddhism back to Confucianism and the Confucian classics. While the Neo-Confucianists based their thinking on terms found in the Confucian classics, it is safe to say that they interpreted these terms in the light of their understanding of some of the dominant concepts of Buddhism. For instance, the interpretation given by a Sung philosopher of *jen* to embrace all under heaven was very likely influenced by the Buddhist conceptions of the universality of life and the all compassionate bodhisattva. Likewise, the Ch'an doctrine that the mind is the Buddha, and that this mind instinctively knows what is right and wrong probably exerted some effect on the thinking of the Neo-Confucianist idealists. Both the Buddhists and the Neo-Confucianists advocated mental discipline that emphasized mindfulness, meditation, and equanimity. Finally, the Neo-Confucianist definition of the sage as one who is master of his emotions and who controls his passions appears very much like a response to the Mahayana ideal of the bodhisattva.

Besides Neo-Confucianism, Taoism was also influenced by Buddhism in more ways than one. The Taoists borrowed from the Buddhist liberally in such fields as the composition and organization of the Taoist canon, iconography, and doctrines. The most pronounced of such borrowings occurred in the Taoist canon, where the Taoists took over entire Buddhist sutras, changed some proper names, and then included them in their canon. In their haste to copy as many texts as possible, the Taoist copyists sometimes became careless, and consequently in works now found in the Taoist canon, we find passages to the effect that the Buddha's teaching is foremost in the world, and that the host of Taoist immortals and saints have realized the way of the Buddha. Sometimes, biographies of Lao-tzu contained passages taken almost verbatim from the biographies of the Buddha. In imitation of the Buddhist bodhisattva, the Taoist created a class of transcendent beings known as *t'ien-tsun* or venerable celestials. Likewise the Buddhist concept of karma and rebirth was appropriated, for we are told in a Taoist work that the Taoist saints have achieved their positions through the accumulations of merits derived from their former careers.

In the field of Chinese literature, the practice of Chinese fictional writers in mixing prose and poetry in their works undoubtedly was modeled after that in the Buddhist translations. More important was the element of imagination which the Buddhists brought to the Chinese. Confucian literature was on the whole practical, formal, and restricted, and had very little to do with mythology. When the Chinese came in contact with the rich imaginative literature of Mahayana Buddhism with its colorful and fanciful descriptions of heavens and hells, they were captivated and enthralled, and soon became proficient masters of the art of story-telling. The best illustrations of this proficiency are the long and exciting novels, *Record of a Trip to the West,* *Annals of the Investiture of Deities,* and *Water Margin.* The first is an account of the travels and adventures of a Buddhist monk in the company of a monkey and a pig, who by their extraordinary exploits helped him overcome all sorts of obstacles and dangers. The second is an account of the imaginary battles fought between two dynasties in ancient China, with each side assisted by deities who brought into play the most ingenious weapons, while the third records the thrilling and incredible feats of strength performed by a group of righteous bandits.

Closely allied with literature is language, where a number of new terms coined by the Buddhists have been accepted as part of the Chinese language and are now so widely used that very few Chinese would suspect that such terms are of foreign origin. Such terms as *p'u-sa* for bodhisattva, *t'a* (pagoda) from *thupa,* and *seng* (monk) from *sangha* immediately come to mind when we think of Indian words accepted by the Chinese.

In landscape painting we may see the finest flowering of the Ch'an spirit in Chinese culture. The Ch'an masters hold that the Buddha essence is found in all things, in man as well as in all objects of nature. The landscape artist devotes his time in silent meditation, and when the vision of this spiritual essence comes to him, he paints these objects of nature in the shortest time possible, freely, speedily, and spontaneously. Impelled by the force of his inspiration, he paints automatically without any time for delibera-tion or hesitation, just as a pupil for instance answers the question of his master instantly and freely without any aforethought. When the landscape painter paints his mountains or trees, he does not present their external appearance but seeks rather to express their spiritual significance to him. In order to illustrate the dominant Mahayana doctrine of emptiness or the illusory existence of all phenomena, he paints the mountains as if they are floating in the distant haze, having no real existence, while the vast expanse of water is indicated only by a line or two alongside a boat.

When we come to science, we see some contributions in astronomy, calendrical studies, and medicine. During the T'ang dynasty, treatises on Indian astronomy were translated into Chinese by Buddhist monks, and Indian calendar experts served as officials in the Imperial Bureau of Astronomy. These experts pre-pared the calendar used by the dynasty. In medicine, certain surgical techniques, such as the removal of abdominal walls, operation on the skull, removal of cataracts, were influenced by Indian methods. One of the greatest of T'ang physicians was well versed in the medical literature of the Buddhists, and in his medical treatise, he wrote that in order to become a great physi-cian, one must understand the virtues of love, compassion, and equanimity stressed by the Buddhists. Only out of such under-standing can a doctor treat his patient, whether he be rich or poor, beautiful or ugly, enemy or friend, Chinese or barbarian, with the utmost impartiality, and accord him the same treatment as he would his closest friend.

However, it is in the religious life that Buddhism exerted its greatest influence and this is what we expect. Chinese religious life was enriched and deepened by the worship of compassionate Buddhas and bodhisattvas and the colorful pageantry and rituals accompanying such worship, while the Chinese religious horizon was broadened and extended by the Buddhist message of the unity of all life, tolerance of all creeds, and the universality of salvation. When the Chinese was too heavily burdened by the problems of the world, he could take refuge in the bodhisattva Kuan-yin, who offered him protection and spiritual consolation. Under the guidance of the same deity, he might even be led to the Pure Land to enjoy a heavenly hereafter.

The Indian religion Buddhism was able to render these significant contributions because after its introduction into China it adjusted itself to the Chinese environment and became more Chinese than Indian. The outstanding illustration of such adaptation is the establishment of the Chinese schools of Buddhism such as the T'ien-t'ai, Ch'an, Pure Land, and Hua-yen. The Buddhist *sangha* in China became closely identified with the interests of the state and performed religious ceremonies for the welfare of the state in state supported temples. The religious community was also subjected to the control and supervision of the state through such measures as the granting of ordination certificates by the state, the subordination of monastic officials to the civil authorities, compilation of a registry of monks by a government bureau, and the limitation of the size of the *sangha* by the state. Certain bodhisattvas also assumed Chinese appearances to render them more acceptable. Maitreya the Future Buddha became the fat genial laughing figure who greets visitors to the temple. Avalokitesvara or Kuan-yin became a female deity who received prayers from mothers anxious to have sons. Finally, the religion chose to neglect its anti-social and anti-family emphasis in China, and embraced unto itself the cardinal Confucian virtue of filial piety, which was manifested in the form of temples and pagodas dedicated to the memory of deceased ancestors. By such adaptations to the Chinese environment, and by fulfilling the religious aspirations of the Chinese, Buddhism developed into the most powerful religious force in China.

CHAPTER 8

Buddhism in Japan

IN VIEW OF THE SPREAD OF Buddhism in China during the Period of Disunity (third to sixth century) and of the lines of communication which existed between the Asiatic mainland and the island kingdom of Japan, it is not surprising that Buddhism would eventually find its way across the sea to the Japanese. Very early in history, probably before the Xian era, colonies of Japanese had already been established in the southern tip of Korea, an area that was rapidly being influenced by Chinese civilization. By the early part of the fifth century, Buddhism was already introduced into Korea. From Korea, it was then carried over into Japan by the Korean and Chinese immigrants who served as vehicles for the introduction of various elements of Chinese civilization to the island kingdom. How extensive were these preliminary contacts with Buddhism we do not know, for very few traces have been left in history. The first official presentation of the religion took place in 538 when a delegation consisting of Buddhist priests bringing along such sacred objects as sutras, banners, and images of the Buddha was sent by the Korean prince of Kudara to the Japanese court. Accompanying the presents was a message from the Korean prince which stated that Buddhism is the most excellent of all religions, very difficult to master, the practice of which would bring about endless blessings and even enlightenment.

This was the first inkling that the Japanese had of a religion which was concerned with the welfare of all peoples and not just one tribe or nation, and which consisted of divine figures worshipped with beautiful elaborate rituals.

In spite of its novelty and the beauty of its imagery, the new religion did not receive ready acceptance by the Japanese. The response was mixed, some favored, others were opposed. Outwardly the question was whether or not homage to the new Buddhist deities would arouse the wrath of the native gods worshipped by the Japanese as protectors of the country. In truth, however, the opposition stemmed from a rivalry between two clans for political supremacy. The party opposed to Buddhism was led by military clansmen who were against any innovations introduced from the mainland, and this group was supported by the native priests. In support of the new faith was the party of the diplomats and government administrators, who recognized the necessity of learning from the strong continental neighbor.

While this internal debate was going on, there was a continual influx of Buddhist missionaries from the mainland bringing with them the arts and sciences such as writing, astronomy, medicine, and so forth. The impact of these new branches of learning, and the activities of the increased number of Buddhist missionaries, succeeded in overcoming the opposition, and by the end of the sixth century, the religion was beginning to be accepted by the Japanese. The interest of Buddhism was assisted immensely just at this juncture by a personality who guided and consolidated the new religion with wisdom and insight. This individual was Prince Shotoku, who became regent of the empire in 593 at the age of nineteen.

Prince Shotoku and Buddhism

One of the first acts that Prince Shotoku performed was to proclaim Buddhism as the state religion, and to this end, he called for the establishment of four institutions, temple, asylum, hospital, and dispensary. The temple was to serve not only as a center for religious ceremonies but also as an educational center to study Buddhism. From the very beginning, therefore, Prince Shotoku had the idea that the new religion was to engage not only in religious but also educational and philanthropic activities. He also initiated diplomatic relations with China, and together with the envoys he sent monks and students to study the arts, sciences, and religions of the Chinese. After he had succeeded in carrying out his program of reforms, he proclaimed his fundamental principles in a document known as the Constitution of Seventeen Articles, in which political, moral, and religious ideas were closely interwoven. In the second article, he wrote, "Sincerely revere the 'Three Treasures.' The Three Treasures are the Buddha, dharma, and sangha, the final resort of all beings and the supreme object of faith for all peoples. Should any age or any people fail to revere this truth? There are few men who are utterly vicious. Every one will realize it (truth) if duly instructed. Could any wickedness be corrected without having resort to the Three Treasures?" 30

From this statement we can see that the prince was interested in applying the principles of Buddhism to all phases of national life. Having proclaimed it, he proceeded to implement it by giving lectures on Buddhist texts to his subjects in the palace and temple. His favorite texts were the *Lotus Sutra* and the *Vimalakirti* and his lectures on them have been preserved down to the present. In these lectures he emphasized the idea of universal communion of all sentient beings, and the life of dedication for the salvation of all living creatures. Such a broad, universal, and humanistic ideal had never been enunciated to the Japanese before this, and it inspired in them a much deeper appreciation and comprehension of human life.

Another conspicuous achievement of Prince Shotoku was in the realm of Buddhist art. Under his leadership, the Japanese artists brought forth an art based on the ceremonies and architecture that was most effective in instilling reverence for the religion. Rituals with musical accompaniment, performed in temples decorated with mural paintings and constructed with an eye for the combined effects of roofs, eaves, gables, and pillars, proved to be powerful forces working for the conversion of the Japanese to Buddhism.

As a result of Shotoku's efforts, Buddhist philosophy was being studied, monastic institutions established, beautiful temples constructed, the various arts such as music, rituals, and dancing were cultivated by the Japanese. The whole country was literally transformed by the civilizing influence of the religion which he patronized. It is no wonder that later Japanese sometimes regard him as an incarnation of Avalokitesvara, the Bodhisattva of compassion.

Given the impetus by Shotoku, Buddhism was able to develop unabatedly during the next few centuries. The progress of civilization and national unity prompted the Japanese to establish a national capital at Nara in 710, modeled after the Chinese capital of Ch'ang-an. The flourishing contacts which the Japanese maintained with the mainland brought over to Japan all the latest developments in Buddhism in China. In this manner the different Buddhist schools developed by the Chinese masters were introduced to the Japanese. The most prominent of these schools in Japan at this time was the Hosso or the Idealist School, established in Japan by the monk Dosho (629-700), undoubtedly the most outstanding Buddhist leader of the seventh century. Dosho had gone to China to study under the famous Chinese master Hsuan-tsang and had mastered the Idealist system under him. He returned to Japan to establish the Hosso School, and after him other Japanese monks went to China to study the Idealist system also. During the seventh and eighth centuries, doctrines of the Idealist School were accepted as the standard dogma of Japanese Buddhism.

One of the fundamental doctrines of the Hosso School was that not all beings possess the Buddha-nature. The school held that Buddhahood and spiritual enlightenment were achieved only by a select few. This idea made the Idealist system acceptable to the aristocratic regime of the times, and this alliance between court nobles and monastic officials soon brought about some undesirable results.

While Buddhism was the dominating force in Japan during the eighth century, the indigenous system, called Shintoism, or the Way of the Gods, still maintained some influence over the common people, but now, important movements were taking place. Shintoism was primarily a tribal cult, taken up with the worship of local deities, but under the influence of Buddhism, its ideas and visions began to broaden. The Sun-goddess, the supreme deity of Shintoism and who the Shintoists claim is the ancestor of the Japanese people, was proclaimed to be a manifestation of the Mahavairocana, the Great Brilliant One, and another Shinto god, Hachiman, god of the eight banner or the god of war, and was said to symbolize the eight-fold path.

While these changes were taking place in the religious sphere, the alliance between the nobles and prelates were bringing about some corruption within the monastic order. This alliance resulted in the accumulation of great wealth in the monasteries, mainly in the form of land which the monasteries were able to purchase or to seize through mortgage forfeits. This increase in wealth tempted the Buddhist clergy to strive for temporal powers and one even aspired to the throne. The Shinto priests collaborated or followed the lead of the Buddhists in this quest for wealth and power. The government realized that the power-hungry Buddhist prelates were a threat to the state, and so at the end of the eighth century, the court moved the capital from Nara to Kyoto. This move signaled the end of one period of Japanese history, the Nara period, and the beginning of another, the Heian period, lasting roughly from 800 to 1200.

Now that a new start was made in the new capital, it was felt that a new departure was needed in the form of a new synthesis that would put an end to the competition and rivalry between the different Buddhist schools. The task of achieving this synthesis was attempted by two prominent Buddhist leaders who aimed at establishing a center for Buddhism and gaining the support of the central government. These two were Saicho (767-822) and Kukai (774-835), and their teachings and organizations dominated Buddhism for the next few centuries. They did not attain their objective, mainly because of the rivalry between the two organizations which they established.

Saicho and Tendai Buddhism

Saicho was the descendant of a Chinese immigrant who joined the *sangha* in Nara, but was soon dissatisfied with conditions in that area and returned to his home on Mt. Hiei to live in solitude on the mountain. After the removal of the capital to Kyoto, the government bestowed generous donations to the monastery which Saicho established at Hiei, thus inaugurating an era of close cooperation between the political and religious authorities. Building upon this support of the government, Saicho began to carry out his plan of establishing a new center for Buddhism. Temples, colleges, and sanctuaries were built on Mt. Hiei, and the entire complex was called Chief Seat of the Buddhist Religion for Ensuring the Security of the Country.

In 804 Saicho went to China to study Buddhism, and returned in the following year, bringing back with him the scriptures and teachings of the T'ien-t'ai School (Tendai in Japanese). This brought increased prestige to Mt. Hiei, and before long it became the most powerful center of Buddhist studies in Japan. His opponents were followers of the Hosso School, who held, as we have seen, that the Buddha-nature was the monopoly of a select few, whereas the Tendai emphasized the universality of salvation, that the Buddha-nature was to be found even in the most vicious creature.

In his teachings, Saicho did not depart from what he had learned in China. These teachings have already been discussed in some detail in the chapter on Buddhism in China. However, in the ordination ceremony, Saicho initiated some new interpretations. One of the fundamental tenets of Tendai Buddhism is to enter into the abode of the Buddha. Saicho insisted that this could be done only by taking the vows of monkhood before the Buddha and the bodhisattvas, instead of the traditional method of taking refuge in the three jewels and vowing to observe the commandments. To Saicho, making the vows before the Buddha meant making them to one's own innermost soul or self, since we are all endowed with the Buddha-nature. By making the vows with faith and zeal, one can arouse the innermost wisdom and power that lie dormant within us. The initiation ceremony is therefore the means to awaken the inherent Buddha-nature. To carry out the initiation, Saicho petitioned the governemnt to permit him to build an ordination hall on Mt. Hiei, independent of similar institutions established in the area. This move aroused strong opposition from the Buddhist leaders of the Hosso School, and Saicho had to spend a good deal of time arguing against them. These debates appear to have undermined his health, and he died in 822. Within a week after his death, the government granted his request to establish the independent initiation hall.

The greatest contribution of Saicho lies in his establishment of the great Buddhist center at Mt. Hiei, with its numerous temples, colleges, meditation halls, and sanctuaries. Even after the center degenerated in later centuries, it continued to wield a tremendous influence over the course of the religion.

Kukai and Shingon Buddhism

Kukai shared with Saicho the dream of a unified Buddhism that was to be a synthesis of the divergent schools of his time. Early in his life he dabbled in Confucianism and Taoism, but finding satisfaction in neither, he turned to Buddhism and was soon converted. In 804 he went to China to study Tantric Buddhism. After two years on the mainland, he returned to Japan to found a monastery on Koyasan, about fifty miles south of Kyoto. For the next fifteen years he prepared and trained himself and a small group of disciples, and when Saicho died in 822, he at once emerged into prominence by his appointment as abbot of a great state temple in Kyoto, then as presiding priest of the Inner Sanctuary of the imperial palace. At the peak of his fame, he had himself buried alive while immersed in deep concentration on his beloved Koyasan in 835.

The type of Buddhism advocated by Kukai was Tantric in

nature, called in Japanese Shingon, or the true word. This is the Japanese translation of *mantra* or mystic syllables so prominent in the Tantras. Tantrism is a highly syncretistic system, embracing features taken from Mahayana Buddhism, Hinduism, and possibly even from Persian religions. In its pantheon may be found a host of deities and demons, all considered to be manifestations of the supreme Buddha Vairocana, and manifested by pictures or letters of the alphabet. In order to evoke the mysterious powers residing in these deities, elaborate rituals are performed, consisting of postures of the body, movements of the hands and fingers, and mystical utterances, all of which are rigidly prescribed.

In its attempt to systematize and unify the pantheon, Shingon Buddhism represents the cosmos in two *mandalas* or mystic circles. The ideal aspect of the cosmos is symbolized by the Thunderbolt-element Circle, the center of which is occupied by Vairocana, seated on a white lotus and engaged in deep contemplation. Vairocana as the supreme, primeval Buddha is the source of the cosmos, while all the other existences such as deities, men, animals, demons, and denizens of hell are considered as manifestations of his power. In this *mandala* he is surrounded by his emanations represented by figures and symbols. The dynamic aspect of the cosmos is symbolized by the Womb-element Circle, where all the deities and beings are arranged in accordance with the powers that they represent. In the Shingon rituals, these *mandalas* are placed on the ceremonial dais, and the mysterious powers residing in the figures and symbols are evoked by the worshipper by means of the appropriate posture of the body, gesture of the hands, and invocation of the mystic formulas. The postures and gestures, and the symbols such as the lotus and the thunderbolt, are looked upon as the body of Vairocana, while the ritual utterances and mystic formulas are regarded as the speech of Vairocana.

The contribution of Kukai lies in his success in organizing these elaborate rituals and symbols into a coherent and consistent system. There were certain factors working in favor of Kukai and his school. The Japanese by his time were tired of polemical discussions going on between the different schools on points of doctrine, and they were attracted by the pageantry, splendor, and mystery of the impressive rituals executed by the Shingon School. In the monasteries and the palaces, the incantations, sacrificial fires, fragrance of the incense, the combination of color and light, all presented a spectacle mysterious as well as absorbing to the people. They were also impressed by the mysterious powers of the *mantras* which could be evoked for the torture or the salvation of fellow creatures. By teaching that any gesture or utterance performed properly could enable one to identify himself with the supreme all-creating Vairocana, thereby fulfilling the religious aspirations of the people, Shingon Buddhism became enormously popular with the Japanese, and the school remains one of the largest numerically even at the present time.

The popularity of Shingon Buddhism led to an interesting development within the native Shinto faith. In an attempt to play a greater role in the thought and life of the common people, among whom Shintoism was still influential, Shingon Buddhism took a bold step by announcing that while the deities of the Buddhist pantheon were real and indestructible entities, the Shinto gods were their phenomenal appearances on earth. Thus every Shinto deity was regarded as a manifestation of a Buddhist deity. Such a step was easily justified by the Shingon concept of the two aspects of cosmic life. This syncretic religion was known as Double-aspect Shinto, and it represented an extension of the Buddhist pantheon to the Shinto gods as well as a Buddhist adaptation to native traditions.

Under the external splendor of the Buddhist church during the Heian period, there were increasing signs of deterioration and corruption. The trend begun during the Nara period of the temples acquiring large estates was accelerated during this period. Avaricious priests were determined to amass greater wealth for themselves and their temples, and often used their occult powers to attain these ends. In order to protect their land and other forms of wealth, the temples began to organize their monks into armies of monk-soldiers, but this defensive force was soon converted into an offensive power to grab more wealth and to intimidate the government. Struggle for power, murder, intrigue, and hatred were the dominant features of the times. Amidst such conditions, pious Buddhists believed, just as the Chinese Buddhists had believed five hundred years earlier in China, that the period of the decay of the law was at hand, and that they must seek refuge in the worship of Amitabha and the western paradise. The inception of the final period was put in the eleventh century in Japan, and not in the sixth century as in China, because the Japanese believed that the period of the Pure Law lasted one thousand years.

Jodo Buddhism

The prevailing sentiment expressed in this Amitabha worship was that since the fateful days have arrived, weak and vicious people could be saved only by invoking the name of Amitabha. To the Amitabha followers, Buddhism was a religion of pious devotion, not of mystic ritualism or contemplation. It was the way of grace, the easy way of salvation for sinful people. The one who established a new school of Buddhism, based on this easy way of salvation through the grace of the Buddha, was Honen (1133-1212). The school that he founded is known as Jodo, or the Pure Land.

Honen was born the son of a local chieftain. When he was eight, bandits killed his father, but the dying man requested that the son never think of revenge, for revenge would lead to further revenge. He insisted that his son become a monk. The son followed his father's dying wish, and enrolled at Mt. Hiei for his training. There he learned all the different branches of the Buddhist discipline, and could have become a high church official, but he yearned for something more than fame and authority, and in his search for repose, he turned to worship of Amitabha. He placed his reliance upon absolute faith in the redeeming grace of Amitabha, to be invoked by the formula, *namu Amida Butsu* (homage to the Buddha Amitabha). This faith could overcome all sin, all obstacle to salvation, because the saving power of Amitabha was unconditional. His message received a quick and ready response from a society that was disgusted with the sinfulness and corruption of the world, and fed up with the formal meaningless ritualism. His fame rose so rapidly that his ecclesiastical opponents became jealous of him, and initiated a campaign to persecute him. He was banished in 1207 when he was seventy-four years old, and though he was released after only four years, his health was so impaired that he soon died after release.

Though Honen's religion was a simple one based on faith, some differences of opinion soon arose amongst his followers. The most serious was whether or not this faith is a free gift of Amitabha's grace, having nothing to do with our intention or capacity. Is this faith generated by our own intention or capacity, or is it entirely the gift of Amitabha to us? One group contended that even our faith is not our own act or possession but is the gift of Amitabha. This group became known as Jodo Shinshu, or the True Doctrine of the Pure Land, and its most famous representative was Shinran (1173-1263).

Shinran was at Mt. Hiei when he was converted by Honen. He remained a disciple for six years, and when Honen was exiled, he moved to the provinces where he gave up his monastic robes to work as a common preacher to the country people. He even married and raised a family. He justified this action by saying that celibacy was a sign of lack of faith in Amitabha, because no sin was an obstacle to the saving grace of the Buddha. This was a significant change in Buddhism, for it meant that a person could be a good monk and still live a lay life, and this change is undoubtedly one of the main reasons why the Jodo Shinshu founded by Shinran became so popular in Japan, even down to the present time, when it is the largest sect numerically.

Honen once said that a bad man will be received in the Buddha-land, how much more a good man. Shinran was not satisfied with this and so he said that even a good man will be received in the Buddha-land, how much more a bad man. There is a striking similarity here with the idea expressed in the parable of the prodigal son, or the one sheep in a hundred gone astray. To Shinran, neither wisdom nor folly, neither virtue nor vice count for anything; the most important thing is faith in Amitabha, and this faith is Amitabha's free gift to us. The Jodo School of Honen says that invoking the name of the Buddha and practicing good deeds result in the accumulation of merits and smooth the way to rebirth in the Pure Land, but the Shinshu would abandon all ideas of accumulating merits, and place the sole reliance on the invocation, which should be uttered as an expression of trust and gratitude and not of supplication. Shinran thus went further than his master in departing from traditional Buddhist practices and moved closer to the daily life of the common people.

Nichiren

In contrast to the simple and pure piety of Honen, Nichiren (1222-1282) was a man of deep religious fervor and ardent reform. Whereas Honen's life was one of calm and peace, Nichiren's career was full of perils and crises. Early in his life he was tormented by the problem of what was the pure doctrine of Buddhism. To solve his problem he went to Mt. Hiei and studied there for ten years. When he was about thirty, he finally came to the conviction that the doctrines of the *Lotus Sutra* constituted the true teachings of the Buddha, and that these teachings should be interpreted in the light of conditions pertaining to the period of the decay of the law. All these teachings he reduced to a simple formula, "Adoration to the Lotus Sutra," which he considered to be the embodiment of all the truths of that sutra. By uttering the formula, one achieves enlightenment.

After arriving at this position, Nichiren returned to his native place to initiate his campaign to purify the prevailing Buddhism of his time, and in no time was rewarded for his efforts by being driven out. From his native province he went to the seat of the government at Kamakura, which was beset at this time by a series of natural calamities, earthquakes, pestilence, famines, and storms. Nichiren regarded these calamities as indications that the Buddha had withdrawn his protection from the country because of the prevalence of false doctrines. He put forth his ideas in an essay, *The Establishment of Righteousness and the Security of the Country,* in which he directed the brunt of his attack against the Jodo Buddhism of Honen, whom he regarded as the spirit of hell. However, all the other schools of Buddhism were also attacked, and their leaders denounced as hypocrites and traitors of the country. Only by the suppression of all these sects and by the conversion of the whole nation to the *Lotus Sutra* could order be restored to the land.

Such strong language of course did not endear him to his opponents, and the latter persuaded the government to brand him as a disturber of the peace and to banish him to an isolated peninsula. During this period of exile, he reviewed his life so far and found that everything he had done could be justified in the *Lotus Sutra.* Out of this conviction he formulated the following conclusions: (1) His religion was based on the unique teachings of the *Lotus Sutra.* (2) Mankind during the period of the decay of the law could be taught only by simple expressions and not by complicated doctrines. (3) In this period of decay and degeneration, the only true doctrine was that taught in the *Lotus Sutra.* (4) Japan was the land where the true form of Buddhism was to prevail, and from Japan it would extend to the rest of the world.

Though Nichiren was in exile, his message must have been disseminated widely by his followers, for when he returned after three years of exile, he found that he had more followers than before. This led him to be even more uncompromising, and his enemies even more bitter against him. Finally the government decided to get rid of the fiery reformer by banishing him once more, though the real intention was to have him murdered while on his way to exile. Nichiren must have guessed what the intention of the government was, and was prepared to accept death, when suddenly a ball of fire flashed across the heavens just as his executioner was about to swing the sword. The startled executioner dropped the sword, while the rest of the soldiers were terrified. Thinking that this was a portent from heaven, they decided to forego execution and to carry out the banishment.

Having survived this close brush with death, Nichiren regarded the years after this as his second life, which was to be devoted to an even greater mission. This conviction sustained him during the bitter years of his exile. When he was released from exile, the government was willing to give official sanction to his teachings, on condition that he did not attack the other schools. Being the prophet that he considered himself to be, he refused this condition. But in his declining years, he was no longer the fiery reformer; instead he directed his attention to the establishment of the center which was to propagate Buddhism to the rest of the world. He was firmly convinced that he was the messenger sent by the Buddha to bring about the transformation of the world to Buddhism. However, the hardships suffered during the years of his exile proved too much for the health of the prophet and he died before he could establish the center on the site which he chose on Mt. Fuji.

The combative attitude of Nichiren endeared him to the warrior class, who found in the master's personality and teachings a religious support for their patriotism and martial ideals. The chauvinism and militarism which characterize Japanese policy during the nineteenth and twentieth centuries could be traced to some extent to the aggressive attitude and ideas of Nichiren.

Zen Buddhism

After its glorious history in China, Ch'an or Zen Buddhism was introduced into Japan during the twelfth century by the Japanese monk Eisai (1141-1215), who had been dissatisfied with the scholastic tendencies at Mt. Hiei and went to China to study a new method of spiritual discipline. The most famous leader of the school in Japan, however, was Dogen (1200-1253) for it was he who by his creativity established the school on a firm footing and gave it a peculiar Japanese flavor.

At an early age, Dogen was bothered by a perplexing problem: if one already possesses the Buddha-nature, then why does one have to practice the religious life to gain enlightenment? The search for an answer to this question of the relationship between the innate and acquired enlightenment led Dogen to go from one temple to another in Japan, and finally induced him to sail to China. Again he wandered from master to master until he found one whom he considered worthy, and under the guidance of that master attained enlightenment.

From his master, Dogen learned the technique of sitting in meditation, called in Japanese *zazen*. He felt that this was in line with the genuine traditions of the religion, for the Buddha and the first patriarch of the school, Bodhidharma, had achieved enlightenment by sitting in meditation. In this technique, the disciple sits upright with his legs crossed, and frees his mind from all attachments to externals, from all desires, and from all concepts. He must not even think about how to become the Buddha.

The key to the meaning of the last sentence lies in Dogen's insistence that enlightenment is present in *zazen* itself. To him, practice and enlightenment are one and the same, there is no separation between the two. The practice of *zazen* is regarded as the manifestation of the original enlightenment, and the disciple who is practicing this sitting in meditation will find the Buddha-nature or the Absolute within himself and not outside. Here we see the answer which Dogen arrived at to solve his perplexing problem. He considered the innate Buddha-nature and the practice to acquire that Buddha-nature to be one and the same. *Zazen* therefore embraces both the metaphysical absolute and ordinary phenomena, and constitutes the essence of all Buddhism. When the Zen disciple practices sitting in meditation, he does not do so with the hope of acquiring something new, but he does so "to manifest continuously the enlightenment which is present in the practice." [31]

Zen was introduced into Japan at a favorable moment in her history. The military men and administrators who were in power needed a religion which made for mental firmness and resolute action. These men considered the traditional schools of Buddhism in Japan to be too effeminate or too intricate and mysterious, but in Zen they found a religion with a very simple practice, sitting in meditation, which could be done anywhere, and yet powerful enough to bring about mental tranquillity. Zen therefore gave the warriors the means to harmonize their spiritual aspirations with their practical training. For this reason, Zen Buddhism became exceedingly popular with the samurai or warrior class.

The mind of the warrior is simple and direct, just as the discipline of Zen is simple and direct. In attack, the warrior is single-minded in pressing toward the achievement of his goal, the defeat of his enemy, and in the pursuit of his goal, he must not be distracted by physical, emotional, and intellectual considerations. Likewise the Zen disciple while sitting in meditation is free from all detachments and doubts, and single-minded in his purpose. The sword is the main weapon of the warrior, and Zen has a great deal to do with the art of swordsmanship, not so much with technique as with the mental attitude of the swordsman. This mental attitude is based on the Buddhist doctrine of non-self, or egolessness. As long as the swordsman clings to the idea of an ego, he sees the dualism between the self and the other, he is attached to external elements and becomes emotionally disturbed by them. In this state he is beset by doubts and hesitations, and this hesitation provides the opening for his opponent to finish him. For the master-swordsman, however, his attitude is one of complete self-abandonment, free from intellection and calculation. He moves his sword freely, spontaneously, and automatically, without any interfering calculation or deliberation. There is perfect identification between the doer and his action. In this respect, swordsmanship is akin to the *koan* exercises, where the master poses the problem and the disciple must answer immediately without any deliberation or hesitation.

Even after Zen Buddhism was transplanted in Japan, the Japanese Buddhist monks still made periodic trips to China to seek religious guidance from the the Chinese masters. While in China, these monks were interested not only in their religion but in all aspects of Chinese culture, and when they returned to Japan, they brought back with them paintings, calligraphy, porcelains, jade, lacquer, embroideries, and other items of Chinese art. The presence of these artistic objects in the Zen temples led many of the latter to become centers of artistic achievements. Among these achievements may be included the art of gardening. The most famous Zen garden in Japan is that found in Ryoanji in Kyoto, planned as far back as 1499. The garden is rectangular in form, 102 by 50 feet, and consists of nothing but sand and fifteen stones arranged in five groups and covered with moss. There is no path or stepping stone on the sand, since no one walks on it. It is void of all animal and vegetative life. This garden is the Zen symbol of the pure mind without any conscious thought present. Another artistic contribution is the Zen influence on the tea ceremony, where the spirit of harmony, reverence, purity, and tranquillity that runs through the tea ceremony is the same as that which is essential in a Zen monastery.

In China, only two schools of Buddhism have been active during the past thousand years. In Japan, in spite of attempts of numerous leaders to unify the religion, sectarian differences persist, and in Japan we find more contrasting Buddhist schools or sects than in any other Buddhist country. On the one hand, there are the two main branches of the Pure Land School, the Jodo claiming over four million followers, and the Shin claiming about ten million. Both emphasize faith, but the Shin sect goes further and contends that this faith is given to us by Amitabha. With the priests of the Shin sect, celibacy is a yoke to be cast aside. The spiritual goal lies in producing a peaceful contentment while pursuing the ordinary activities of social life. Contrast this contentment with the militant aggressiveness of the Nichiren sect, whose followers believe that Japan is to be the spiritual center of the world. Nichiren was the religious zealot, supremely confident of the truth of his cause and intolerant of the claims of others. There is yet another contrast. If we enter a Zen monastery, we will find monks seated row by row, cross-legged, clothed in simple robes, body erect from the waist, and concentrating intently on their problems. In this surrounding of stark simplicity and austerity, the dominant atmosphere is one of tranquillity and silence. If we should go from a Zen to a Shingon temple, we enter into another world. We are immediately ushered into grounds where altars, statues, pictures, banners, and symbolic utensils are everywhere, prepared for the performance of all kinds of rituals. The ringing of bells, the beating of gongs, the singing of music, resound through the grounds and buildings. Upon entering the temple, one sees priests dressed in the most brilliant robes waving their hands, manipulating their fingers, and reciting mysterious formulas. While all this is going on, fumes from the burning incense waft the audience into a state of euphoric stupor, so that the mystery of the sacraments becomes even more mysterious. These diverse practices and tenets only serve to remind us that Japanese Buddhism is really a vast system, held together by certain fundamental beliefs, namely, belief in the Lord Buddha as the savior of mankind, belief in the equality of all sentient beings, belief in the universality of life, and belief in the attainment of perfection through different paths.

CHAPTER 9

Buddhism in Tibet

BEFORE BUDDHISM was introduced into Tibet, the Tibetans believed in a form of shamanism called Bon. Not much is known about this primitive belief. From the meager Tibetan and Chinese records available, we learn that the Bon world was filled with spirits both good and hostile. Such spirits roamed about in the mountains and valleys or lived in trees and rocks. When they were propitiated they tended to be friendly but when they were annoyed, then they became hostile and sent pestilence or sickness to the people, and sometimes even devoured children. To propitiate these spirits there was a group of exorcists and priests who when necessary fell into trances to communicate with them. Animal sacrifices were resorted to on certain occasions, such as the swearing of the oath of fealty and the signing of treaties. According to the Chinese chroniclers, the people sacrificed sheep, dogs, monkeys, horses, oxen, asses, and even human beings. The human victims were first seized by the hands and feet, then they were cut open and their hearts torn out. After this the blood and flesh were scattered to the four corners. At the oath of fealty, the participants were warned that if they broke their oath, their bodies would be cut into pieces like those of the victims. Such were some of the beliefs and practices of native Bon religion

189

which confronted Buddhism when it was first introduced into Tibet during the seventh century.

The First Phase

Tibet at that time was ruled by a king named Srong-btsam-sgam-po, who had already married three Tibetan princesses to bring about a confederation of the Tibetan provinces. With this achieved, he turned his attention to India, where he obtained through his ambassador the hand of a Nepalese princess, Khri-can, daughter of King Amśurvarman of Nepal. According to the Tibetans, this princess brought along some images of the Buddha when she went to Tibet, and in this fashion was responsible for the introduction of Buddhism into the country. Having concluded this alliance with the Nepalese, Srong-btsam-sgam-po then turned his attention to the direction of China. He had heard that some Turkish tribes had asked for and were given the hands of some Chinese princesses in marriage, and he requested the T'ang ruling house to accord him the same treatment. After an initial refusal, the T'ang emperor acceded to this request and offered in 641 Princess Wen-ch'eng of the imperial family to the Tibetan king. In an attempt to enhance her status, the Tibetan sources say that the princess was a daughter of the emperor. Some accounts claim that this Chinese princess brought along with her an image of the Buddha, and that this was the first time the Tibetan king became acquainted with Buddhism. However, this is not likely, for the Nepalese princess Khri-can preceded the arrival of Wen-ch'eng in the Tibetan court, and furthermore as early as 632 or soon thereafter, King Srong-btsam-sgam-po in an attempt to further his knowledge of Buddhism, dispatched Thon-mi Sambhota with a mission of Tibetans to Kashmir to study the Indian system of writing. This event suggests that the king was already acquainted with Kashmir as a center of learning and that there had been previous contacts with the region. After a sojourn of some four years in Kashmir, the mission returned to Tibet and devised the Tibetan alphabet of thirty letters modelled after the Indian system.

Tibetan chronicles tell us that the new religion made great advances during the reign of King Srong-btsam-sgam-po. They claim that the king built temples throughout the kingdom, made Buddhism the state religion, and encouraged the Tibetans to follow the principles of the religion. Such accounts are however the embellishments of later Tibetan writers intent on glorifying the king. The truth of the matter is that during this initial period of introduction, Buddhist activities were at a minimum. Srong-btsam-sgam-po did establish the foundations of Tibetan civilization, unify the country, and introduce the rudiments of art and literature. After his death, very little more was heard about the newly introduced religion until the next century, when another of the Tibetan kings married a Chinese princess named Chin-ch'eng in 710, who brought along with her some elements of Chinese civilization as well as some Chinese Buddhist monks.

The growing influence of Buddhism in the royal family soon aroused the hostility of the nobility, who allied themselves with the native Bon priests to block the progress of the new religion. In 740-41, a pestilence swept the country, lightning struck the royal palace, and floods damaged the harvest. All these misfortunes were regarded as signs that the Bon spirits were displeased with the invasion of Buddhism, and they provided the pretext for the nobles to start a campaign against the religion. Though the Tibetan king was favorable to Buddhism, he was unable to stop the opposition of nobles, and he felt obliged to consult with Santarakshita, an Indian monk then in Tibet, as to what he should do. The Indian monk suggested that Padmasambhava, a Tantric master, be invited to Tibet to subdue the hostile Bon spirits. This was done and Padmasambhava arrived in Tibet in 747.

Padmasambhava is undoubtedly a historical individual, although the Tibetans have built up a host of legends about him that cannot be accepted. In his youth he was adopted by the king of Udyana in northwest India as a son, and when the boy grew up, the king retired from public life and entrusted the rule over his kingdom to his adopted son. Padmasambhava had no desire to continue as ruler, however, and left his home and kingdom to become a Buddhist monk. He concentrated on Tantric Buddhism and soon learned all the secret doctrines and the mysterious powers associated with that aspect. After his arrival in Tibet, he used these powers to subdue the Bon demons who were hostile to Buddhism. An example of his triumph over the local demons is his victory over the Bon mountain spirit. This spirit took the form of a white yak standing on the side of a hill, with snow swirling out of his mouth and nose. Padmasambhava seized him by the mouth with an iron hook, bound him with a noose and iron shackles. The demon was thus forced to swear an oath of allegiance to the Tantric master. After being subjugated, these local demons were included in the Tibetan Buddhist pantheon and became protectors of the religion. In all, Padmasambhava remained in Tibet some eighteen months, although some Tibetan accounts exaggerated this figure to fifty years. He built the monastery in Samye, just thirty miles from Lhasa the capital, and that monastery has had a continuous existence since that time.

The subjugation of the local Bon demons by Padmasambhava is usually interpreted to mean that Buddhism triumphed over the native Tibetan religion. Though the resistance of the Bon priests and their allies the nobles was broken for the time being, those two groups were by no means silenced permanently, for their opposition still plagued Buddhism from time to time.

The main development of Buddhism was now to take place in the Samye Monastery under the abbotship of Santarakshita. The first seven Tibetan monks were ordained there under his regime, and Indian masters were invited to Tibet to translate the Sanskrit texts into Tibetan and to train capable Tibetan youths for the work of propagating the religion. Since Padmasambhava was a Tantric master, Tantric Buddhism was heavily favored by the monks at Samye. Certain features of Tantrism, such as the employment of the skull as a drinking vessel and the leg bone as a trumpet, the spreading of human bones to denote a holy spot, and dancing with a wreath of human bones as ornament, were considered repulsive by the Tibetans, and they denounced the religion as an evil brought to Tibet from India.

Besides the Indian monks and translators working in Tibet

during the eighth century, there were some Chinese monks who were also active in translation activities. Such Chinese monks, who were mostly followers of the Ch'an School of Buddhism in China, were in Tibet as an aftermath of the marriage of the Chinese princesses to the Tibetan kings. The presence of these Chinese monks led to a historic debate between them and the followers of Santarakshita, under the leadership of Kamalasila, held at the end of the eighth century before the Tibetan king. The leader of the Chinese who debated against Kamalasila was named as Hva-shang in the Tibetan records, as Ta-ch'eng or Mahayana in the Chinese sources.

As a representative of the Ch'an School, Hva-shang contended that the attainment of Buddhahood did not take place gradually but instantly and intuitively, that conscious striving for enlightenment was of no avail, and that one should abandon all deliberate action and take refuge in inactivity. Kamalasila argued that complete abstention from all acts is impossible. The very decision to take refuge in inactivity is in itself an activity of the mind already. Complete absence of thought or of deliberate action can take place only when an individual is unconscious or drunk. Kamalasila also asserted that it is impossible to attain Buddhahood suddenly, that it is necessary to strive for moral improvement gradually, and that only after the proper degree of advancement has been achieved can one attain enlightenment. The Indian monks present at the debate supported Kamalasila's contentions, and according to the Tibetan accounts of the debate, Hvashang was forced to admit defeat, and he and his followers were expelled from the country.

This debate and the defeat of the Chinese were of great significance to the development of Tibetan Buddhism. The result determined that henceforth the Tibetans were committed to Mahayana Buddhism in its Indian garb, and not the Chinese versions. In addition to Tantric Buddhism, the Madhyamika system, founded by Nagarjuna and introduced into Tibet by Santarakshita and Kamalasila, was to become dominant in the land. As this system in its early development involved some consideration of the Prajna sutras and the Abhidharma literature of the

Sarvastivadin School, the Tibetans also paid a good deal of attention to those fields of Buddhist literature. Tantric Buddhism, after its introduction into Tibet by Padmasambhava, took over some of the deities and practices of the native Bon faith in an attempt to overcome some of the native resistance. This mixture of Tantrism, Mahayana Buddhism, and Bonism make up the Tibetan religion commonly called Lamaism, or the religion of the lama, a Tibetan word which means the superior one.

During the early ninth century, Buddhism received strong support from King Ral-pa-can, who ruled from 817-836. This king is chiefly remembered for his efforts to systematize and standardize the Tibetan translations. Since the introduction of the religion, a considerable body of literature had been translated into Tibetan from a number of foreign languages such as Sanskrit, Khotanese, and even Chinese. Coming from different traditions and backgrounds, the translators used a variety of expressions to translate the technical terms of the religion. Mistakes in translation also were common. The primitive Tibetan language likewise was not flexible enough to express some of the subtle ideas of Buddhist philosophy. The task of effecting improvements in the literary style and technical terms was entrusted by the king to a commission of Indian and Tibetan scholars. These scholars established a system of standard terms to be followed by all translators, and they also went through the existing body of literature to make the necessary changes in form and terminology.

Besides promoting reforms in Buddhist literature, the king also encouraged Buddhism by decreeing that throughout the land, seven families should be jointly responsible for the support of one Buddhist monk. Monks were appointed to official positions, and nobles were required to conform to Buddhist practices and beliefs.

This promotion of Buddhism by Ral-pa-can evoked strong opposition from the nobility, who organized a conspiracy to murder the king and to install an anti-Buddhist ruler on the throne. This ruler, Lang-dar-ma, ruled from 836-842, and his reign was marked by a series of measures all aimed at suppressing Buddhism. Temples and monasteries were razed, the valuable paintings kept in them destroyed, famous Buddhist translators were killed, and monks forced to return to laity and marry. Lang-dar-ma was finally murdered by a fanatic Buddhist monk, who claimed that he did so out of compassion for the ruler, in order to prevent him from committing further offenses against Buddhism and thus accumulate bad karma.

The persecution of Lang-dar-ma struck deeply into the leadership of the Buddhism in Tibet, and for a time, it looked as if the religion would disappear from the scene. However, a few Tibetan monks did manage to flee from Tibet to the borders of China, and when conditions became more favorable, these monks returned to Tibet to work for the revival of their religion. Even so, progress was slight until the first part of the eleventh century, when the Indian monk Atisha was invited to go to Tibet. Atisha arrived in 1042, and his coming marked the beginning of a new period in Tibetan Buddhist history.

The Second Phase

Until his death in 1053, Atisha worked actively to restore Buddhism. So effective were his efforts that the foundations of the religion were firmly laid for the remarkable expansion that was to follow. Though he was a follower of the Tantras, he strove to maintain a proper balance between religious discipline, mysticism, and Tantric practices. Everywhere he went in Tibet, he conferred the mystic initiation on his pupils, translated sutras, and built monasteries. It was Atisha also who was responsible for the introduction of the sixty-year cycle in Tibetan chronology, with the first year of the first cycle being set at 1027 A.D.

One of the most remarkable Tibetan monks of the eleventh century was Mar-pa, who was considered a bodhisattva even though he married and accumulated riches through his mastery of the *mantras*. For a fee of ten ounces of gold, he agreed to protect the rich and influential Tibetans from evil and demonic forces, and this brought him a sizable income annually. Besides his wife he kept eight other female disciples whom he considered to be his religious consorts. He reared a family and also engaged in agricultural pursuits. To the ordinary people, he appeared to be leading a worldly life, but to his disciples, he was a Buddhist master of the Tantras, for on different occasions he was said to have projected his own soul into a dead body and to take that body as his own, a practice known as "entering the dead." This was the most difficult of the occult arts of Tantrism.

Of the numerous disciples who studied under Mar-pa, the most famous was Milarepa, 1040-1123. His father died when he was seven. Before his death, the father had entrusted the family property to a brother with instructions that the brother take care of the property until Milarepa came of age. The brother however kept the property as his own and forced Milarepa, his mother, and his sister to work like slaves. When Milarepa's mother asked for the return of the property, the unscrupulous brother-in-law claimed that the property was his own and that he had merely loaned it to Milarepa's father. He then drove the widow and the two children out to fend for themselves. This so angered the widow that she and Milarepa devised a scheme for revenge. Milarepa was to become a wizard.

After long months of training, Milarepa became proficient enough as a wizard and returned to the village of his evil uncle with the intention of destroying him and his family. He found the uncle celebrating the marriage of his son, and by the exercise of the black art which he acquired, caused the roof of the house to collapse, killing all the occupants within.

Now that the revenge had been exacted, Milarepa underwent a conversion. Instead of directing the forces and powers that he had acquired to evil ends, he decided that they should be channeled to beneficial goals, and once this decision was taken he searched for a master to teach him a new life. He found this master in Mar-pa. Mar-pa at once detected the great potentialities of Milarepa, but first subjected him to the most gruelling ordeals to test him. Milarepa was beaten, deceived, insulted, made to build a house and then ordered to tear it down, sent on journeys and then recalled for no apparent reason. Twice

Milarepa ran away from his master and twice he returned, until he finally learned all that the master could teach him.

With his Tantric training completed, Milarepa returned to his native village expecting to find his mother there, but found instead only a broken down house with some bones left. His sister had also gone away. So Milarepa, minus all his earthly possessions, sought refuge in a cave to devote his life to ascetic practices. He ate only what he could find near his refuge, he wore little or no clothing at all, he was filthy and unkempt and appeared like a ghost, but detached as he was from the world around him, he felt a profound peace of mind. His sister finally found him in his wretched condition and tried to persuade him from his ascetic practices, but to no avail. More years of practices in solitude enabled him to raise his body at will and to produce bodily warmth, so that even in the coldest weather he did not freeze. While not meditating and practicing austerities, he composed poems and sang songs in which he described the supreme joys of a mystic who had renounced the world and found refuge in the Buddha.

The new zeal in the religion brought about by the activities of Atisha, Mar-pa, Milarepa, and others during the eleventh century resulted in the Tibetans taking a deeper and more genuine interest in Buddhism, and not just in the magic and exorcisms of the Tantric masters. Huge monasteries were now being built in the land, and different schools were being established. The nobility were gradually becoming aware of the power and prestige that went with the monastic robe, and many of them sought to become abbots of the great monasteries. Even after they became abbots, they still retained their temporal powers, which they sought to extend by absorbing some rival monastery. Some of the monasteries became virtual fortresses, from which the abbot sallied forth with his army of monks now turned into soldiers to conquer some neighboring institution. By the time the Mongols appeared on the scene in the thirteenth century, the struggle had narrowed down to a fight between a few powerful surviving monasteries, one of which was the Sa-skya (Fallow Land) Monastery.

Sa-skya Monastery

This Sa-skya Monastery was founded by a Tibetan named hBrog-mi, a contemporary of Atisha, in 1073. The abbots of this monastery were permitted to marry, and the line of succession was hereditary. The most famous of the abbots was Sa-skya Pandita, better known as Sa-pan (1182-1251), because he handled the negotiations which resulted in the submission of Tibet to the Mongols. He was a learned monk, versed in the languages of India, and was looked upon as an incarnation of the bodhisattva Manjusri.

In 1239, a Mongol army under the generalship of Godan advanced into Tibet, and after pushing to a point northeast of the capital Lhasa, it retired. The withdrawal did not mean that the Mongols had renounced the conquest of Tibet, but merely that they were ready to negotiate after having impressed upon the Tibetans the futility of fighting.

The Tibetans chose Sa-pan, abbot of Sa-skya Monastery, to handle the negotiations. The meeting with Godan took place in Lan-chou in northwest China in 1246. Tibetan historians aver that the Mongol general became favorably inclined toward Buddhism when an ailment which he had was cured by Sa-pan. It appears more likely that this favorable attitude arose out of Godan's fear of the mysterious powers manifested by Sa-pan while uttering the *mantras*.

After the negotiations, Sa-pan wrote a letter to the civil and religious authorities in Tibet, in which he praised the Mongol Khan, calling him a bodhisattva who had the deepest faith in Buddhism. To persuade the Tibetans to abide by the terms of submission, he mentioned that the Mongol armies were beyond count, and that the whole world had submitted to their power. The Mongols in turn offered Sa-pan the golden patent, which enabled him to act as the Mongol vice-regent in Tibet. Sa-pan's work was completed by his nephew, hPhags-pa, who obtained from the Mongols firm recognition that the Sa-skya abbot was supreme over all Tibet in all matters temporal and spiritual. The peculiar practice in Tibet of a religious figure being the head of the church and state thus started with the Sa-skya abbot during the thirteenth century. For the Mongols it was a satisfactory arrangement, for it relieved them of the necessity of stationing an army of occupation in Tibet, while assuring at the same time their control of the Tibetans through the office of the Sa-skya abbotship.

Unfortunately for the Mongols, their hopes were not fully realized. The abbots of the other powerful monasteries in Tibet were dissatisfied with so much power concentrated in the hands of the Sa-skya abbot, and they refused to obey his decrees. Their numerous attempts at revolt had to be suppressed by Mongol force. With the fall of the Mongol dynasty in China, the power of the Sa-skya abbot declined further. When the succeeding Chinese Ming dynasty assumed power, it still wanted to maintain friendly relations with Tibet, but instead of favoring one monastery, the Chinese accorded recognition to the abbots of all the important monasteries.

While the different monasteries during the fourteenth century might be vying for political and religious paramountcy, they did have one thing in common. The abbots and monks of these monasteries were all interested in the acquisition of more temporal powers and wealth, their minds were concentrated on their ecclesiatical properties and worldly pleasures. Such being the case, religious discipline became lax, monks indulged in marriage and wine, indolence and complacency became rampant. The monastic order was more intent on preserving its temporal involvements and pleasures than in living the pure religious life taught by the Buddha. The time was ripe for a reformer to purify the religion and check the widespread decay within the order. Such a reformer was Tsong-kha-pa, 1357-1419.

The Yellow Sect and the Dalai-lama

Tsong-kha-pa entered the monastic order at seven as a novice. At sixteen he began the systematic study of the writings of the Indian masters beginning with Nagarjuna, then proceeding with

logic, prajna philosophy, the *Abhidharma,* and finally the *Vinaya.*
His study of the *Vinaya* led him to realize the low state of decay
and laxity into which the Tibetan clergy had degenerated, and
prompted him to think about ways to reform the church. By the
time he was ordained at twenty-five, he was already a master of
the different spheres of Buddhist learning as well as in such
secular fields as medicine and mathematics. The results of his
scholarship are embodied in a great number of works, the most
famous of which is entitled *Steps to Enlightenment,* completed
in 1403.

The great scholarship and the pure religious life of Tsong-
kha-pa soon attracted large numbers of disciples, who banded
together to form a new school, the dGe-lugs-pa (Virtuous)
School. In 1409 the school built its first monastery, dGah -ldan
(Joyful, pronounced Gandan), and within a decade after that,
the hBras-spung (Heaps of Rice, in 1416) and Se-ra (1419).
Tsong-kha-pa advocated a return to the traditional Buddhist way
of life as prescribed in the *Vinaya,* such as celibacy, prohibition
of wine and meat, and rigid monastic discipline. He also wanted
to restrict or modify some of the Tantric magical practices. Although he antagonized some of the older sects in Tibet, he won
wide and immediate approval from the populace, who were tired
of the laxity and corruption prevalent among the followers of the
older sects, and who were inspired by the fresh ideas and religious
zeal of the new school. Because its followers wore yellow robes
and hats, the new sect was also called the Yellow Sect.

After Tsong-kha-pa died in 1419, leadership of the sect passed
on to his great disciples. The third in the line of succession was
dGe-ldun-grub-pa, a nephew of Tsong-kha-pa who assumed
leadership in 1438, and who played an important role in con-
solidating the hierarchy of the Yellow Church. Apparently he
was the one who first developed the incarnation theory as a rigid
dogma to be followed strictly. According to this theory, after the
leader of the sect dies, he will be reincarnated in the body of a
newly born baby, and the task of the church is to find and
identify the baby. The dogma further declares that the grand
lama or leader of the sect is the reincarnation of Avalokitesvara,

the protective deity of Tibet. dGe-ldun-grub-pa is now called the first Grand Lama of the Yellow Sect.

The rapid growth of the Yellow Sect evoked the opposition of the older sects, the most powerful of which was the Red Sect. This sect had the support of the king of Tsang, the strongest province in Tibet. Confronted with this opposition, the leaders of the Yellow Sect began to look elsewhere for support, and in this search they turned to the Mongols. The Mongols had been converted to Lamaism once before by Sa-pan and his nephew hPhags-pa, but that conversion had not lasted and the task had to be done over again. In 1578, the third Grand Lama of the Yellow Sect arrived at the court of Altan Khan of the Mongols, not only to propagate the faith among the Mongols but also to negotiate an alliance with them. Valuable gifts such as a *mandala* made of 500 ounces of silver and a golden bowl filled with precious gems were made by the khan to the Grand Lama, and in return the latter called upon the Mongols to give up their bloody practices and take refuge in Buddhism. The khan then conferred on the prelate the title Dalai-lama (*dalai* is the Mongol word meaning great ocean), Holder of the Thunderbolt, while he in turn received the title, Ruler of the Gods and King of the Dharma. The title Dalai-lama about which we hear so much thus originated with the third Grand Lama of the Yellow Sect. He became the third Dalai-lama, and the title was then bestowed retrospectively on his two predecessors.

As a result of this mission, the Mongols were converted to Lamaism and thereafter became fanatical followers of the Yellow Sect.

When the third Dalai-lama died, he was reincarnated in the grandson of Altan Khan. This birth of the fourth Dalai-lama among the Mongols was probably the result of some intrigue, but it served its purpose, for the ties that bound the Mongols to the Yellow Sect were drawn even closer. With the advent of the fifth Dalai-lama, this alliance between the Yellow Sect and the Mongols was carried to the final conclusion. Faced with increasing opposition from the Red Sect and the ruler of Tsang, the fifth Dalai-lama called upon his Mongol allies to intervene in Tibet in 1641. In the military campaign that followed, the Tibetan armies were quickly defeated and the king of Tsang killed. With Tibet subjugated, Gusri Khan of the Mongols established the fifth Dalai-lama as the religious head of the entire Buddhist community, while he himself took on the title of King of Tibet. The relation between the two was that of patron and priest, the patron supported the religious position of the priest, while the priest supported the temporal position of the patron. There was no precise definition of the superiority or inferiority of the one to the other. When Gusri Khan died in 1655, his successors showed little interest in the administration of Tibet, with the result that the fifth Dalai-lama, who was a powerful and determined character, drew all powers into his hands. Tibet now became the priest-state, with the Dalai-lama being not only the spiritual but also the temporal ruler over the entire country. Such a situation was to endure down to the invasion and subjugation of Tibet by the Chinese Communists in 1959.

The fifth Dalai-lama is also remembered for two other deeds. He built the imposing palace called the Potala, which was to serve as the residence for all the Dalai-lamas following him. This was an enormous structure, thirteen stories high. The central part of the building contained the ceremonial halls, chapels, and the mausoleums of deceased Dalai-lamas, all covered with gold and precious stones. The western wing contained the quarters for one hundred seventy-five monks, while the eastern wing housed the meeting halls of the National Assembly, government offices, and school for officials. The apartment of the Dalai-lama was on the top floor. The Potala was also an enormous storehouse, with rooms filled with priceless treasures dating back a thousand years of Tibetan history. The regalia of past kings and lamas, gifts from Mongol and Chinese emperors, arms and armor used by the soldiers of the past, religious paintings and scrolls, and scriptures written on palm leaves, all these were stored in the Potala. Some of the scriptures were written with ink of powdered gold, silver, iron, copper, conch shell, turquoise, and coral, each line written with a different ink. In the basement were storerooms filled with stocks of butter, tea, and cloth to be distributed to the army, monasteries, and officials. In one section was a prison for wrong doers of the high ranks.

The other deed for which the fifth Dalai-lama is remembered is his confirmation of the abbot of the Tashilunpo Monastery (located in Shigatse west of Lhasa), who had been his tutor, as the second grand lama in Tibet, with his successor to be chosen in the same manner as the Dalai-lama. He also declared him to be the incarnation of Amitabha and bestowed on him the title, Panchen-lama. This title is a combination of a Sanskrit and a Tibetan word, "pan" being derived from *pandita,* the wise one, and "chen" from *chen-po,* great. Thus we have two grand lamas, the Dalai-lama as the supreme spiritual and temporal ruler of the land, and the Panchen-lama, the spiritual head of one monastery.

In view of his accomplishments, the fifth Dalai-lama is probably the greatest of all those who held the position. The Tibetans acknowledge this by calling him the Great Fifth. He put an end to internal strife in Tibet, he unified the country, and he led the Yellow Sect to its triumph over the other sects. However, his act in calling upon the Mongols to intervene led to consequences which he could not have foreseen. Once the Tibetans recognized the right of the foreign patron to intervene in Tibetan affairs, they exposed themselves to the shifting political changes outside Tibet. In succeeding centuries, the Manchu Dynasty, Nationalist China, and finally Communist China, all asserted their influence over Tibetan politics.

The Great Fifth died in 1682, but before this, he appointed his own son as regent. It is commonly believed that the regent-son withheld the announcement of the Dalai-lama's death in order to get the workmen to finish the Potala. Because of this situation, the sixth Dalai-lama, when he was enthroned in 1696, was already a grown-up boy familiar with the pleasures of the world. Even after he was proclaimed the Dalai-lama, he wrote love poems and indulged in sensual pleasures in disguise. Despite his unorthodox behavior, the Tibetans still accepted him, and attempted to justify his activities by explaining that the person who shared in the pleasures of the world was not the real person of the Dalai-lama but was only his apparition, his phantom body. This is in accord with Buddhist Mahayana doctrine that the transcendental Buddha creates numerous apparitional bodies who are born among mankind to act as man does. When the Manchu emperor K'ang-hsi tried to treat the libertine sixth Dalai-lama as not the true incarnation of the fifth, he was vigorously opposed by the Tibetans, and in the end the emperor had to accept the position of the Tibetans.

Since the Dalai-lama was always in the minority when chosen for the position, the administration of the government was in the hands of regents chosen either by the previous Dalai-lama before his death, or elected by the national assembly summoned for the purpose. The institution of the regency was therefore standard practice in Tibet. If the regents were men of integrity, then they ruled the country with honor and justice until the Dalai-lama became of age. However there have been numerous instances of ambitious and power-hungry regents who mysteriously did away with the young Dalai-lamas in order that they might perpetuate their powers. For a period of about a century and a half, from 1750 to 1895, the Dalai-lama actually held authority for only seven years. The eighth Dalai-lama was the only one who reached maturity, but he was not interested in temporal affairs and the regency continued to rule. The ninth and the tenth died before reaching maturity, the first one being murdered and the other dying amidst suspicious circumstances. The eleventh and the twelfth were enthroned but they died soon after. It is only when we come to the thirteenth Dalai-lama who was enthroned in 1895 that we have an incumbent who lived out his natural life.

The presence of two grand lamas in Tibet raises an interesting question. The Dalai-lama is the incarnation of Avalokitesvara, while the Panchen-lama is the incarnation of Amitabha. In the Buddhist hierarchy, Amitabha is superior to Avalokitesvara, and if we follow the axiom that the master is always superior to the pupil, one can argue that the Panchen-lama should occupy a position superior to that of the Dalai-lama. Such an argument does not take into consideration the realities of the Tibetan scene. The Tibetans hold that Amitabha exists only on the spiritual plane, that he exists only in the mind of the Buddhist devotee immersed in meditation, and that he has never lived on earth as a Buddha. Amitabha therefore has no contact with the world, and it is only his minister Avalokitesvara who descends to the world of living beings to save them. The Panchen-lama as the incarnation of Amitabha remains true to his nature only if he remains in the spiritual realm.

The presence of the two grand lamas did provide a ready made situation for foreign powers to manipulate. In 1729 the Manchu dynasty in China initiated moves to set the Panchen-lama up as the political rival of the Dalai-lama and offered him control over a wide area in central and western Tibet, but the Panchen-lama refused to be involved in the move. What was started by the Manchus was taken up again by the Chinese government and the British in India during the early twentieth century. This gave rise to considerable antagonism between the sixth Panchen-lama and the thirteenth Dalai-lama, who was a vigorous and determined individual bent on asserting his political and spiritual powers. The Panchen-lama was obliged to leave Tibet in 1923 to spend the rest of his years in exile in China. Until his death in 1937, he was the center of endless machinations by the Chinese, who tried to persuade him to return to Tibet with the aid of Chinese troops. After his death in 1937, three boys were discovered as his probable incarnation. One died very early. Of the remaining two, the one born in the Chinese province of Ching-hai was proclaimed as the true incarnation by the Nationalist Government during its last days on the mainland. When the Communists occupied the area in 1950, the young Panchen-lama quickly turned over to the new regime, and ever since that time, the Chinese Communists have been building him up as the counterforce against the Dalai-lama. After the Dalai-lama fled to India for refuge in 1959, the Panchen-lama was proclaimed by the Chinese Communists to be the spiritual head of all Tibet. However, as long as the Dalai-lama lives, it is safe to say that he will always be regarded as the supreme temporal and spiritual ruler of Tibet.

Method of Choosing the Dalai-lama

The Tibetans choose their Dalai-lamas not by election or by hereditary succession. Instead they follow a system that has no parallel in the world. As the Dalai-lama is the incarnation of Avalokitesvara, the compassionate bodhisattva who has vowed to save all sentient beings, it follows that he should not die as long as his mission is not completed. However, the Dalai-lama does die as any normal human being when his material body decays. To the Tibetans, this death merely means that the bodily tabernacle has returned to the heavenly field, but the Dalai-lama himself, true to his vow, will return to continue his mission by taking a fresh human abode. Consequently the Tibetans believe that they have been governed not by fourteen different Dalai-lamas, but by fourteen successive appearances of the same spiritual entity among mankind. They also believe that their system of selection enjoys the advantages of both the hereditary principle and the elective system. With each Dalai-lama a new start is made, so that there is no danger of one class or one family seizing power and clinging to it indefinitely. And since the new Dalai-lama may be found in any family, the whole of Tibet participates in the search and there is an element of the democratic process here. How and where to find the new Dalai-lama in his new incarnation is the major problem for the whole divination machinery of the Tibetans.

As soon as a Dalai-lama dies, the most important lamas in the land gather to initiate the search. One of the first things they do is to look for signs or indications given by the deceased, a word, a gesture, a written line, or some objects kept around him. In the case of the third Dalai-lama, he was still in Mongolia when he approached death, and the Mongol princes who surrounded him pleaded with him to be reborn as a Mongol to continue his mission. The third said he had the same idea, and after he died, his incarnation was found in a Mongol family. Sometimes such signs were lacking, and recourse had to be taken to other measures. Outside of Lhasa is the state oracle at Nechung Monastery, which is also consulted in the preliminary stages of the search. The oracle may reveal the names of the parents, or the appearance of the house in which the child is to be found. The names of the parents do not reveal much, for many Tibetans have the same names. Another site that is consulted is a lake about five days journey to the south of Lhasa. This lake is the favorite haunt of the patron goddess of the Dalai-lama. The best time to consult the lake is the fourth month of the year, and the most auspicious day is the fifteenth day of the month. The Tibetans believe that it is possible to see a vision of the shape of future events above this lake. During the search for the thirteenth Dalai-lama, a group of lamas sat on the hillsides watching the lake. At first they were disappointed, for the lake was frozen over. Soon, however, a wind arose which blew the snow away, exposing an icy surface that shone like a mirror. On the lake, the lamas claimed that they saw the vision of a house and a peach tree in bloom. That same night, one of the lamas dreamt that he saw a mother with a child about two years of age in her arms. Armed with these signs, the lamas proceeded with the search, until one day they saw a peach tree in bloom, even though it was not the season for flowers. This miraculous blossoming was regarded as an auspicious portent. Close by the tree was a house, and inside the house was a woman with a child resembling those seen in the dream. In this manner the thirteenth Dalai-lama was found.

In 1935, two years after the death of the thirteenth Dalai-lama, the searching party for the fourteenth Dalai-lama decided to consult the lake, hoping to see a vision above it. This time the lamas first saw three syllables, "ah-ka-ma," then a three-storied monastery with gilded roof and turquoise tiles. To the east of the monastery was a road leading to a bare pagoda-shaped hill. Facing the hill was a house with peculiar eaves. The vision of all this the lamas claimed to have seen above the waters of the lake. The meaning of these signs was debated for a long time by the learned lamas, and they finally decided that the incarnation was to be found east of Lhasa. This decision was soon confirmed by one of those miraculous episodes that the Tibetans delight to recount.

The embalmed body of the thirteenth Dalai-lama had been placed in the Potala, waiting for a special tomb to be built. For several mornings, the lamas on watch found that the head and body of the dead man, which originally pointed toward the south, were pounted toward the east. The search was directed therefore to the region indicated.

By 1937 the search had already considered two candidates. One died before he was examined in detail, and the second fled at the sight of the approaching lamas in the searching party. The search now led to northeastern Tibet, then under the control of the Chinese, and finally to a village near Kumbum Monastery. In the village the party saw a house with turquoise tiles. The leader of the party asked whether there was any child in the house and was told that there was one about two years old. The real leader now disguised himself as a servant to a junior monk who acted as the leader. After entering the house, they found the child, and when he saw the disguised lama, he wanted to sit on his lap. He also asked for the rosary which the disguised lama was wearing, a rosary that had belonged to the deceased Dalai-lama. The disguised lama promised to give the rosary if the child could guess who he was, and the child replied correctly that he was a lama of Sera Monastery. The lama spent the rest of the day watching the child, becoming more and more convinced that the search party was nearing the end of its search. When the party started to leave, the child insisted on going with the group. A few days later the entire search party of senior lamas arrived for the conclusive tests. In these tests, a number of objects used by the previous Dalai-lama, such as the rosary, liturgical drum, bell, thunderbolt, and walking staff, together with exact duplicates of them, were placed before the child. The child was to pick out the genuine object, the one actually used by the deceased. In every instance the child chose the right one until he came to the walking staff. He first picked up the wrong one to the consternation of the search party, but then he paused, looked at it, and finally he picked the right one. The lamas wondered about the hesitation later, and found that the staff picked up first had been used by the deceased Dalai-lama for a time and then given away to a friend.

As for the letters seen above the lake, "Ah" was interpreted to stand for Amdo, the name of the district, while "ka-ma" referred to the monastery of Karma Polpai Dorje which stood on the mountain above the village. Years before, the thirteenth Dalai-lama had visited the monastery and stayed there. In this fashion the Tibetans see the vision above the lake fulfilled.

The search for the incarnation of the thirteenth Dalai-lama was at an end. The new incarnation was born in 1935, two years after the death of the previous Dalai-lama, in a well-to-do farming family. Though the incarnation had been found, almost two years were to transpire before he was finally able to leave his native village for Lhasa to be enthroned, the delay being caused by negotiations over the demand of the Chinese governor of the region for 300,000 Chinese dollars before he would release the child. The negotiations finally settled, the trip to Lhasa was made in 1939, and the enthronement ceremonies took place in 1940 in the Potala.

The ceremonies consisted of the chanting of prayers, presentation of gifts from Tibetan monastic and lay officials, and representatives of foreign governments, debates between learned monks on subtle religious questions, dramatic performances, dances, the conferring of blessing by the Dalai-lama on all those present, and the recital of historical accounts concerning auspicious years in the past. Though the entire ceremony took several hours, the young child just over four and a half years old sat through it all with dignity and composure.

After enthronement the education of the Dalai-lama began. He followed the traditional system of Tibetan education, which meant that he studied Sanskrit, dialectics, arts and craft, metaphysics, and philosophy. His philosophical studies embraced the *Prajna-paramita*, Madhyamika, *Abhidharma*, and the *Vinaya*. Tantric philosophy was studied separately. The pupil first learned to read and write by imitating the teacher. His regular religious education began when he was twelve. He started by memorizing one of the Prajna sutras, and engaged in dialectical debates under the tutelage of his teachers. At thirteen he was formally inducted into the monasteries at Drepung and Sera near Lhasa, where he engaged in public debates over the Prajna sutras. Whatever spare time he had from now on was devoted to the study of Buddhist philosophy.

When he was twenty-four, he took the preliminary examinations in each of the three monasteries of the Yellow Sect in Lhasa. These examinations were all in the form of congregational debates. Each student faced a number of opponents who chose whatever subjects they wanted to debate with him. One had to be ready for anything and everything, for the examination was really a free-for-all. The favorite method of the opponents was to quote from the words of the Buddha and the works of Indian and Tibetan masters to refute the contentions of the one examined. In this preliminary examination, the young Dalai-lama had to defend his views against an array of fifteen learned scholars as well as refute their arguments. One year later he appeared for the final examination. This was held in three sessions. In the morning he was examined on logic by thirty scholars, who took turns in engaging him in dialectical discussions. In the afternoon, fifteen scholars took part in the discussion on Madhyamika and Prajna philosophy. Finally, in the evening, thirty-five scholars examined him on the *Vinaya* and the *Abhidharma*. During each session, hundreds of lamas attended and listened attentively. When it was all over, the examiners decided that the youthful Dalai-lama had passed successfully all the examinations and conferred on him the degree, Master of Metaphysics.

CHAPTER 10

Buddhist Literature

THE SOURCE OF OUR knowledge concerning the Theravada aspect of Buddhism is the Pali canon, committed to writing during the first century B.C. in Ceylon. Thus a period of roughly four centuries elapsed between that event and the nirvana of the Buddha, during which time the dhamma was transmitted mainly by the spoken word. This oral transmission required a prodigious memory on the part of the teachers, but such a talent was and still is not lacking in Asian countries, even in the modern world of tape recorders and records. From the earliest days of her history, scholars in India, China, Ceylon, or Burma have memorized their classics and recited them whenever the need arose. The traditional Chinese scholar for instance carried all his historical facts and bibliographical tools in his head, and looked condescendingly upon those western trained students who have to consult indices to find what they want. In 1955 a Burmese monk qualified for the highest degree, Holder of the Tipitaka, by memorizing the entire *Vinaya* or *Book of Discipline,* which in its present printed form consists of five volumes, each one averaging 300 pages.

According to the Ceylonese, this Pali canon was introduced to the island of Ceylon by Mahinda, son of King Asoka, in the middle of the third century, B.C., and that they had preserved it with rare fidelity since that time. For this reason, the Ceylonese

Buddhists claim that their canon is a faithful reproduction of the words of the Buddha, and that the Buddha himself spoke in Pali. These two claims deserve closer examination.

The question of Pali will be considered first. What is Pali, and was it spoken by the Buddha? Pali is a literary language used exclusively by the Buddhists. In its development into a literary language, it probably represented a sort of compromise among various spoken Indian dialects. If we study carefully linguistic forms preserved in the Pali canon, we can still detect traces of word forms and grammar which are foreign to Pali. Any literary language, however, must have been based on one predominant dialect, and numerous attempts have been made by scholars to determine what that dialect was. Some have suggested Magadhi, the dialect of the kingdom of Magadha, while others have pointed to a central Indian dialect prevalent in the region of Ujjeni, but so far there has been no definite conclusion. Nor is it certain just when Pali as a literary language first came into usage, though it is usually suggested that the time was after Asoka (third century B.C.), since there is no mention at all of Pali in the Asokan inscriptions. When the Ceylonese Buddhists claim that the Buddha spoke Pali, they must first show that he spoke Magadhi, and that Magadhi was the basis of Pali. Neither of these can be proven definitely. Despite the claims of the Theravadins, we must conclude that since Pali is a literary language, it is not the tongue spoken by the Buddha.

If this is true, then what was the original language spoken by the master? Here again there is no definite answer. The Buddha was an Easterner, that is to say, he lived in the eastern portion of the Ganges Valley. When he spoke, we may assume that he spoke one of the eastern dialects. But from our present vintage, it is impossible to determine just what that dialect was. His disciples also used their own dialects in the recitation of the dhamma. Very likely the dialects used in the main cities which the Buddha visited in his travels did not differ from one another in any great respect, so that it was not too difficult for a speaker to switch from one to the other. Instead of Pali, therefore, the Buddha in all likelihood spoke several of the local dialects prevalent in eastern India.

As to the second claim of the Theravadins, that their canon was a faithful preserver of the teachings of the master, it must be pointed out that approximately two hundred years elapsed from the time the canon was introduced into Ceylon to the time it was reduced to writing. Again, from the time of the Buddha to the time when Mahinda introduced the canon into Ceylon, there was also a period of some two hundred years, making a total of over four hundred years in all. It stands to reason that during such a long interval, changes must have crept into the tradition during the oral transmission. New materials would have been added, or commentaries would have become mixed with the main story, thus giving rise to the contradictions that we sometimes find, and to the frequent juxtaposition of early and late materials. However, these minor deficiencies are usually dismissed by the Pali advocates as being inconsequential, and they adduce the following evidence to bolster their claim of the authenticity of the Pali canon.

The first witness that they bring forward is the contents of one of the Asokan inscriptions, which recommended seven titles in the canon for study; six of the seven have been identified with titles in the present Pali canon. Their second witness consists of the inscriptions carved on the balustrades of the Bharhut and Sanchi stupas, two famous centers of Buddhist art in central India that date back possibly to the second century B.C. In these inscriptions there are found such epithets as sutta reciter, knower of the five collections, and knower of the pitaka. Their presence might be taken to mean that already during the second century B.C. there existed a body of texts known as the three pitakas or baskets, and that one was divided into five collections. As for their third witness, the Pali advocates refer to the contents of sutras written in Sanskrit. This Sanskrit literature represented an independent tradition, since it was not translated from the Pali, and yet a comparison of some Sanskrit and Pali texts shows a remarkable degree of literary agreement between them, with entire passages using the same terms and breathing the same spirit. This is claimed by the Pali adherents to be a good indication of the antiquity and fidelity of their canon.

Interesting and important though these arguments are, it is well to keep in mind the counterarguments advanced against the Pali advocates. The opponents of the Pali school contend that the very lateness of the compilation of the Pali version (1st century B.C.) is a strong point against its antiquity and fidelity, and they would argue in favor of paying more attention to the Buddhist Sanskrit texts, which are preserved either in the original Sanskrit or translated into Chinese or Tibetan. This group is fascinated by the richness and variety of the Sanskrit materials, which they claim stemmed from the same earlier tradition as did the Pali. According to them, the Pali compilers incorporated into their canon only those parts of the earlier tradition which were in accord with their views and practices, and neglected those which were at variance. Accordingly the Pali canon is neat and systematic, and shows the handwork of the Pali theologians. The Sanskrit compilers on the other hand tried to preserve all the traditions that were floating around, and hence the Sanskrit texts are characterized by an amazing and bewildering irregularity, richness, and complexity. There was no systematic organizing and editing of materials here, the compilers cast their nets far and wide and included everything, early and late.

It is because of such considerations that some scholars are now inclined to make a distinction between the Buddhism taught in the Pali canon and that taught by the master himself. These scholars would advocate that the former should be called monastic Buddhism, the Buddhism that was decided upon and accepted by the Pali theologians in Ceylon during the 1st century B.C. when they compiled the Pali canon. As opposed to this, the original teachings of the Buddha would be called primitive or pre-canonical Buddhism. The problem, however, is to find out what those original teachings were, and this has proven to be one of the most intractable of puzzles tackled by Buddhist scholars. We shall not impose on the good will of the reader by going into the intricacies of the problem, but shall proceed with our discussion of the Pali canon.

The Pali Canon

As now constituted, this canon consists of three parts, the *Vinaya* or the *Book of Discipline,* the *Suttas* or *Discourses of the Buddha,* and the *Abhidhamma* or *Higher Subtleties of the Dhamma.*

The *Book of Discipline* contains the rules which govern the conduct of the monks and nuns in the Buddhist order. They cover such things as the admission of monks and nuns, their daily activities, their communal life during the rainy season, their food, clothing, and shelter, and their relations with the laity.

The discourses constitute the best sources for the Buddhist dhamma, and comprise some of the greatest literary pieces in Buddhist literature. They are divided into five collections, entitled the *Collection of Long Discourses, Middle Length Discourses, Kindred Sayings, Gradual Sayings,* and the *Minor Anthologies.* In the first, each sutta is a long independent work, treating a variety of subjects which are sometimes not connected with the teachings of the master. For instance, one discourse is a detailed discussion of the philosophical views in vogue during the time of the Sakya sage, as well as the arts and crafts, games, and occupations indulged in by the people. Another sutta discusses the subject of caste, while a third contains a list of the duties of the laymen. Probably the most important discourse in this collection is the Sutta on the Great Decease, which described the last three months of the earthly life of the Blessed One.

For the study of the dhamma, however, the best source is the *Collection of Middle Length Discourses,* which discusses every point of the doctrine over and over again. In the third collection, *Kindred Sayings,* there is a feeble attempt on the part of the Buddhists to classify the suttas according to different categories. They were divided according to a chief point of doctrine, or a class of demon or deity, or some prominent disciple of the master. The fourth collection, *Gradual Sayings,* consists of a classification according to numerical categories; that is to say, Section One consists of suttas dealing with things of which only one exists, Section

Two, of things in which there are two, and so on until Section Eleven.

There is still a 5th collection, entitled *Minor Anthologies,* which consists of a number of miscellaneous works, some of which belie the adjective minor, since two of them are probably the earliest pieces of Buddhist literature, while the *Book of the Jatakas* or the *Birth Stories* is the longest item in the whole canon. The two are the *Dhammapada,* or *Religious Sentences,* and the *Sutta-nipata, Section on Discourses.* The former is by far the text most often quoted by Buddhists and non-Buddhists alike, for the 423 stanzas that it consists of embody better than any other piece of literature the spirit of the master's teachings, summoning as they do all men to a life of strenuous mental and moral discipline. For this reason, the *Dhammapada* is most highly esteemed in all the Theravadin countries in southeast Asia, and is used as a textbook which must be memorized by all novices who desire the higher ordination. The *Sutta-nipata* is most valuable for the study of primitive Buddhism, for we find here not the life of the settled monasteries, but of monks and hermits still following the eremetical ideal. The Buddhism that is presented here is not yet an established monastic system, but only an ethical religion stressing the simple virtuous life. The recluse is called upon to adhere to the moral virtues, to subdue his desires for sensual pleasures, to turn his mind away from material possessions, to have no dealings in gold and silver, and to eat only moderately; in short, he is told to lead a perfectly honest and moral life. The theme, let him wander alone like a rhinoceros, is repeated again and again.

The longest item in the whole collection of suttas, the *Jatakas* or *Birth Stories,* contains the stories of the former rebirths of the Buddha. In these stories, the Buddha is referred to as the bodhisatta, since he was not yet enlightened, and he is presented sometimes as the hero, sometimes a secondary character, and at times a mere spectator. The story usually begins with the words, "At such and such a time, the bodhisatta was reborn in the womb of so and so," and this permitted any story to be converted into a Buddhist *jataka* by merely changing some human being, animal, or deity in it into the bodhisatta.

As now constituted, a birth story consists of the following parts:

(1) the introductory story, or story of the present, which tells the occasion for the relation of the *jataka* in question.

(2) the story of the past, which is in prose and recounts the experience of the bodhisatta in a former rebirth. This is the most important portion of the *jataka*.

(3) stanzas, which form a part of the story of the past.

(4) a short commentary, which explains the words in the stanzas.

(5) the connection, in which the Buddha identifies the characters of the past with those of the present.

Of the 547 *jatakas* in the collection, probably more than half were of non-Buddhist origins. The explanation for this might be that the Buddhist monks, drawn as they were from all classes of society, were familiar with the popular anecdotes, fables, and fairy tales circulating among the common people, and they felt that they could use these tales to spread the religion among the masses by merely converting one of the characters in the stories into the bodhisatta.

As edifying tales to entertain audiences, these birth stories have no equal, but they are also important for a number of other reasons. They are valuable for the information which they provide concerning the early history of Buddhism as well as the political, social, and economic conditions in India before the Christian era. They served as the inspiration for numerous scenes in the sculpture decorating the stupas at Bharhut and Sanchi in central India. Finally they are important for their connection with world literature, for directly or indirectly, they have influenced the literature of many other peoples. When Buddhism broke out of the confines of India and became a world religion, it diffused these birth stories far and wide, on the one hand to countries such as Persia and Arabia, and thence to eastern and western Europe, and on the other hand to the countries of the Far East. Let us look at some of these stories which appeared in more than one garb.

In *Jataka* 67, there is the anecdote of a woman whose husband, son, and brother were to be executed. Offered a choice of the life of one of the three by the king, the woman chose her brother. When she was asked the reason for her strange choice, she answered that she was still young and could easily find a husband, and beget a son, but since both her parents were dead, she could never obtain a brother. Now this same anecdote is to be found in the *History* of Herodotus and the play *Antigone* by Sophocles. According to Herodotus, Darius the king of Persia seized Intaphernes, his children, and kindred, put them in chains and condemned them to death. The wife of Intaphernes then came and stood weeping and wailing at the palace gate. Darius was touched by pity for her, and gave her the boon of the life of one of her kinsmen. She pondered a while, and replied that since the king granted the life of one alone, then she would choose her brother. The king was astonished by this, and asked her why she passed over her husband and children who were dearer to her. She replied in the same manner as in the Indian *Jataka* story. This pleased Darius so much that he spared the life of not only her brother but also her eldest son.

In *Jataka* 546 there is the story of the judgment of the wise man. A woman took her small son to a nearby stream to bathe him, and when she was finished, she placed him on the banks, while she herself went into the water. Along came another woman who was so attracted by the child that she kidnapped him. The mother gave chase and finally caught up with her, but the kidnapper now claimed that the child belonged to her. To settle the argument, the two women brought the dispute before the wise man. He drew a line on the ground, laid the child across the middle of the line, ordered one woman to hold the hands of the child, and the other the legs, then commanded them to pull the child across the line. When the women pulled, the child cried, whereupon one of the women (the real mother) immediately released her hold on the child. The wise man awarded the child to her, saying that only the real mother would love the child so much as to release her hold when he cried. This story reminds one of the Biblical account of the judgment of Solomon, and it is also widely known in China, where it served as the theme of the play, The Circle of Chalk.

In the first of the above two examples, it is not at all certain as to whether Sophocles and Herodotus were acquainted with the contents of the Buddhist birth story; the chances are that they were not, and that they derived their versions from sources other than the Buddhist. However there is no question concerning the source of a very popular Christian tale of the middle ages, the story of Barlaam and Joasaph.

According to the story, the King of India, an enemy and persecutor of Christianity, had a son named Joasaph who the astrologers predicted would become a Christian. To prevent the son from learning about Christianity, the father built a magnificent palace in a remote district to serve as the dwelling place of the son, and surrounded him with people who were forbidden to mention anything about Christianity. One day, after Joasaph had grown up, he asked for permission to go out, and during the trip saw a blind man and a leper. When he asked about the cause for their appearances, he was told that the cause was illness, and that everyone was subject to illness. On a second excursion, he was confronted with the sight of an old man, and when he asked what the end of this was, he was told that death was the end. The young prince was exceedingly distressed by these sights, and he now plunged himself into deep meditation. While in this state, he was visited by the hermit Barlaam in disguise, and from the latter he became acquainted with Christianity and was soon converted. After Barlaam left, Joasaph tried to live the life of a hermit in the palace.

When the king heard about the conversion of his son, he immediately took measures to draw him away from the religion, first with menaces, and then with persuasion. A magician named Theudas suggested that the prince be tempted with female wiles, but the prince remained firm and resisted all the temptations. Instead, he was able to convert Theudas to the new faith. He then left the palace to live in the forest with Barlaam. It was said that he fled the palace at night with a personal attendant until he reached the edge of the forest, then he sent the attendant back with the horse and his valuables. Four angels then took him to heaven where he acquired further wisdom, after which he returned to earth to convert all those whom he met. He died after giving blessings to his favorite disciple Anand.

Readers will recognize at once that this story of Joasaph is based on none other than the life of the Buddha. The prediction of the astrologer reminds one of the prophecy made by Asita after seeing the bodhisatta. In both cases, the king tried to isolate the young prince from the outside world, and in both cases, the prince saw the same signs. The adjectives describing the old man in the two versions are almost identical, old, shrivelled in the face, weak on the knees, bent, grey-haired, toothless. The suggestion of Theudas to tempt the prince with women finds its counterpart in the attempts of Mara and his daughters. The names used in the story also indicate their Indian progenitors. The attendant of Joasaph was named Zardan in one version and Zandani in another, and this is an echo of Chandaka the attendant of the bodhisatta. The name Theudas is derived from the Indian word Devadatta, the cousin of the Buddha. Anand was the favorite disciple of Joasaph, while Ananda was the favorite of the Buddha. The names of the two Christian heroes, Barlaam and Joasaph, also betray their Indian origins. Barlaam is derived from Bhagavan, meaning the Blessed One, while Joasaph in Arab becomes Yodasaph, which is none other than the word bodhisatta.

During the middle ages, this legend, which was but an adaptation of the Buddha legend, became extremely popular in Christendom, both east and west. As a measure of its popularity in Eastern Christendom, it was translated into Syriac, Arabic, Ethiopian, Armenian, and Hebrew, while in Western Christendom, it was translated into Greek, Latin, French, Italian, German, English, Spanish, Bohemian, and Polish. Because of this popularity, Barlaam and Joasaph were regarded during the middle ages as pious Christians who actually lived and preached, and they finally rose to be saints in both branches of the church. In the catalogue of Christian saints, *Catalogus Sanctorum* of Peter de Natalibus, dated 1370, the names of these two are included. In the eastern church, August 26 was set aside as Saint's Day for them, while November 27 was designated in the west.

It is interesting to note that in this tale of Barlaam and Joasaph there is also included the famous Indian parable of the man in the well. According to this parable, a man out hunting was pursued by a unicorn and in trying to flee, fell into a well. As he was falling, he stretched out his arm and caught hold of a small tree growing on the side of the well. He thought that he was now safe, but upon closer scrutiny, he found that two mice, one white and one black, were gnawing at the roots of the slender tree to which he was clinging. He now looked down into the well and what did he see but a monstrous dragon with mouth open waiting for him to fall. He then examined the place where his feet were resting, and saw four serpents surrounding him. Now he looked up at the tree he was holding, and saw some honey dripping down from one of the branches. Immediately, the unicorn, mice, dragon, and serpents were forgotten, and his mind became intent only on securing the honey.

The Indians explain this parable as follows: the unicorn is death, the deep well is the world, the small tree is man's life, gnawed at its roots by day and night (the white and black mice), the dragon is the jaws of hell, the four serpents are the four great elements that compose the body. Surrounded by all these horrors and dangers, man forgets all and thinks only of the pleasures of life.

Such interesting and charming Buddhist tales and fables as these have made their way into the literature of both east and west, and have provided pleasure to uncounted numbers of people who have heard or read them. Sometimes the story of their migrations from the remote Indian villages to the great centers of eastern and western civilizations is more interesting than the tales themselves. For example, the origin of the proverb, "Don't count the chickens before they are hatched," has been traced by scholars step by step through different translated versions clear back to a collection of Indian fables used for the instruction of young princes. Fascinating though these tales and their migrations may be, we must take leave of them, and summarize our discussion of the suttas.

As we read the Buddhist suttas, we note three outstanding characteristics. There is first the repetition. It seems that the authors were so pleased and impressed with the excellent dhamma that they repeated it tirelessly and endlessly, without any feeling that such repetitions were tedious and wearisome. We must keep in mind that in the early stages, instruction in the dhamma was done exclusively by oral means, and constant repetition served to impress the meaning of the law in the minds of the listeners. Thus the repetitions would be like the recurring theme in a musical composition. Secondly, the suttas are primarily in the form of dialogues between the Buddha and another person, with the conversation carried out in a polite, refined, and skillful manner. In dealing with opponents, the Buddha did not attack their positions directly, but by skilful questioning, won them over to his position. In the third place, there is the profuse use of similes and parables. Now similes do not constitute an argument, but they have a remarkable effect upon the minds of audiences, and consequently the Buddha resorted to them frequently. In one sermon, the Blessed One attacked the views of the brahmans concerning their method of attaining emancipation through union with the supreme Brahma. He asked them whether any one of them had seen the supreme Brahma, and when they answered that none had, he replied that they were like a chain of blind people following a leader who was also blind, or that they were like a man who said he loved a girl, but when asked about the girl, could not tell what her name was, where she lived, and what her family was like. A more famous parable was that of the blind men and the elephant. Some brahmans and ascetics were arguing about the indeterminate questions, and this was reported to the Buddha. The Blessed One then told the story of some blind men who were arguing about the appearance of an elephant. The king had the blind men assembled, and commanded that an elephant be led among them. Each of the blind men then touched one part of the elephant, and when they had finished, they were asked what the elephant was like. The one who touched the head said it was like a pot, the one who touched the ear said it resembled a basket, the tusk a plow share, the trunk a pole, the tail a broom, and the body a wall. Each one held to his own point of view, and the result was one protracted quarrel. According to the

Buddha, the brahmans and ascetics were like the blind men who knew only one part and not the whole.

The third basket of the canon is the *Abhidhamma* (sometimes translated as *Higher Subtleties of the Dhamma* or *Metaphysics*) which consists of seven separate works. The *Abhidhamma* is concerned with phenomena, and for the purpose of describing phenomena, it uses two methods, analysis and investigating the relations of things. The relations of things are treated in minute details to show that even in a single moment of consciousness there is involved a multiplicity of factors. A moment of consciousness is therefore considered in its relations with all its factors, functions, and energies, as well as its external relations to other moments of consciousness. By showing that even in the briefest moment of consciousness, there is an intricate network of relationships, the idea of a static world is attacked and the truth of impermanence emphasized.

However, we are also taught that the things presented by investigation are not isolated, self-contained things, but are conditioning others and are being conditioned by others. They occur in temporary combinations which are constantly in the process of integration and disintegration. However, disintegration does not mean complete disappearance of all the components, for some of them always survive and are repeated in the next composition. In this manner, there is an uninterrupted flow of the stream of life.

When we analyze an object, we look at it as it is existing at the present moment. A moment's reflection will reveal however that the present is something very elusive, for as soon as we talk or think of a thing as being present, it is already past. We thus have to conclude that thought does not have a present but a past object. In his analysis, a person therefore has to take into consideration that the object is never static but is constantly moving from the past to the present to the future, so that instead of looking upon the present moment as static and real, we must consider it as illusory, and that only motion and change are real.

Of the seven books in the *Abhidhamma*, probably the most important is the *Kathavatthu*, translated as *Points of Controversy*.

It enjoys the unique distinction of being the only text in the Pali canon ascribed to a particular author, Moggaliputta Tissa, who as president of the third council during the reign of Asoka was commissioned to write the work as a refutation of heresies which had cropped up. These heresies had to do with questions of theology and philosophy, such as the following:

Is there an individual soul which is real and absolute?
Is it possible for householders to become arhats?
Do followers of the Buddha share in his supernatural powers?
Can the arhats backslide?
Can animals be reborn as deities?

All these questions were answered in the negative, and those who answered them in the affirmative were adjudged heretics.

What we have been discussing so far constitutes the Pali canon, the source of our knowledge concerning Theravadin Buddhism. The three constituent parts of this canon make up what is commonly referred to as the Tripitaka, or the Three Baskets. Besides the Tripitaka there are two works in Pali which are held in such high regards that even though they are extra-canonical, they wield just as much authority as the canonical literature. These two works are the *Questions of Milinda* and the *Path of Purity*.

The *Questions of Milinda* was probably written first in Sanskrit somewhere in northern India, but this original is now lost, and what now exists is the Pali translation of that original, made in Ceylon at an early date. The original text itself probably dates back to the 2nd century A.D. There are two Chinese versions of the text, but whether they are translations made from the original Sanskrit or the Pali is something difficult to determine.

The text is in the form of a dialogue between King Milinda and the Buddhist monk Nagasena, with the latter answering all the questions put to him by the former concerning a number of fundamental problems and dilemmas in Buddhism. Milinda, king of the Yonas has been identified with Menander the Bactrian king who ruled over the extensive Greco-Indian empire in northern India during the 1st century B.C. In Plutarch's *Lives*, it is recorded that after his death, several Indian cities quarreled over the disposition of his ashes, which were eventually divided among them, with each city erecting a stupa over its portion. This is generally taken to mean that he was converted to Buddhism. Coins bearing the name Menander and showing the Buddhist wheel of the law have also been found. It is interesting to note that this great ruler, whose military exploits must have been considerable in view of his vast empire, is remembered by the Indians in their literary traditions not as a conqueror but as a seeker of the religious truth. His partner in the dialogue, Nagasena, is introduced as a learned monk who mastered the Tripitaka in three months, indeed an incredible feat.

The *Questions of Milinda* might well be considered as one of the great literary masterpieces in Pali because of the elegance of its language and the charm of its style. There are some passages in it which are among the most eloquent in the whole field of Pali literature. In order to arouse the interest of the reader, there is a skillfully devised prelude that is concerned with the previous lives of the two chief characters. As for the subject matter, the first three books, which probably constituted the original portion of the work, deal with such items as the nature of the individual, the ethical principles of the religion, the character of karma, the removal of the impurities, and the attainment of salvation. Beginning with Book 4, however, the discussion turns to dogmatics, which are of interest only to the scholars of the canon. These remaining portions, Books 4-7, take up the dilemmas faced by King Milinda concerning such questions as the omniscience of the Buddha, the duration, time, and place of nirvana, the numbers of Buddhas in the past, the qualities of the arhat, and the spiritual rewards of a layman. Since the subject matter of this second half is different from that of the first half, it is commonly assumed that this portion was added on later, an assumption that is strengthened by the fact that it is absent in the Chinese translation of the fourth century.

It might be worth our while to consider a few of these dilemmas, just to find out what questions were bothering Milinda. In the 45th dilemma, Milinda said that it is a cardinal doctrine of Buddhism not to kill any living thing, yet the Buddha in one of his previous existences had living creatures slain and offered for sacrifice. How would Nagasena explain this? The monk replied that in that particular incident, the bodhisatta was temporarily out of his mind because of love for a woman, and hence should not be held responsible for the slaying of living creatures. One must conclude from this that the plea of temporary insanity was not something concocted by the lawyers of our times, but was already invoked almost two millenniums ago by the Buddhists. In the 52nd dilemma, Milinda said he had learned that all the doctrines taught by the Buddhas were one and the same. If that were the case, why did the Buddha say that there could not be two Buddhas living on earth at the same time? To this question, Nagasena explained that the world system could not bear the goodness of two Buddhas living at the same time. Again, if there were two Buddhas, disputes would arise between followers of the two, and the results would be disastrous for the dhamma. Furthermore, in the canon there were many passages designating the Buddha as the chief among men, the highest of mortals, the peerless one. Now if there were two Buddhas, all such passages would no longer be true. In dilemma 63, Milinda asked whether or not arhats could be guilty of offenses. Nagasena answered yes and no, and in elaboration of this, he said that there were two kinds of crimes, first, the breach of the moral law such as killing, stealing, unchastity, lying, covetousness, and malice, and second, breach of the ordinary rules of conduct, concerned with eating, sporting in water, use of ornaments, etc. The arhat was incapable of infractions against the moral laws, but might be guilty of offenses against the ordinary rules of conduct, because it was not within the province of the arhat to know everything. This admission of Nagasena is a clear indication that the arhat ideal was no longer as lofty as it once was. Milinda was also puzzled as to why the Buddha admitted his cousin Devadatta into the order when he knew clearly that the latter harbored evil designs. Nagasena replied that the master knew Devadatta would suffer torment for endless aeons because of his karma, but out of his infinite compassion and wisdom took him into the sangha in order that his torment would become limited. Finally Milinda asked how would one know that the Buddha lived? In answer to this, Nagasena replied that one knew the existence of ancient kings through the royal insignias, crown, or slippers which they left behind. In like manner one would know of the existence of the Buddha through the insignias which he left behind, and through the qualities of the arhat which formed the subject of his discourses. Just as one could infer the ability of the architect from the sight of a beautiful city, so could one infer the existence and ability of the Buddha through the city of righteousness that he built. Thus one by one the learned Nagasena answered the questions put by Milinda, and resolved the dilemmas so skillfully that the king finally acknowledged him as master.

Besides the *Questions of Milinda,* the other extra-canonical work which stands pre-eminent in the minds of the Theravadins is the *Path of Purity,* the masterpiece by the most famous of all Pali commentators, Buddhaghosa (fifth century A.D.). Unfortunately, we know very little of the man himself, his life and his career, even though he has left behind such a voluminous record through his commentaries. From the meager notices about him, it appears that he was born a brahman who went through the usual brahman education, but was later converted to Buddhism by a monk who convinced him of the superiority of the Buddhist doctrine. As he was most eloquent in the exposition of the dhamma after his conversion he was named Buddhaghosa, the Voice of the Buddha. He then went to Ceylon to study the doctrine and the commentaries there, and when he was convinced that he had mastered the meaning of the dhamma, he sought permission from the elders of the Ceylonese church to translate the Ceylonese commentaries from Ceylonese to Pali. To demonstrate his competency to the Ceylonese elders, he wrote this work, *Path of Purity,* which is the fullest exposition of the three fold discipline, moral conduct, concentration, and intuitive wisdom. The work thus serves as the best and most authoritative summary of Theravada Buddhism. After reading this work, the elders deemed that he had passed the test successfully, and installed him in the capital where he carried on his stupendous task of putting the commentaries into Pali. The sheer bulk and quality of his labor meant that he must have shut himself in his cell for years, drawing upon his vast knowledge of astronomy, geography, grammar, history, anthropology, fauna, flora, manners and customs, Vedic lore, and Indian history. So well did he write in Pali that one modern writer has rendered the following verdict concerning his contribution: "In place of the archaic, stilted, sometimes halting sutta speech, almost puritanical in its simplicity, groping about often for want of words to express ideas and conceptions then fresh to the minds of the users of this or that dialect, Buddhaghosa left behind him in his works a language rich in vocabulary, flexible in its use, elegant in structure, often intricate in the verbiage of its constructions, and capable of expressing all the ideas the human mind had then conceived. Sonorous, long-winded sentences took the place of the direct simple composition of the suttas. The Oriental mind, fascinated by the ornamentation of its structure, soon began to use more extensively than before the Pali language now grown into adolescence. And we find one author after another beginning his works with the proud boast that he is compiling his works for the benefit of learners in Pali." [32]

Our discussion of Pali literature comes to a close with these remarks on Buddhaghosa and his works. From the time the teachings of the Blessed One were first transmitted by the words of his disciples to the time when Buddhaghosa, who lived during the 5th century A.D., wrote his authoritative commentaries, there elapsed a period of close to a thousand years, when the words of the Buddha were first preserved by the memory of his followers, then recorded in writing, and finally commented upon by numerous Ceylonese scholiasts who paved the way for the Voice of the Buddha. Of this Pali canon, the *Vinaya pitaka* or the *Book of Discipline* and the *Suttapitaka* or the *Discourses* are available in English translation, while four of the seven books in the *Abhidhammapitaka* have been rendered into English. The two extracanonical works mentioned above are also available in English, but the bulk of the commentaries are accessible only to those who read Pali. Herein lies the unfinished task for future students of Buddhism.

Mahayana Literature

In Theravada Buddhism, there is a unified canon written in Pali, and if we wish to investigate any feature of that aspect, we can easily consult the rules of discipline, the sermons, and the higher discussions to find what we want. Everything is neat, systematic, and precise. The same cannot be said for Mahayana literature. In the first place, there is no body of literature that we can point to as constituting the Mahayana canon. In reality, there is no Mahayana canon, the reason being that Mahayana Buddhism is not a unified system. There are only separate sutras which are called Mahayana sutras, originally written in Sanskrit, the literary language of the Indians. However, many of the Sanskrit originals have been lost in the land of their origin, and are preserved chiefly in their Tibetan or Chinese translations. In order to study Theravada Buddhism, one needs only to know Pali, but in order to become proficient in Mahayana Buddhism, one must be familiar not only with Pali, but also Sanskrit, Tibetan, and Chinese.

There are certain features common to all the Mahayana sutras. In the first place, these sutras are usually preached by the Body of Communal Enjoyment of the Buddha, and the audience consists not only of men and gods, but also of innumerable Buddhas, bodhisattvas, and their retinues. Secondly, the scene of the teaching is often in some Buddhist heaven, where natural law is transcended and marvels of profound symbolical significance take place. Finally the mode of instruction is usually intuitive. There is little attempt at argumentation, for the Buddha is not endeavoring to convince his listeners but to awaken their intuitive wisdom.

The earliest literature that we can call Mahayana is the Prajna or Wisdom literature. This Wisdom literature consists of a huge body of texts preserved in Sanskrit, Chinese, and Tibetan, and whose composition is spread over a thousand years, divided into four periods:

(1) composition of basic texts, ca. 100 B.C.–100 A.D.
(2) expansion of basic texts, ca. 100 A.D. to 300.
(3) restatement of doctrine in shorter sutras, ca. 300-500.
(4) Tantric influence and composition of commentaries, 500-1200.

The basic Prajna text is undoubtedly the *Perfection of Wisdom in 8,000 Lines.* Each line consists of thirty-two syllables. This basic text was compiled about 100 B.C. by some unknown author or authors. The problem of chronology and authorship is one that shall plague the students of Mahayana literature continually. No names are appended to some of the most important Mahayana sutras, and so we do not know who the author or authors were. It is likely that in most cases a number of authors are involved in the composition of a long sutra. As for the time of composition, there is again no indication in the work itself, and one can only assign tentative and probable dates. The difficulty of dating is compounded by the fact that a long sutra was not completed at one sitting, but the composition must have been carried on over long periods of time, with later portions grafted on to the earlier portions. Consequently, it is well to keep in mind that whatever dates we give are only approximate.

About the beginning of the Christian era, the basic Prajna text was expanded considerably, the longest of which extended to 100,000 lines. The sheer bulkiness of these long texts proved to be an impediment, and in the third phase, the tendency was to reduce these lengthy texts with their interminable repetitions to more manageable proportions. The best products of this shortening process are the *Heart Sutra* and the *Diamond Cutter Sutra.* In the final phase, the process of condensation was carried even further, this time under the influence of Tantrism into *mantras* or mystic syllables. The extreme of this condensation was achieved in the text, *The Perfection of Wisdom in One Letter,* in which the first letter of the alphabet, A, was considered to be the epitome of wisdom.

In these Prajna sutras, the main teaching is that the real nature of all the dharmas or elements of existence is empty or void. In the chapter on Mahayana Buddhism, there is already an extended discussion of this basic doctrine. These Prajna texts provide the background for the emergence of the literature of the two important schools of Mahayana Buddhism, the School of the Middle Path and the Idealistic School.

There are also a number of individual Mahayana sutras that served as the basic texts of Buddhist schools in China and Japan. One of these is the *Pure Land Sutra,* which describes in minute details the Western Paradise presided over by the Buddha Amitabha, and the steps required to attain rebirth in that paradise. According to the long version of the sutra, good works as well as faith are necessary, but according to the abridged version, only faith in the saving powers of Amitabha is sufficient. Because this short version teaches the easy path to salvation, it is one of the most popular Mahayana scriptures in the Orient. The school based on this sutra is the Pure Land School in China, the Jodo and Jodo Shin in Japan. The Hua-yen School in China (the Kegon School in Japan) has as its basic scripture the *Avatamsaka* or *Garland Sutra,* which teaches the fundamental truth that the myriad things in the phenomenal world are but manifestations of the absolute, and this being so, they are mutually related to one another. Thus the unity of life is affirmed. Within the Avatamsaka, there is a portion entitled *Dasabbumika sutra,* or *Sutra on the Ten Stages,* which is the most detailed discourse on the ten stages of the bodhisattva. The truth of the interpenetration between the absolute and phenomena is also taught in the *Saddharmapundarika,* or the *Lotus of the Good Law,* the basic scripture of the T'ien-t'ai School in China (Tendai in Japan). This sutra is by far the most important of all the Mahayana texts; in fact it may be called the basic Mahayana scripture, for it is studied by practically all the Mahayana schools. Its popularity rests on the comprehensiveness of its statement of Mahayana doctrines and on its inspiration to Buddhist art in the whole Far East.

The first part of the sutra deals with the work of the Buddha Sakyamuni on earth as he preached his goal of universal salvation for all sentient beings and the means to reach that goal. By practicing charity, being patient, cultivating the spiritual life diligently, making offerings to the Buddha, building stupas with gold, silver, sandalwood, clay, or even sand, carving or painting images of the Buddha, reciting a verse, or merely uttering a word of devotion, one will be able to attain salvation. For Sakyamuni is the father of all beings, and the truth that he teaches is the universal truth which can be realized by all beings, just as the rain is one in essence but can enable all plants to grow and flourish according to their capacity and nature.

The second half of the sutra aims to reveal the true nature of the Buddha, who is now declared to be eternal and everlasting, who is neither born nor dies, but lives from eternity to eternity. Sakyamuni is but a creation of the eternal Buddha, manifested among mankind in order to convert them. The eternal Buddha has done this countless times in the past and will continue to do so in the future. The task of the true Buddhist is to recognize the eternal primeval nature of the Buddha, and when he becomes aware of this, he realizes that his own nature is as eternal as the eternity of the Buddha. It is this teaching of the everlasting life of the Buddha and of ourselves as followers of the Buddha that has inspired boundless faith and given strength to devout Mahayana adherents in the Far East.

Besides this doctrine of the eternal Buddha, the *Lotus Sutra* also stressed the concepts of universal salvation, of the ever-compassionate bodhisattvas, and of the skillfulness in means with which the Buddha chooses the method of preaching in accordance with the needs and conditions of the audience.

Finally there are those Mahayana sutras which do not form the basis for any particular school, but which are read and studied just the same by numberless Mahayana Buddhists. Undoubtedly the most popular in this category is the *Vimalakirti-nirdesa*, or the *Sutra Spoken by Vimalakirti*. The principal figure in the sutra is Vimalakirti, a contemporary of the Buddha who was thoroughly versed in Mahayana philosophy, a generous philanthropist, and living in the world as a layman. On one occasion he became sick and the Buddha wanted to send someone among his monks to inquire after his health. One by one, these monks who had already attained arhatship begged off, saying that they were not equal to the task of meeting the sick layman, and relating a previous encounter in which they were shamed by his arguments. The implication of these stories is unmistakable; the Mahayana is clearly superior to the Hinayana, for some of the wisest Hinayana arhats are not equal in wisdom and learning to the ordinary Mahayana lay philosopher Vimalakirti. Finally, Manjusri, the bodhisattva who is the epitome of wisdom, consents to visit the sick man, and during the interview the two carry on a spirited conversation on many points of Mahayana doctrines; the career of the bodhisattva, the perfections, true non-attachment, and non-duality.

This dialogue between Manjusri and Vimalakirti is the theme of many of the sculptural reliefs in Yun-kang and Lung-men in north China. Episodes in the sutras were also taken out and expanded into popular ballads and stories, which were then recited to the multitudes attending the temple festivals. Undoubtedly the figure of Vimalakirti had much to do with this popularity of the sutra. Here was a layman who had surrounded himself with all the pleasures of life but who was also a faithful and wise disciple of the Buddha, and thoroughly disciplined in his conduct. He was indeed a devout Buddhist but he was also one who could be taken as an ideal Confucian gentleman whom the Chinese could emulate.

We come now to one of the most beautiful pieces of religious poetry in Mahayana literature, the *Bodhicaryavatara*, or *Entry into the Life of Enlightenment*, written by Santideva (7th century). In words charged with emotion and inspiration the poet describes his feelings after he had taken the vows to follow the career of the bodhisattva, he prays to all the Buddhas that they might deliver all beings from ignorance, and he offers his own self to aid others in the quest for salvation. "May I be a balm to the sick, their healer and servitor, until sickness comes never again; may I quench with rains of food and drink the anguish of hunger and thirst; . . . . may I become an unfailing store for the poor, and serve them with manifold things for their need. My own being, and my pleasures, all my righteousness in the past, present, and future I surrender indifferently, that all creatures may win to their end. If I must surrender all, it is best to give it for fellow-creatures. I yield myself to all living things to deal with me as they list; I have given them my body, what shall I care? Let them make me do whatever works bring them pleasure, but may never mishap befall any of them by reason of me. If the spirit of any be wroth or pleased with me, may that ever be a cause for them to win all their desires. May all who slander me, or do me hurt, or jeer me, gain a share in enlightenment. I would be a protector of the unprotected, a guide of wayfarers, a ship, a dyke, and a bridge for them who seek the further shore; a lamp to them who need a lamp, a bed to them who need a bed, a slave for all beings who need a slave." [33] The poet then described the duties which the bodhisattva must perform after making the resolution. In the performance of these duties, the bodhisattva should make no distinction between himself and his neighbor but should identify himself absolutely and entirely with the other. Just as a man should love his hands and feet because they are members of his own body, so should he love all sentient because they are all members of the same world of the living. He then closes the poem with these words, "As long as the heavens and earth abide, may I continue to overcome the world's sorrow. May all the world's suffering be cast upon me, and may the world be made happy by all the merits of the bodhisattva." [34]

As in the case of the Hinayana literature, only a minute portion of the vast volume of Mahayana literature has been translated into western languages. We have mentioned but a few of the more significant sutras. Make no mistake, the volume is colossal. Just the collection of Chinese translations of the Prajna Sutras takes up four volumes of the most recent Taishō edition of the Buddhist canon, each volume about the size of a copy of the *Encyclopedia Britannica,* and numbering about a thousand pages. The English translation of the *Lotus Sutra* runs to about two hundred fifty printed pages. As for the *Avatamsaka,* the original Sanskrit version is said to consist of about one hundred thousand stanzas of four lines each, and one of the Chinese translations, which is more correctly an abridgement of the original, has eighty chapters, or about four hundred fifty printed pages in the Taishō edition. It is impossible to translate this mass of literature;

indeed there is no need to do so, for often these sutras owe their length to the interminable repetitions within them. However enough of them have been made available for students of Buddhism to realize that as far as depth of philosophical inquiry, richness of imagery, pageantry of colorful personalities, scope of imagination, complexity of themes, and variety of human emotions are concerned, the Mahayana sutras are far superior to the Hinayana. They are indeed some of the finest products of the human imagination.

CHAPTER 11

Buddhist Art

PRIMITIVE BUDDHISM was aniconic, in the sense that the original *sangha* did not have any image of the Buddha. In the great Buddhist monuments in central India, the stupas or funeral mounds at Sanchi and Bharhut, the storytelling reliefs depict the Buddha by means of symbols. Thus the great renunciation of the Buddha is represented by a parasol and two footprints, while the horse he is supposed to be riding is riderless. In order to illustrate the legend that the Buddha ascended to one of the Buddhist heavens to visit his mother, there is a stairway, with footprints at the top and at the bottom. The elephant is the symbol of conception, lotus the symbol of nativity, tree the symbol of enlightenment, and the wheel the symbol of the preaching of the law.

Historians have usually connected the absence of the Buddha image with the doctrine of nirvana. Nirvana being the immeasurable absolute, how is it possible to depict one who has entered into nirvana with lines and forms? Reference is also made to an important canonical passage which purports to forbid the visible image of the Buddha after nirvana. In the *Sutta on Brahma's Net,* we read, "The outward form, brethren, of Him who has won the Truth, stands before you, but that which binds it to rebirth is cut in twain. So long as his body last, so long do gods and men behold him. On the dissolution of that body, beyond the end of his life, neither gods nor men shall see him." [35] It is held that on the basis of this sutta the artists at Sanchi and Bharhut did not attempt to create a visible image of the master.

A number of objections may be raised against this explanation. It assumes that the village artisans who created the art at Sanchi and Bharhut knew about the doctrine of nirvana and its implications, and therefore refrained from making an image. Such an assumption is hardly tenable. Moreover, if the theory were correct, there should be portrayal of the Buddha in his final rebirth up to the moment of nirvana. Such is not the case. In the stupa reliefs, illustrations of the previous rebirths of the Blessed One in which he is visibly represented are found, but as soon as we come to the final rebirth, he vanishes, leaving only symbols to denote his presence. If the connection with the doctrine of nirvana is denied, then how is this absence of the visible image to be explained?

At present two explanations have been advanced to account for this aniconic feature. The first was put forth by the pioneer of Buddhist art studies, the French scholar A. Foucher. According to Foucher, Buddhist pilgrims from the very beginning came to worship at the four holy sites of Buddhism. At these sites, humble artisans made little souvenirs depicting the holy places in a stylized way, and sold them to the pilgrims. These were the first humble products of Buddhist art. By natural association, these representations of the holy sites were soon looked upon as the symbols of the four incidents which took place at the sites. With the passage of time, it became the accepted practice that events in the life of the master could be represented by these four symbols. Thus the wheel first signified the place, Benares; then the incident which took place at Benares, the preaching of the first sermon; and finally the chief figure involved in the event, the Buddha himself.

Critics of this explanation have pointed out that the first stage in the process imagined by Foucher is understandable; that is to say, the change from the representation of the place to the representation of the event. Thus the stupa at Kusinara represents nirvana, while the tree at Gaya represents enlightenment. However, they also point out that it is much more difficult to imagine the second change, how the original symbol came to represent the principal individual, i.e. the wheel as the symbol of Buddha preaching the first sermon. The problem is complicated by the fact that the same symbol, such as the wheel, is sometimes used in an entirely different episode, not that of the first preaching of the law.

It is because of these difficulties presented by Foucher's explanation that a second explanation has been advanced. According to this view, the Buddhist artists who created the art at Sanchi and Bharhut believed that the Buddha from the moment of his final birth was a transcendental being which could not be represented by portraits. For a fuller explanation of this view, it is necessary to devote some attention to the development of the Buddha cult, which began to take shape soon after the demise of the Blessed One. This cult is centered not so much on the teachings of the master as on his nature and personality.

While the Buddha was still living, he was regarded as a teacher, but soon after he died, the cult which arose developed a new trend in the conception of the master. He was now looked upon as a unique personality who had destroyed the imperfections of life, such as ignorance, cravings, and wrong views. He was like the lotus, in the sense that he was born and dwelled in the world but was untouched by the imperfections of the world. He was regarded neither as a man nor a god, but a sort of superman, endowed with such supernatural faculties as divine vision, divine hearing, ability to read other people's thoughts, ability to recall his own and other people's rebirths of the past, and magical prowess such as flying over the air and walking over water. He was also endowed with certain physical characteristics, such as a protuberance on the head, extra-long tongue, golden colored skin, and the sign of the wheel on his hands and feet. This was the first shift in the conception of the Buddha within the cult.

During the Asokan era, some more changes began to emerge. While the monks in the monasteries carried on their traditional forms of worship such as the fortnightly assemblies, liturgical chantings, scripture reading, and doctrinal debates, the members of the Buddha cult and the lay followers of the religion developed some new rituals and ceremonies, the most important of which was stupa worship.

Originally the stupa was a burial mound which existed prior to Asoka, but by the time of Asoka, it had already assumed its familiar shape. It consisted of a low square or circular base surmounted by a hemispherical dome. At ground level the stupa is encircled by a balustrade, with four gates at the four cardinal directions. Between the balustrade and the dome there is a path used for circumambulation by worshippers, who walk around with the stupa at their right. On top of the dome is a square box, and on top of the box is a mast encircled by a series of circular disks one above the other.

After the death of the Buddha, his remains were cremated and the relics after the cremation were gathered and distributed to a number of Indian towns, whose inhabitants there erected stupas over them. Since the stupa contained the relics of the master, it was looked upon as the outward and visual symbol of the Buddha, and was worshipped accordingly. Such worship of the stupa probably arose during the Asokan era, and was one of the prominent features of popular Buddhism. Legend has it that King Asoka built 84,000 stupas throughout his empire, but this figure is very likely just a stereotyped manner of indicating a large number. The number of people participating in such stupa worship must have been fairly large and they made up a colorful pageantry, with their pennants, flowers, and musical instruments as they circumambulated the stupa.

Of the stupas which were the centers of such worship and festivals, two have been brought to light by the archeologists, the great stupas of Sanchi and Bharhut, which were completed probably during the second century B.C. The reliefs on these stupas are considered the best example of early Buddhist art. Generations of Indians must have participated in the construction of these structures, somewhat in the manner of cathedral building in medieval Europe.

The gateways and their pillars constitute the chief points of interest in these stupas, for on them are carved elaborate bas-reliefs illustrating the previous births of the Buddha. This decorative art is undoubtedly the best indication of the state of popular Buddhism and the Buddha cult of the age, not the Buddhism of the monastic tradition. It is an art created by the village artists who were not too skillful in their craftsmanship and not too conversant with the traditions of their religion. In composition, events happening at different places and at different times were carved in the same relief, with the main figure being repeated to indicate the shifting of the scenes. In the eastern gate of Sanchi, for instance, there is a scene of the great renunciation. To the left of the relief is the city and moat. Issuing from the gate is the horse Kanthaka, with its hoofs supported by deities. The groom Chanda is holding an umbrella, the symbol of the Buddha. In order to indicate progress, this scene is repeated four times in succession toward the right of the relief. Then at the parting of the way, Chanda and the horse are seen returning to the city, while the further journey of the Buddha is indicated by footprints surmounted by an umbrella. In the reliefs, we find scenes depicting domestic animals, villagers, and rural life, and from the nature of such scenes, it is believed that the village artists did not receive any expert instruction from the monks.

While the village artists were mainly interested in decorating the stupa, they also included many symbols of the Buddha in the reliefs, especially when such reliefs contained illustrations of episodes taken from the birth stories. The absence of the Buddha figure in this stupa art would appear to be inconsistent with the contents of the birth stories since it is clearly stated there that the Buddha was heard and seen. In many scenes, deities are depicted with great technical skill and imagination, so that it could not be argued that the artists did not have the craftsmanship to produce the Buddha figure. It is evident that the omission of the Buddha image must be attributed to the emergence of some new attitudes concerning the personality of the Blessed One.

We have already mentioned the early change in the concept of the Buddha, the change from man to superman. However, in this change, the humanity of the Buddha was not questioned, for he was still subject to the operation of karma. Now during the time of Asoka another change must have taken place. As a result of this change, the Buddha emerged as a supermundane figure, but in order to conform to the ways of man, he voluntarily created an apparition of himself on earth to carry out his mission among mankind. We have seen that such a concept was held by the Mahasanghika School. This same concept is also found in a Pali discourse in which the Buddha described his previous existences. However, what is described is not the life story of a person but of the eternal unchanging Buddha personality untouched by karma.

This was the concept of the Buddha held by the village artists as they worked on the Buddha legend in the Sanchi and Bharhut stupas. To them, a man or a deity could be represented by visible images, but they felt that they could not represent the personality of one who is eternal and who is said to be formless. Consequently, the artists preferred to remain silent whenever the legends called for the presentation of the image or the figure of the Blessed One. Instead they represented the Buddha with a parasol, a wheel, a lotus, a stupa, or footprints. Such symbols not only signify the transcendence of the Buddha, but they were also instruments of magic to assist the followers to communicate with the divine object of their religion. For the devout worshippers, the symbols did not take the place of the Buddha but were the Buddha himself.

This aniconic feature of early Buddhist art was soon transformed by the introduction of the *bhakti* or devotional element into the religion. *Bhakti* means faith and devotion to the Lord, accompanied by prayer, worship, and propitiation.

When stupa worship became prominent among the Buddhists, this devotional element found an avenue of expression, and in the worship of the stupa, the Buddha as the Lord of Compassion is invoked. This element of devotion soon demanded the presence of some image that could be the object of worship. It is true that the symbols and relics could serve the purpose, but as time passed, the worshippers felt that a more tangible image was needed. It was undoubtedly in response to this psychological background that the concrete image of the Buddha emerged. This background is presented clearly in a legend entitled Upagupta and Mara, found in the collection of stories called *Divyavadana*, or *Heavenly Stories*.

Upagupta was the spiritual preceptor of King Asoka, and according to the legend, was such a persuasive monk that he even succeeded in converting Mara the evil one. It occurred to Upagupta that if Mara, who was also a skillful actor, could create by magic an exact duplicate of the body of the Buddha, the sight of that body would immeasurably strengthen his (Upagupta's) faith in the Blessed One. Mara consented to do this with the understanding that the monk would not prostrate himself before the created image. When the monk agreed, Mara disguised himself to look exactly like the Buddha, and reappeared before Upagupta, who was so overwhelmed by the sight that he immediately prostrated himself. When the monk was reminded of his promise, he replied that he was worshipping the Buddha himself, and not Mara.

Such a legend is indicative of the psychological urge that existed in the monastic community for a concrete image of the Buddha that could serve as the object of worship and devotion. This urge finally led to the creation of the Buddha image in Gandhara in northwest India and in Mathura in central India. The question as to where it was first created is a problem that has aroused considerable controversy among the art historians.

Those who give the priority to Gandhara contend that the first image was created by the Greek artisans who had become Indianized about the beginning of the Christian era. These artisans had to decide how to treat the person of the Buddha who was the object of emotional attachment. To them it did not matter whether the Buddha was a man or a god, for to them there was only one way of representing either, and that was to present the Buddha in a human form. As a model they chose the Greek god Apollo and Indianized it. This was the beginning of Buddhist art in Gandhara, a region which was exposed to various kinds of foreign influence, Greek, Roman, and Persian. In order to satisfy the great demand for artistic representation of the Bud-

dhist deities, many workshops were established in the area. However, those who staffed these workshops were mere craftsman,
and these mediocre artisans, while conversant with the contents
of the Buddhist legends, created images of the Buddha that were
mechanical, without character, and lacking the inner serenity of
the Blessed One. Such images were endowed with curly hair,
mustache, ornaments, and draped with robes that resembled the
Roman toga, while the arhats and the monks were bearded like
the classical philosophers of Hellenism.

The advocates of Gandharan priority contend that the Gandharan Buddha with its foreign features was not satisfactory to
the native Indians, who felt that the image of the master should
portray the inner spirit and the dynamic power of the founder of
the religion. As a protest against this mode of representing the
Buddha, the Mathura school of Buddhist art emerged in central
India.

Those who give the priority to the Mathura school do not consider the above conclusion to be correct, and base their view on
the following grounds. Since very early times, Mathura was a
center of Indian art, for some of the earliest examples of Indian
sculpture have been found in the vicinity of Mathura. In this
Mathura sculpture, the head of the Buddha is shaven and never
covered with curls, and there is no mustache. The robes cling
very closely to the flesh. The seat is always the lion and not the
lotus. The broad masculine chest and shoulders give the impression of enormous pent-up energy. The Mathura Buddha is also
characterized by a simple dignity and a radiant expression, probably to indicate the inner contentment of the Blessed One. In
conformity with the standard textual descriptions, the Buddha is
presented with a lion-shaped torso and tapering arms and legs.
Such qualities of the Mathura Buddha connect it intimately with
the figures of the indigenous yakshas or tree deities, and it stands
in marked contrast with the Gandharan Buddha with its cold,
vapid, and lifeless expression. The Mathura advocates would
therefore argue that the emergence of the Mathura Buddha was
not in the nature of a protest against the Gandharan Buddha, but
was a natural continuation of native developments in sculpture

evolved in response to the Buddhist desire for a concrete image of worship.

What are the dates for the emergence of the Gandharan and the Mathura Buddhas? This is the focal point of contention. It is now generally accepted that the earliest dated image of the Buddha in Gandhara is that found on the Kanishkan reliquary. This treasure was discovered through excavations in Peshawar in northern India, and consisted of a small box made of metal and dated the first year of King Kanishka. The lid of the reliquary is the main item of interest, for on top of it is a standing statue of the Buddha, flanked by two figures. On the side of the box are inscribed some more images of the Blessed One, as well as an image of Kanishka himself. Now Kanishka was the third king of the Kushan Dynasty, established by an Indo-European tribe called the Scythians who had settled in central Asia across the borders of northwestern India during the second century B.C. In the first century B.C. they founded an empire that embraced much of northern India and central Asia. Kanishka was the third Kushan ruler. His dates are by no means certain. After considerable controversy it is now generally held that he ascended the throne in either ca. 78 A.D. or ca. 144 A.D. If we accept the earlier chronology, then the statue of the Buddha on the Kanishkan reliquary would be dated ca. 78 A.D. The fact that this particular statue is dated would imply that the practice of making the Buddha image must have existed prior to that time. Coins minted during the reign of Kanishka also have the image of the Buddha on one side, together with the Greek inscription "Boddo." Were there any Buddha images before Kanishka? Maybe there were, but none have been found so far.

The date of the earliest Mathura Buddha can be arrived at only by conjecture. Even before Mathura became a Buddhist center, it already had a flourishing community of Jains, followers of another Indian religion, Jainism, that emphasized austerities and asceticism. After Buddhism was established there, it is likely that Buddhist and Jain art became closely related. An image of the Jain founder was known to have existed in 57 B.C., according to an inscription on a Jain stupa in Mathura. In examining the art objects of that early period, it is difficult to distinguish between the two religions unless there are definite inscriptions, for the architecture, stupas, and symbols are very similar. Since Jain images were known to exist ca. 50 B.C., it is not too hazardous to surmise that images of the Buddha must have been in use in Mathura also at about the same time. If this guess is correct, then the earliest Mathura Buddha could have been created during the second half of the first century B.C. and would have antedated the Gandharan image, that it originated on Indian soil and was conceived to meet the needs of devotional Buddhism. The emergence of the Buddha image was therefore another aspect of the newly developing Mahayana Buddhism. The creation of the concrete image resulted in Mahayana Buddhism becoming a much more attractive religion as far as the masses are concerned, for now these faithful and devout followers have visible objects as the focus of their devotion and worship.

Buddhist art also proved to be of considerable assistance in the spread of the religion. Wherever the Buddhist missionaries went, they carried along with them images of the founder of their religion as well as the symbols which have been developed in India. Many of the monks were also skilled craftsmen in the creation of such artistic objects, and very often they transmitted their skill to their newly won converts in different parts of Asia. Consequently we find centers of Buddhist art in practically all the countries that Buddhism penetrated. Just across the borders of India are the colossal figures of the Buddha in Bamiyan, Afghanistan, carved out of the sandstone, with one towering as high as 175 feet. Along the central Asiatic routes from India to China, in oases whose names have disappeared from our maps, traces have been discovered of this Buddhist art showing Greek, Roman, Indian, and Iranian influences. Finally at the end of the line, in the northern section of the great Chinese empire, these Buddhist monks and their Chinese collaborators carved out of the rocks masterpieces of Buddhist sculpture which may still be seen today, bearing mute testimony of the emotional fervor generated by devotion to the religion founded by the Sakyan sage. The most important of such centers are Tun-huang in northwest China, and

Yun-kang and Lung-men in north China. In these centers are statues and images of Sakyamuni, Maitreya, Amitabha, Avalo-kitesvara, Manjusri, and a host of lesser Buddhist deities. The gigantic task of chiseling the figures out of the hard rock was sponsored not only by the ruling class and the aristocracy but also by the common people. Even in these far-away centers of Bud-dhist sculpture in China, Indian influences may still be seen. The imposing figures of the Buddha in Yun-kang were undoubtedly modelled after those in Bamiyan. Treatment of the hair betray Indian as well as central Asiatic influences. For instance, some of the Buddhas in China have wavy hair, after the manner of the Gandharan Buddha; others follow the Mathura Buddhas in having spiral locks, while still others are bald, after the fashion of images in central Asia. The huge numbers of such statues and images of Buddhist deities are probably the best indication of how closely identified Buddhist art was with the development of the religion in China.

At the other end of the Buddhist world, in the countries of southeast Asia, we also find Buddhist art and architecture playing a dominant role in the religious life of the people. The landscape of Burma and Thailand for instance, is dominated by the Bud-dhist temples and the stupa, which is now transformed from its dome-like shape in India to a pinnacle shape spire. One of the finest examples of the reclining Buddha, or the Buddha attaining nirvana, is said to be that found in Polonnaruva in Ceylon, dating back to the eleventh century. In Java may be seen what is com-monly acclaimed as the finest masterpiece of religious art in Asia, the Borobudur, built by the Sailendra Dynasty during the eighth and ninth centuries. Conceived as a symbol of the world structure, this imposing stupa is filled with sculptural reliefs illustrating the life of the Buddha as recounted in the *Lalita-vistara*, a Mahayana biographical scripture. As the pilgrim per-forms his circumambulation, he can follow through these reliefs the footsteps of his master in his final journey to enlightenment. In Cambodia today, only the ruins of the fabulous Angkor Wat may be seen, but these ruins are sufficient to show us the degree of excellence and proficiency attained by the Indian and Buddhist artists and architects as they built the palaces and decorated them with themes taken from Indian and Buddhist sources.

In the Buddhist temples of southeast Asia, where Theravada Buddhism is predominant, the images to be found in them are almost exclusively those of Gautama Sakyamuni. In some temples in Thailand, he is accompanied by two followers, Sariputta and Moggallana, who preceded him to nirvana. Even though there may be several images in the same temple, such images are still those of Sakyamuni. He is usually presented in a seated or standing position, and in rare instances, in a reclining position.

In temples belonging to the Mahayana tradition, such as those found in China, then images of not only the Buddha but also the bodhisattvas and the lesser deities are to be found. As soon as one enters the premises of the temple, one is confronted by two fierce figures, the generals Heng and Ha, two legendary warriors who fought each other in ancient China. How these two non-Buddhist figures got included in the Buddhist pantheon is indeed a puzzle. Both are armed with clubs, and stand on both sides of the entrance into the temple. After entering the courtyard, one is greeted by a jovial image in a sitting posture, with a mountainous belly protruding prominently. This is the Laughing Buddha, the Chinese version of Maitreya the Future Buddha. There is no longer any traces of Indian art in this figure, for he has become entirely Chinese in appearance. On both sides of the Laughing Buddha are the four Heavenly Kings, who rule the four corners of the universe, and protect the temple as well as the followers of the law. As one proceeds further into the temple, he will enter the Great Hall, in which may be found the main altar. The altar may be occupied by a single image of Sakyamuni, or he may be flanked by two other Buddhas, Amitabha the presiding Buddha of the Western Paradise on his right, and Bhaishajyaguru the Healing Buddha on his left. Along the gables of the Great Hall there are podiums built for images of the sixteen arhats. In the Chinese temple the arhats do not command great respect and their images are mere accessories to the arrangement of the Great Hall.

The main altar is screened from behind by a partition, and

behind this partition there is another altar, facing the opposite direction. The most common deity honored here is the bodhisattva Avalokitesvara, or Kuan-yin, in female form. In this appearance, the bodhisattva is worshipped mainly by women who desire to give birth to male offsprings. In some temples, instead of Kuan-yin, there is the Pure Land trinity, with Amitabha in the center, flanked by Kuan-yin in the male form on his left, and Mahasthama the bodhisattva representing force on his right.

The images of the Buddha aways show him with stylized positions of the fingers and hands called *mudras* or hand-gestures. One of the most common of such gestures, called the earth-touching or *bhumisparca-mudra,* shows the Buddha in a seated position, right arm hanging over right knee, hand with palm turned in, and all the fingers extended downward with the third finger touching the throne. The left hand is on the lap, palm upward. This gesture has reference to the episode when the Buddha called upon the earth goddess to witness that he had resisted the temptation of Mara the Evil One. Another common gesture is that of the turning of the wheel of the law. Here the right hand is at the breast, with the tips of the index and thumb touching one of the fingers of the left hand, with the palm turned inward. There is also the gesture of meditation, where the hands lie on the lap, right on the left, with all fingers extended and palms turned upward. Finally we might mention the gesture of protection, with the right hand elevated, slightly bent, hand lifted, palm turned outward and all the fingers turned upward. The left hand hangs down with palm turned outward.

In countries like China which already has a long artistic tradition of her own, the advent of Buddhist art broadened and enriched the outlook of the native artists by the introduction of new techniqus, new themes, and new artistic values. In areas of inferior civilization where artistic traditions were lacking, as in the countries of southeast Asia, Buddhist art served as a great civilizing influence, opening the eyes of the people to new canons of line and form, beauty and proportion, and showing them how it is possible, by appropriate objects and symbols, to deepen and strengthen their religious aspirations. Together with the message of the Buddha and the religious festivals and ceremonies, Buddhist art provided the magnet that attracted the masses to become followers of the Sakyan sage.

CHAPTER *12*

Buddhist Ceremonies
and Festivals

IN PREVIOUS CHAPTERS we have discussed at some length the
two fundamental components of a religion, the body of teachings
left behind by the master and the community of monks who are
the agents to carry out those teachings. Compared to the total
population of a community, the number of monks represents
but a small minority, so that those in the community who would
be introduced to the religion by the monks would be rather small.
Through ceremonies and festivals, however, Buddhism is able
to reach much larger segment of the population. By the display
of religious symbolisms, by the performance of religious drama,
and by the lectures and debates which sometimes accompany the
grand festivals, the basic teachings of the religion are disseminated
to a much wider audience.

For the people at large, these ceremonies and festivals provide
an opportunity to participate in the activities of the religion and
thus feel a personal attachment to it. By the collective expression
of interest and participation, the people feel that they are sharing
something in common in the quest of some basic goals and ideals;
they no longer feel that they are mere spectators in a religion
practiced only by the ordained monks, but are instead active co-

250

workers drawn together by the unity and solidarity of a common faith. By participating in the ceremonies and festivals they feel that they are sharing in the experiences of the founder and the heroes of their religion, and such a realization creates in them the sense of continuity with their past.

Finally, ceremonies and festivals provide the participants with some diversions from the humdrum routine of their everyday lives. On such occasions, they can forget their toils and worries for the day, and shed off the restraints that regulate their daily lives. With their fellow-men, they can go out to enjoy themselves, dancing, singing, shouting, playing musical instruments, beating drums, and making a lot of noise in general. Ordinary men are not machines who slave from cradle to grave, but are creatures endowed with feelings and emotions, and the religious ceremonies and festivals provide them with an outlet for the expression of such emotions.

Throughout the year, there are a number of ceremonies and festivals that figure prominantly in the lives of the Buddhist devotees. For the clerical order, the most important ceremonies are those connected with the ordination of monks and the fortnightly assemblies held on the first and fifteenth days of the month. These have already been described in some detail in the chapter on the monastic community. In Tibet, numerous ceremonies have proliferated, due very likely to the introduction of Bon practices into the religion. Here we shall concern ourselves with only one, the ceremony of guiding the consciousness after death. The ceremony is performed by the monks for the benefit of one who has just died, and is instigated in the first place by his family, sometimes with the good intention of influencing the form of the next rebirth of the deceased, but sometimes also with the idea of prevailing upon the spirit not to cause trouble for the living.

In the ceremony, a name card is used as a substitute for the deceased. At first, a lotus-shaped *mandala* with six petals, one for each of the six modes of existences, is drawn by the officiating monks. Since it is assumed that the deceased would be reborn in any of the six modes, his name card is moved around the various lotus petals of the *mandala*, beginning with the lowest mode of existence or hell. As soon as the name card is placed there, mystic syllables are uttered by the monks, calling upon Avalokitesvara to remove all the torments of heat and cold from the body of the deceased, and to purify the evil effects of wrath by the nectar of knowledge. The spirit of the dead person is then told that his tormentors in hell have been appeased by offerings of food, and that the gates of hell are now closed to him. As the name card is moved to each successive sphere of existence, (hungry ghost, animal, man, titan, and deity), the name ceremony is repeated, with the necessary changes made in the names of the particular Buddhas and the nature of sufferings in each sphere. After the sphere of the deities has been closed to the deceased, then the lotus shaped *mandala* is pushed away, and the Rite of the Intermediate State recited. Food, drink, clothing, and a large number of desirable objects are now offered to the deceased to take care of his needs in the intermediary state between successive rebirths. As these offerings are being made, the spirit of the deceased is called upon, if he should be reborn in another body, to practice the perfections of charity, good qualities, tolerance, zealous activity, concentration, and wisdom. After these exhortations, the spirit is then told that he is in the Buddha field of Avalokitesvara, and that he should remain in that sphere protected by the bodhisattva. The name card is then destroyed, and the ceremony ends with the utterance of the concluding *mantra*. Through the performance of this ceremony, the spirit of the deceased is freed from phenomenal existence and is assured of rebirth in a pure Buddha field.[36]

In Ceylon there is a ceremony which can be held anytime, since it is for the purpose of exorcising evil spirits, curing sickness, or blessing a new house. This ceremony is called *pirit*, from the Pali *paritta*, which means protection. There is a *Pirit-pota* or *Book of Parittas* containing selections from the Pali canon that are to be recited during the ceremony.

If an evil spirit is to be exorcised, the *Metta-sutta* and the *Ratana-sutta* are to be recited for seven days. During the recital, a relic of the Buddha is placed in a casket and set on a platform.

The presence of the relic is to indicate that the Buddha is present. On another platform sit the officiating monks who recite the suttas continuously day and night. From twelve to twenty-four monks participate, divided into teams of two who recite for two hours each. In addition, the whole group of monks are assembled three times a day, sunrise, midday, and sunset, to chant verses taken from the canon. If after this seven day recital, the evil spirit leaves the patient, well and good, but if the spirit does not leave, then the most powerful of the suttas, the *Atanatiya-sutta* in the *Collection of Long Discourses* is recited. Whenever this is done, then certain precautions must be taken. The monk who recites this sutta should abstain from meat or any food prepared from flour. His residence should not be near a cemetery, so as to avoid harassment from the evil spirits living there. When he goes from the monastery to the home of the patient, he should be protected by men carrying weapons and shields. Instead of reciting the sutta in open air, he should do so within a tightly closed room, guarded at all times by men bearing arms.

After the patient has vowed to follow the precepts, then the recital begins. If the spirit leaves, the service comes to an end, but if the spirit persists in remaining within the patient, then the latter is taken to the monastery, and laid down on the courtyard, which is swept clean and decorated with flowers and lamps. Verses of blessings are now recited, and a full assembly of the deities convened. The patient is asked for his name, and after that the evil spirit is addressed by that name. The spirit is now told that since the merits arising from alms-giving, the offerings of flowers and lamps, and the recital of the verses of blessings have been transferred to him, he should be thankful and leave the patient. If after all this the spirit still refuses to leave, then the deities should be invoked and informed of his obstinacy, and the *Atanatiya sutta* again recited.[37]

Worship of the stupa is another ceremony that is commonly observed in Buddhist countries. Members of the clerical order and lay devotees may join together in this ceremony. Since the stupa contains within it some relic of the Blessed One, it is looked upon by the worshippers as the visual manifestation of the Buddha. To set the sacred structure apart from the profane world, the stupa is surrounded by a high balustrade of stone. At the cardinal points of the compass, the balustrade is pierced by four gateways which are said to correspond to the course of the sun across the sky, sunrise, zenith, sunset, and nadir. The birth of the Buddha is represented by the eastern gate, enlightenment by the southern, preaching the law by the western, and nirvana by the northern. Between the balustrade and the dome is a wide circular path to be used for the circumambulation of the stupa.

On days when the worship of the stupa is carried out, the worshippers in colorful procession and bearing flowers, pennants, and incense, enter the circumambulatory path by the eastern gateway, and then proceed to walk around the dome in a clockwise fashion, always with the dome at the right. In this manner, they really follow the career of the Buddha as they walk past the southern, western, and northern gateways.

The Tibetan version of this circumambulation is the walk which the Tibetans usually take on the holy path around the city of Lhasa during the fourth month of the Tibetan calendar. During that month, all Tibetans who can possibly spare the time make the circumambulation for the purpose of acquiring merits. For the more devout Tibetans, it is not enough just to walk around; they would negotiate the entire distance by falling prostrate on the ground, get up, and then repeat the process. About a week is necessary to complete the round of about six miles. In order to protect their hands and knees, such people use leather gloves and knee pads.

Besides these ceremonies, there are numerous festivals which are observed throughout the Buddhist annual calendar and in which all elements of society, the rulers, the aristocracy, the common people, the rich and the poor, monks and laymen all join together to participate in the celebrations. In some instances, as in the case of imperial China under the T'ang dynasty, such celebrations were really state functions to celebrate imperial birthdays, held in the Buddhist temples to ensure that the forces of the spiritual world would protect the imperial family from evil influences. The occasion for the festivities may be certain events in the life of the Buddha. In every Buddhist country, the birthday of the Buddha is celebrated from the earliest days to the present. In some instances, the festival may be focused on a relic of the Buddha, such as the tooth in Kandy in Ceylon. In other instances, it may be centered on some Buddhist practice, such as the bestowing of robes to the monks at the end of the rainy retreat. In China and Japan, one of the most popular festivals in the past was the celebration of the festival of the dead, an event connected with the search of Moggallana for his mother.

The celebration of the Buddha's birthday is called the Vesakha festival, Vesakha being the name of the month in which the Blessed One was born. This is one of the earliest Buddhist festivals, and probably the first description to be found in literature is that furnished by the Chinese pilgrim Fa-hsien, who witnessed the event in India during the early fifth century. Here is his description of the celebration.

"Every year on the eighth day of the second month they celebrate a procession of images. They make a four-wheeled car, and on it erect a structure of five storeys by means of bamboos tied together. This is supported by a king-post, with poles and lances slanting from it, and is rather more than twenty cubits high, having the shape of a tope. White and silk-like cloth of hair is wrapped all around it, which is then painted in various colors. They make figures of devas, with gold, silver, and lapis lazuli grandly blended and having silken streamers and canopies hung out over them. On the four sides are niches, with a Buddha seated in each, and a Bodhisattva standing in attendance on him. There may be twenty cars, all grand and imposing, but each one different from the others. On the day mentioned, the monks and laity within the borders all come together; they have singers and skillful musicians; they pay their devotions with flowers and incense. The Brahmans come and invite the Buddhists to enter the city. These do so in order, and remain two nights in it. All through the night they keep lamps burning, have skillful music, and present offerings. This is the practice in all the other kingdoms as well. The Heads of the Vaisya families in them establish in the cities houses for dispensing charity and medicines. All the poor and destitute in the country, orphans, widowers, and child-less men, maimed people and cripples, and all who are diseased, go to these houses, and are provided with every kind of help, and doctors examine their diseases. They get the food and medicines which their cases require, and are made to feel at ease; and when they are better, they go away of themselves." [38]

In China, the occasion was usually celebrated on the eighth day of the fourth moon, and sometimes on the eighth day of the second moon, of the lunar calendar. The celebration was marked by two events, the procession of the Buddha images and the bathing of the Buddha. The latter ceremony was based on the tradition that the Buddha was bathed with scented water poured down by the gods as soon as he was born. As for the procession of the images, these were first concentrated in one central temple on the seventh, and on the following day, they were transported through the streets of the city, amidst the cheering and shouting and the laughter of the multitudes, who set off firecrackers, burned incense, scattered flowers, or waved pennants.

One of the most famous of relics is the tooth of the Buddha now kept in Kandy. From the time of its earliest introduction to Ceylon in 371, the presence of the tooth had served as the inspiration of an annual festival. In the beginning it was kept in the Abhayagiri Vihara in the capital Anuradhapura, and in the middle of the third month, according to Fa-hsien, it was brought out for public procession and view.

Ten days before the procession was to take place, a man chosen because of his stentorian voice and eloquence would ride around the city on a richly decorated elephant and proclaim the following message to the inhabitants of the city. He said that the Buddha in his previous lives had sacrificed his own life many times for the benefit of others; he offered himself as food to the hungry tigress in order that the latter might not eat her newly born cubs, he tortured himself in order to save a dove from a hungry hawk. After numerous lives of self-sacrifice, he entered nirvana. Ten days hence, the tooth of this Buddha would be brought out for public display. All the inhabitants of the city should prepare for the event by cleaning and adorning the streets, scatter flowers, and burn incense.

With the proclamation out of the way, the king then placed on both sides of the processional path the five hundred bodily forms of the Buddha, each one representing one of the previous rebirths of the Blessed One. The figures were beautifully painted and lavishly decorated, and very lifelike in color and appearance. Then on the appointed day, the tooth was brought out and paraded along the principal thoroughfare, where practically all the inhabitants had gathered to pay their respects to the relic. After the tooth was returned to the Abhayagiri, the celebrations continued for ninety days there, with the clergy and laity coming in without ceasing, day and night, to burn incense, light lamps, and perform ceremonies.

At present, the festival of the tooth is held in Kandy in the month of August, and lasts about ten days. Elephants still figure prominently in the festivities. A stud of elephants is kept in the Temple of the Tooth, let out during the rest of the year for heavy work, but during the day of the procession, these elephants come into their own. Along the route of the procession, which has been swept clean and gaily decorated for the occasion, the team of mighty elephants march along majestically, led by the biggest and mightiest of them all, carrying the precious relic, to be seen by the huge crowds lining up both sides of the route. The lead elephant is covered with rich and spectacular decorations, consisting of gold, silver, and jewelled embroidery, and covered with fragrant flowers. Beside the basket in which the tooth is contained, there is also an image of the Buddha. The sacred elephant is ridden by a Kandyan headman wearing a glorious uniform, and flanked on both sides by two smaller elephants. The procession of the elephants and the others in the parade extends for about a mile, and all along the route, there is just one confusing bedlam. The crowds yell, blow conch shells, bang cymbals, blow screeching pipes, and beat tom-toms, creating a kind of rhythm that seems to galvanize the devil dancers in their splendid garb into more violent contortions and movements. All in all the spectacle is a superb exhibition.[39] Such an exhibition is still held annually in Ceylon.

Just as fervent and delirious were the celebrations in China when Buddhism was enjoying its heyday. In T'ang China, four temples in the capital claimed to have specimens of the Buddha's teeth, which were put on display for one week during the second or the third lunar month of the year. When this happened, then all sorts of offerings, such as medicines and foods, rare fruits and flowers as well as different assortments of incense were presented to the relics. Sometimes the worshippers made offerings of grains to feed the monks in the temples, or they tossed showers of coins toward the hall where the tooth was enshrined.

The most famous of the relics was a finger bone kept in a temple west of the capital of Ch'ang-an. Whenever this relic was taken into the capital and put on public display in a temple, then the populace in the capital literally went wild in their celebration over the event. On such occasions the multitudes burnt their heads and roasted their fingers, or threw away their clothes and scattered their money. Officialdom and the grand families donated unlimited wealth to the monastery, while the common people vied with one another to make their offerings to the relic, giving up the earnings of a lifetime. Streets in the capital were jammed with people milling about trying to get to the temple to see the relic. On one occasion, a soldier cut off his left arm and as he reverenced the relic, his blood sprinkled all over the ground. Others walked on their elbows and knees as they approached the sacred spot. To celebrate the event, some rich families poured mercury to form pools, set up gold and jade as trees, and competed with each other to establish Buddha images. In the streets, the people added to the confusion by blowing conch shells and horns, or striking cymbals. Singers and dancers also roamed the streets, adding to the gaiety of the occasion. After the public display, the emperor would welcome the relic into the palace chapel and place it on a couch with curtains made of golden flowers, a mat made of dragon scales, and a mattress made of phoenix feathers. All in all, the ceremony of reverencing the relic was the occasion for the most gorgeous show in the capital.

In India, Ceylon, and the countries of southeast Asia, the monsoon rains during the summer months render it impossible for the monks to move about with ease and convenience. From the very beginning of his mission, the Buddha requested the monks to go into retreat during the rainy season. During the retreat, the monks are to reside in one locality to carry on their studies and meditation. At the end of the retreat, there is a *kathina* or robe ceremony, at which time robes which had been donated to the community of monks by devout laymen would be distributed to the monks. In Thailand, this occasion is celebrated as a state ceremony, with the king of the land playing a dominant role. By his participation in the ceremony, the king indicates the royal support for the integrity and prosperity of Buddhism. This support is concretely manifested by the lavish gifts which the king makes to the *sangha*. Following the example of the king, the nobles and common people throughout the realm likewise display their generosity toward the *sangha* by their gifts. Thus every temple and monastery in the land is benefitted during the celebration of the *kathina* ceremony.

In Thailand, the celebration takes place annually from the middle of the eleventh month to the middle of the twelfth month in the Thai calendar, corresponding roughly to the October-November period. The monsoon rains have ceased, and the retreat is at an end. During the period of celebration, processions of one sort or another may be seen every day, either on land or on water. On the water, the boats are gaily decorated, carrying bands which blare forth their notes, and passengers dressed in their best garments.

The principal monasteries in the capital are designated as the royal monasteries, and as such are under special royal protection and receive gifts directly from the king. However, such royal monasteries have become so numerous that the king cannot visit them all, and so nobles who represent the king are sent to the more distant ones to present the gifts. The king may proceed either by land or by water to the royal monasteries. If by land, he goes by palanquin and is accompanied by his retinue in a colorful and dignified procession to the temple. If by water he proceeds to his destination on a royal barge together with the accompanying noblemen, with the gifts to the temple being carried on another royal barge. The entire procession may include some thirty or forty barges; in earlier days, it is said that about a hundred and fifty barges participated.

Upon arrival and debarkation, the king walks to the temple on foot over a carpet spread out for the occasion. At the door of the temple, he takes over a complete set of monastic robes from one of his courtiers and enters the temple. He proceeds to where the image of the Buddha is located at the far end of the temple. The monks in the monastery are seated in the vicinity row by row. The king places the robes on a specially prepared table on which are placed five golden vases of flowers, five golden dishes of parched corn, five golden candlesticks, and five incense sticks. The number five signifies the three Buddhas of the past, Sakyamuni the Buddha of the present, and Maitreya the Future Buddha. The king pays homage to the image of the Buddha three times, and each time he repeats the formula, "Homage to the Blessed One, the arhat, the fully enlightened Buddha." The abbot of the monastery then repeats the formula three times. After the recitation has been completed, the king offers the robes to the monks, who signify their acceptance by crying out, "Excellent, excellent!"

The abbot now addresses the congregation of monks, saying that the king has honored the community by condescending to come to the monastery and offering the robes personally to the monks, and leaving it to the community to decide who among the monks are to receive the robes. The abbot then distributes the robes to those who are in need, with special robes reserved for those who have attained distinction in their study of Pali. The monks then pronounced a short blessing to the monarch:

"May you live over one hundred years in the fullness of vigor, free from disease and happy; may all your wishes be fulfilled, all your works accomplished, all advantages accrue to you; may you always triumph and succeed, O Paramindra (the king's name), august Sovereign. May it be so forever! We beg to tender (to you) this blessing." [40]

Once more the king pays homage to the image of the Buddha and then leaves.

The same procedure is repeated in all the temples that the king visits to present his gifts. Roughly about half an hour is spent in each institution.

After the royal *kathina,* then boat races are held. Formerly when Ayuthia was the capital, the royal family sponsored the regatta and the royal barge participated in the races. The prevalent prophecy was that if the royal barge lost, then there would be prosperity for the kingdom, but if it won, then calamities would prevail. At present the races are no longer sponsored by the royal family and are entirely a Buddhist affair. Such races give the young men who had been staying in the monasteries for three months an opportunity to work out their excess energy and to have a lot of competitive amusement at the same time.

In Burma, another stronghold of Theravada Buddhism, the end of the rainy season is also celebrated with the great feast of the year, held on the day of the full moon in October. The festival is centered in the great pagoda of the capital, and on the festival days throngs of people come and go, male and female, old and young, rich and poor, all dressed in their finest clothing. Under the brilliant clear sunlight, the crowd of people moving along presents a motley of blazing colors.

The festival lasts seven days, but the most important day is that of the full moon. On that day, the throngs participating in the festivities are the densest and the offerings the most numerous. The mass of people going up the steps of the pagoda is like a flood squeezing through the dragons at the gate to enter into the broad platform. All day long the crowds gather and wander about. Even when the sun sets, there is no pause; instead the tempo increases when the moon rises in the east. As the moon rises, the pagoda takes on a new appearance, for now it is lighted and decorated with thousands of little lamps, and the facades of the shrines are also lighted up. The lamps are hung in long rows or circles to fit the places they decorate. They are really little earthenware jars filled with coconut oil and lighted with wicks. People now flock to the pagoda to see the lamps. The streets near the pagoda are also brilliantly lighted and are equally crowded with happy and laughing people. To entertain the good-natured throngs, dramatic performances in the open air, dances, and marionette shows are staged, lasting far into the night. Only when the moon has fallen low on the horizon and the oil lamps have died out one by one does the crowd disperse and the great festival ends.[41]

The last festival that we shall describe is the Ullambana festival, called *Yu-lan-p'en* in Chinese and *Urabon* in Japanese. This was one of the most popular Buddhist festivals in China, and is still so considered by the Japanese. The celebration takes place on the fifteenth day of the seventh moon of the lunar calendar, but in Japan the festivities begin on the thirteenth. As far as is known, the festival was first held in China in 538, and in Japan in 606. In 733 the celebration became an annual event in Japan. During the early stages of the celebration in China, the sacrifices offered were made to the Buddha and the *sangha* on behalf of the ancestors up to seven generations back. During the T'ang dynasty, a change took place. The sacrifices in the ceremony were now addressed to the spirits of the dead ancestors and the hungry ghosts. This change was brought about by the famous Tantric monk Amoghavajra, and as the change was congenial to the practice of ancestor worship in China, the annual ceremonies became exceedingly popular in that country. The nature of the celebration also changed during the same period. Instead of being just a ceremony for the departed souls, the festival became an occasion in which the rich temples in the capital put on public display their rare possessions. In some instances, rich laymen also used the temples as exhibition halls to display their exquisite and rare objects. On such occasions, the atmosphere of the temples resembled that of a fair, with the multitudes jamming the temple grounds to view the exhibitions and to enjoy the dramatic performances which were also presented.

It is held by both the Chinese and the Japanese that the spirits of the departed come back to this world during this celebration of the Ullambana festival. The Japanese accordingly clean their family shrines, prepare altars before the shrines, and offer special meals to the spirits. Rush mats are spread out on which are placed noodles, millet, gourds, melons, and eggplants. On the thirteenth day, welcome dumplings are placed on the altar. On the fourteenth day, potato salad and eggplant mixed with sesame seeds are offered. On the fifteenth, steamed rice wrapped in lotus leaves and farewell dumplings are presented. Every day, incense is burnt, together with offerings of flowers, tea, and water. On the thirteenth day, lights are placed in the cemeteries and before the houses so as to light the way homeward for the spirits. On the fourteenth, priests are invited to say prayers for the departed. On the last day, lights called farewell fires are again lighted outside to send the spirits back to their abode. In communities near rivers and lakes, those families which had suffered the death of some member would make miniature sailboats and load them with provisions and lighted lanterns, and then send them adrift in the current. The lights of the farewell fires and on the drifting boats vanishing in the dark signify continuity with the departed.

The purpose of the ceremonies performed during the festival is to benefit the spirits of the departed ancestors and relatives, but the merit of having staged the ceremony and made the offerings also is said to bring longevity and happiness to the living donors.

The basis for this Ullambana ceremony is found in a sutra entitled *Ullambanapatrasutra*. According to this sutra, after Moggallana, one of the closest disciples of the Buddha, had attained arhatship and the supernatural powers, he wished to deliver his parents from whatever evil deeds they might have committed. He surveyed all the modes of existences, and finally found his mother as a hungry ghost, with an immense belly but a minute head, so that she was perpetually suffering from hunger. In his compassion he gave her a bowl of rice, but the rice turned into flames as soon as it touched her mouth. Overcome with grief, he returned to the Buddha to ask for help. The Buddha replied that the evil karma of the tormented mother was so great that neither he nor any other deity was in a position to help save her from her agony; only the supernatural powers of all the monks acting in unison could help her. The Buddha also told Moggallana to provide, on the fifteenth day of the seventh month, food, drink, and utensils not only for the sake of his departed parents, but for all living beings who may be suffering. Through such a service and offering, the parents in this world and in the world of death could be delivered from woe and torment. This was accordingly done by Moggallana. At the same time, the Buddha also ordered all the monks in the order to pray on behalf of Moggallana's mother. As a result, the suffering mother was delivered from her state as a hungry ghost. Moggallana then asked the Buddha whether or not this festival should be continued in the future for the generations to come. The Buddha replied that all those who are filial and grateful to their parents and ancestors should celebrate this festival.

During the period of the *urabon* in Japan, bon dances, or *bon-odori*, which are really folk dances, are held in the country villages, and may still be seen today. They provide a delightful pastime for the young people, who gather in the compound of the local temple and dance until midnight. The dance is simple and performed amidst the clapping of hands. Common folk songs are also sung without the accompaniment of musical instruments. Any one can participate. There is no need for special dress or for any dancing skill. The main requirement is that everything, the clapping of hands, the movement of the steps, and the singing, be done in unison. Since the dance is a ceremonial dance, the clapping of the hands is considered an act of worship, the same as joining the hands in prayer. During the dance, *nembutsu,* or invoking the name of the Buddha, is also practiced. Probably the most revealing description of the bon dance is that written by Lafcadio Hearn, who witnessed the scene in the courtyard of an ancient temple.

"In the center of the court is a framework of bamboo supporting a great drum; and about it benches have been arranged. . . . There is a hum of voices, voices of people very low, as if expecting something solemn; and cries of children betimes, and soft laughter of girls. . . .

"Suddenly a girl rises from her seat, and taps the huge drum once. It was the signal for the Dance of Souls.

"Out of the shadow of the temple a processional line of dancers files into the moonlight and as suddenly halts—all young women or girls, clad in their choicest attire; the tallest leads; her comrades follow in order of stature; little maids of ten or twelve compose the end of the procession. . . . All together glide the right foot forward one pace, without lifting the sandal from the ground, and extend both hands to the right, with a strange floating motion and a smiling, mysterious obeisance. Then the right foot is drawn back, with a repetition of the waving hands and the mysterious bow. Then all advance the left foot and repeat the previous movements, half-turning to the left. Then all take two gliding paces forward, with a simultaneous soft clap of the hands, and the first performance is reiterated, alternately to right and left; all the sandaled feet gliding together, all the supple hands waving together, all the pliant bodies bowing and swaying together. And so slowly, weirdly, the processional movement changes into a great round, circling about the moonlit court and around the voiceless crowd of spectators.

"And always the white hands sinuously wave together, as if weaving spells, alternately without and within the round, now with palms upward, now with palms downward; and all the elfish sleeves hover duskily together, with a shadowing as of wings; and all the feet poise together with such a rhythm of complex motion, that, in watching it, one feels a sensation of hypnotism. . . . And this soporous allurement is intensified by a dead hush. No one speaks, not even a spectator. And, in the long intervals between the soft clapping of hands, one hears only the shrilling of the crickets in the trees, and the *shu-shu* of sandals, lightly stirring the dust. . . . And there comes to me the thought that I am looking at something immemorially old, something belonging to the unrecorded beginnings of this Oriental life, . . . to the magical Age of the Gods; a symbolism of motion whereof the meaning has been forgotten for innumerable years. Yet more and more unreal the spectacle appears . . . ; and I find myself wondering whether, were I to utter but a whisper, all would not vanish forever, save the gray mouldering court and the desolate temple, and the broken statue of Jizo, smiling always the same mysterious smile I see upon the faces of the dancers.

"Under the wheeling moon, in the midst of the round, I feel as one within a circle of charm. And verily this is enchantment; I am bewitched, bewitched by the ghostly weaving of hands, by the rhythmic gliding of feet, above all by the flitting of marvellous sleeves—apparitional, soundless, velvety as a flitting of great tropical bats. No; nothing I ever dreamed of could be likened to this. . . .

"Suddenly a deep male chant breaks the hush. Two giants have joined the round, and now lead it, two superb young mountain peasants nearly nude, towering heads and shoulders above the whole of the assembly. Their kimonos are rolled about their waists like girdles, leaving their bronze limbs and torsos naked to the warm air; they wear nothing else save their immense straw hats and white tabi, donned expressly for the festival. . . . They seem brothers, so like in frame, in movement, in the timbre of their voices, as they intone the same song:

"Whether brought forth upon the mountain or in the field, it matters nothing; more than a treasure of one thousand ryo, a baby precious is." . . . And after the silence, the sweet thin voices of the women answer:—"The parents who will not allow their girl to be united with her lover; they are not the parents, but the enemies of their child."

"And song follows song; and the round ever becomes larger; and the hours pass unfelt, unheard, while the moon wheels slowly down the blue steeps of the night.

"A deep low boom rolls suddenly across the court, the rich tone of some temple bell tolling the twelfth hour. Instantly the witchcraft ends, like the wonder of some dream broken by a sound;

the chanting ceases; the round dissolves in an outburst of happy laughter, and chatting, and soft-vowelled callings of flower-names which are the names of girls, and farewell cries of "Sayonara!" as dancers and spectators alike betake themselves homeward, with a great koro-koro of getas." [42]

CHAPTER 13

Buddhism in the Modern World

IN THE PRECEDING PAGES, we have surveyed the progress of Buddhism, from its inception in a tiny kingdom nestling at the foot of the towering Himalayas to its present position as the dominant faith in east and south Asia. In every land where Buddhism has been introduced, the religion has displayed remarkable elasticity in adapting itself to local conditions and in responding to new needs. Probably no other missionary religion has this characteristic to such a remarkable degree. Its introduction to foreign lands was not achieved through conquest of arms but by the conquest of ideas. Yet wherever it went, it was able to accommodate itself to the ideas of the new land and the new people, and in the process of accommodation became practically a new religion. Witness the difference between the atmosphere of a monastery in Ceylon with that of one in Tibet. Where the Ceylonese scene is one of serenity and peace and leisure, with the Buddha wearing the smile of the bliss of nirvana, the Tibetan temple presents a scene of violence, grotesqueness, fascinating mystery, and militant suspicion, dominated by the image of Kala or Death, terrifying the visitor with his ferocious appearance, eyeballs bulging out, weapons in hand, a garland of skulls on his forehead, and his consort ecstatically embracing him. The Theravadin Buddhists place the highest value on morality as an indispensable means of achieving enlightenment, but the Tibetan Buddhists regard as one of their greatest teachers and saints Marpa, the teacher of Milarepa, who killed living beings, told lies, stole property, and enjoyed carnal relations. The Buddhists of Ceylon and Burma follow strictly the last injunction of the Buddha, to work out one's own salvation with diligence, but the Pure Land School in China and Japan teaches that one should depend entirely on the saving grace of Amitabha for salvation. In their absolute dependence upon Amitabha, the priests of the Shin School in Japan marry and raise families, claiming that the grace of Amitabha will even erase the sin of sexual intercourse.

This elasticity of Buddhism is undoubtedly one of the sources of strength of the religion. By being ready to change and to adjust itself to new conditions and new ideas, the religion has managed to keep itself alive. It is never bothered by inconsistencies, nor is it bound by loyalty to an authoritarian past, but it is always free to develop new ideas and institutions to meet new needs, and is not afraid nor too proud to learn from even its rivals. This elasticity of the religion is a great asset as it faces the problems of the modern world. In the remaining pages, we shall discuss briefly some of the problems that confront Buddhism, problems that have to do with Communism, science, race, and war and peace.

Buddhism and Communism

According to the Marxist theory of economic determinism adopted by the Communists, such integral parts of human society as laws, education, ethics, arts, or the position of individuals are all determined by the methods of production. From the very beginning, the history of man was characterized by class struggle, with the owners of wealth on the one hand and the laboring class on the other. In a capitalistic society, all wealth is created by labor, but labor never receives its full share, because the exploiting capitalist gives the worker only enough for his subsistence while keeping the rest for himself. Inequality is thus inherent in the capitalist system. The only solution to this inequality is to destroy the capitalist class and establish a socialist society in which private ownership of the means of production is abolished.

As opposed to the Marxist view of inequalities in society, the Buddhist contends that such inequalities always exist and are due to something basic and fundamental in human nature. For an understanding of human personality, Marxism is of very little help. It fails to explain for instance why members of the same family, brought up under the same social and economic circumstances, differ so much from one another in their personalities. Buddhism offers a rational explanation of such differences by its doctrine of karma and dependent origination. The human personality is not the product of material causes or governed by external circumstances. It is the manifestation of the fruits of our past karma. In the present life, the individual cannot do much about his present state, since this is the result of past action over which he has no control. But the particular way he acts in the present life is entirely under the direction of his own free will. Whereas Marxism would like to suppress this human personality and individuality to the needs of the state, Buddhism would insist that individuals are individuals, free to follow their own choice. Buddhism accepts the inequality of individuals and tries to show how this inequality arose; Marxism ignores such individual differences and treats everyone as belonging to one level.

Communism is opposed to any system that does not accept the dominance of matter over mind. Its central philosophy is materialistic, for it assumes that if man gets all the material wealth he craves for, he will be happy. Buddhism and modern psychology, however, agree that it is impossible to satisfy the cravings of man for material goods. The more he gets, the more he wants. There is a delightful old Russian fairy tale which provides a good illustration of this. There was once an old fisherman who caught a fish. The fish begged for its life, saying that it was a magic fish who could grant the fisherman anything the latter wished for. The fisherman decided to take the chance, asked the fish for a fine house, released the fish, and went home. As soon as he reached home, he found a huge mansion on the site of his old cottage. The old fisherman and his wife lived happily in the house for a while, but soon the wife felt that such a beautiful house did not match the old worn-out furniture which they had, and so she asked her husband to go and ask the fish for some new furniture. The fisherman did accordingly, and the wish was immediately granted. Now with the new house and furniture to enjoy, the desires of the old couple were satisfied for the time being. Pretty soon, the wife felt it was too much work taking care of the house and furniture, and so servants were asked for, then gardeners, coachmen, then more money to spend. All these wishes were granted, but still the couple were not happy. With plenty of leisure and nothing to do, they began to quarrel. No matter how many things they had, they had a vague dissatisfaction about the whole business. Finally, they decided that all these possessions had become a burden, and that there was nothing like the old simple cottage with nothing to worry about. So the old fisherman went back to the sea and asked the magic fish to take back everything, saying that he now knew there is no end to desires.

The Buddhist way of life is opposed to that of the Communist. Instead of stressing the fulfillment of material desires, Buddhism advocates the abandonment of all attachments to material wealth, knowing that the desires for earthly things can never be happily satisfied.

Communism insists on the struggle between classes, between the exploiter and the exploited, the landed and the landless, the capitalist and the laborer, the bourgeois and the proletariat. Buddhism on the other hand strives for a universal brotherhood based on the conception that all mankind are possessors of the Buddha-nature, and therefore we should treat each other with compassion, loving friendship, and sympathy. It is against all extreme views, and directs its efforts and attention toward the harmonization of all dualisms instead of emphasizing them.

Between two systems which are so opposed to one another in so many respects, it would be difficult to find some common meeting ground. Communism is committed firmly to the destruction of all religions, since it regards religion as the instrument which the bourgeois uses to exploit the working classes. Just as firmly is Buddhism opposed to the materialistic and atheistic philosophy that is the basis of Communism. If there is one point on which the two systems could possibly agree, it would be in their attitudes toward property. The Communists seek for the goal of public ownership of all land and the means of production, while the Buddhists stress the communal ownership of property in the *sangha*. In the communes of Communist China, for instance, the individual is fed, clothed, and sheltered by the state, and in return for this, the individual turns over all the fruits of his labor to the state. Such a situation is similar to that in a monastery, where the monk has nothing that he can call his own. The Communist can say to the Buddhist that he is merely applying on the national scale what the Buddhist practices on a limited scale in his monastery.

Can Buddhism exist under a Communist regime? So far, the experience of the Buddhist organization in Communist China furnishes us with some information to answer this question. Under the Communist proclamation of freedom of religion, Buddhist temples continue to function in the metropolitan areas and to carry on some semblance of religious services. As for those temples in the country areas and on high distant mountains, it is not certain just what has happened to them, for travel to such areas has been severely restricted to outsiders. Undoubtedly many if not all of such temples have been taken over by the regime and converted to secular uses, with the monks living in them defrocked and returned to the laity. The temples which function in the cities are state-operated organizations, with the resident monks being state employees. To the Chinese Communists, there are certain advantages in their policy of permitting Buddhism to continue. For one thing, the presence of such temples in those large cities where foreign visitors are wont to travel preserves the facade of religious freedom claimed by the Communists. For another, they can present a more friendly image of themselves to the countries in southeast Asia where Buddhism is the dominant religion.

The Buddhists themselves claim that they can still practice their religion as they wish. However, this may be wishful thinking. To the impartial observer, it is clear that the religion is functioning only because it suits the purposes of the state, and because the Buddhists are committed to support the official policy of the country. The Buddhists in the land are organized into the Buddhist Association of China, whose purpose is to bring all Buddhists together to participate in the national patriotic movement under the leadership of the People's Republic, to eliminate all imperialist agents and reactionary elements, and to support the government in establishing a socialistic society. The true nature of the association is clearly seen in its attitude during the Tibetan crisis in 1959, when it came out strongly in favor of the government's action, even though this resulted in the suppression of Lamaism and the destruction of Tibetan monasteries. From this incident, it appears that the Buddhist Association of China does not speak the message of the Buddha, the message of love and compassion, tolerance and unity. It is no different from any other secular organization permitted to function by the government and following faithfully the policy of the government. Under such circumstances, it does not appear that Buddhism is functioning as a religion any more. To the Communists, it is just another social action organization, such as the association of writers, or artists, or musicians. In the light of such experience in Communist China, the prospects of Buddhism continuing as a religious force in countries dominated by Communism do not appear to be very bright. It would seem that the Chinese Buddhists have stretched the elasticity of Buddhism a bit too much just to keep alive in Communist China. Yet even here one cannot be too certain as to what the outcome for the religion will be. During its long history in China, Buddhism has often submitted itself to the needs of the state, and allowed itself to be controlled and supervised by the secular authorities. Even when it was most powerful in China during the T'ang dynasty, it consented to hold birthday celebrations of emperors and memorial services for the deceased in the monasteries and temples, occasions which had nothing to do with Buddhism. Before admittance into the order, candidates had to submit themselves to examinations set by the secular authorities, and ordained monks could be defrocked by order of the government. Numerous institutions which could be called national temples were constructed and maintained by the state, with the subsistence of the resident monks also provided for by the state. So state control of Buddhism is not something new to Buddhism in China. The resilience and the elasticity of the religion have been such that even under these strict controls the religion survived and prospered. It is possible that Buddhism, by bending under the present storm, may eventually be able to survive the pressures of Communism.

Buddhism and Science

Buddhists and Buddhist scholars are generally united in expressing their belief that Buddhism does not recognize any conflict between their religion and science, that Buddhism has no difficulty accepting the findings of modern science, and that the Buddha was the only teacher who resorted to scientific methods to approach the questions of ultimate truth. They base this belief on the one hand in the general attitude of the Buddha. In one of his sermons, the Buddha cautioned his followers not to accept any opinion or conclusion just because it is found in the scriptures, or because a majority of people hold to it, or because it is a traditional belief, or because it is enunciated by a teacher. His attitude is that of the modern scientist, to doubt, to assume nothing, to examine everything dispassionately, and to test all by empirical experience. If after such testing an idea or practice is found to be efficacious or workable, then it is to be accepted. The attitude of the Buddha, like that of the scientist, is one of open-mindedness, lack of prejudice, and tolerance.

In the second place, it is held that specific doctrines of Buddhism are derived scientifically and in harmony with scientific principles. The advocates of this viewpoint contend that Buddhism is naturalistic and not supernaturalistic, for it does not have the concept of a supreme creator of the universe. Rather, it holds to the view that the universe comes into being and passes away in accordance with natural law, and that man is not the special creation of a supreme creator but is only a part of the total scheme of life which includes other forms.

With reference to some of the fundamental doctrines of Buddhism, such as the four noble truths and dependent origination, these were not revealed to him, but were discovered by him after a period of observation and experimentation. He first tried out some of the extant methods followed by other religious teachers of his times, such as the pursuit of sensual pleasures and submission to austerities and asceticism, but these were found wanting and he abandoned them. It was only after years of such experimentation that he finally arrived at the central truths of his religion.

There are also certain views propounded by the Buddha which have been corroborated by modern science. For example, Buddhism and science agree that the principle of cause and effect is the ultimate explanation of the phenomenal world, and hold in accordance with this principle that change and impermanence are universal with all events and things. The Buddhist also holds that ours is not the only world system in existence, that there are countless numbers of such world systems in various stages of evolution and devolution, and that these world systems are as equally capable of supporting life as our system. It is true that the Buddhists did not arrive at this viewpoint through observation with scientific instruments but spun it out in a brilliant flash of the intuition, yet they anticipated the findings of modern astronomy by more than two thousand years. In concluding that the material world is not something solid and enduring, but is a flux of constantly changing elements, the Buddhists have also come up with a truth now accepted by the modern physicists.

In the minds of some modern scholars, however, the scientific nature of Buddhism has been exaggerated. Such people contend that instead of being open-minded and tolerant, the Buddha is authoritarian, for he claims to be omniscient and infallible, and that his path is the only path leading to salvation. Nor can the Buddha be said to be scientific when he consciously excludes from his field of inquiry the whole range of the indeterminate questions, and when he fails to give precise definition to such fundamental concepts as nirvana and *sunyata* or emptiness. The Mahayana Buddhists especially claim that enlightenment consists of an intuitive awakening, and there is nothing scientific about this. Science is interested in acquiring knowledge for the sake of knowledge, but Buddhism is interested in acquiring knowledge for the sake of salvation. In motive and method, therefore, Buddhism is not scientific.

Where is the truth to be found as to whether Buddhism is scientific or not? The serious Buddhist would probably answer that it is somewhere in between these two opposing viewpoints. It is not entirely scientific, nor is it entirely unscientific. Like all great systems of religion or thought which have evolved over long periods of time, it has taken unto itself features which are sometimes contradictory. The Buddha himself was undoubtedly openminded and tolerant, but his later followers, in their attempts to regard him as superman and a transcendental being, looked upon him as omniscient, infallible, and the authoritative source of all truths. Taking full account of the arguments of the opponents, it is still safe to say that Buddhism in its teachings and methods is closer to science than any of the other leading religions of the world. There is no question that the elasticity of Buddhism will enable it to accommodate itself to the findings of modern science.

Buddhism and Race

What was the attitude of the Buddha toward race and race relations?

Strictly speaking, there is no answer to this question. At the time the Buddha preached, the problem of race relations did not exist, for he was not preaching to different ethnic groups in Indian society. His listeners were all Indians. However, the Indian society of the time did consist of different castes, and the prejudices and discriminations between the castes have often been regarded as analogous to those that exist between races in the present world. The members of the lower castes were considered to be black, ugly, deformed, biologically inferior, and intellectually deficient. The practical results of such discriminatory attitudes against the lower castes consisted of: (1) Denial of political equality. No member of the lower castes or outcasts was considered capable of holding office. (2) Denial of economic equality. Since the lower castes were deemed biologically and intellectually inferior, they were considered capable of performing only menial tasks, such as being the servants of others. Servitude was considered to be innate in the lowest caste. (3) Denial of social equality. As slaves or servants, the lower castes were denied any opportunity of advancement. They could not receive an education, and any brahman who instructed a lower caste was penalized. They were denied any contacts with the upper castes, they could not walk on the same streets nor use the same wells as did the latter. (4) Denial of equality before the law. A member of the lower caste who killed someone belonging to the higher castes had to pay with his life, but a brahman who killed an outcast escaped punishment.

Such discriminations against the lower castes in India during the time of the Buddha remind one of the disqualifications which the colored people have to suffer in the world today. In fact, the very same arguments are used by racists to keep the colored people in bondage. If these were the prejudices that existed between the castes during Buddha's lifetime, then the attitude of the Buddha in combatting the inequalities between castes could be taken as representing the attitude of Buddhists toward the problem of race relations. To be sure, caste is not the same as race, but the inequalities between the castes are substantially those that exist between races, hence there is some justification in assuming that the Buddha, were he alive today, would have taken the same attitude toward racial inequality as he did toward caste discriminations.

In combatting the caste prejudices of his day, the Buddha emphasized first of all the unity of all mankind. On biological grounds he sought to prove that all mankind is one species and that there is no generic difference between one caste and another. Among mankind there are no such distinguishing characteristics as those between trees, worms, fishes, flowers, or beasts. The shape and form of men, their organs, heads, hands, feet, nails, nose, eyes, ears, and so forth are all similar. Since the highest caste, the brahmans themselves, accept the idea that all mankind issued from one source, the ultimate, impersonal, supreme Brahma, how can there be differences among men? The names of the different castes are merely conventional designations for different occupations. The one who trades is a merchant, the one who governs is a king, and the one who fights is a warrior. One is not born a merchant, a king, or a warrior, but becomes one by occupation.

Besides the biological argument, the Buddha also adduced the religious argument to reinforce his claim that all mankind is one species. Regardless of caste, all man can lead the moral life leading to salvation, all men are subject to the operation of the iron law of karma and rebirth. The king of Kosala once asked the Buddha whether or not there is any distinction between the strenuous religious discipline to attain salvation practiced by the different castes, to which the Master replied emphatically that there is no distinction as to the nature of their religious discipline and salvation. To the Buddha all men regardless of caste can attain salvation, and it is in the degree of spiritual progress that a man attains that he is classified as superior or inferior. The inferior ones have not yet reached the goal but they do not remain in that status, for they can make progress. Consequently the Buddha admitted into his community of monks members from all castes, even those who were beyond the pale of caste, such as slaves, scavengers, barbers, and robbers.

Faced with the racial inequalities that exist in the world today, Buddhism reaches back to the teachings of the Buddha and takes the same stand as the master did against the iniquities of the caste system of his day. Buddhism stands for racial equality and against all discriminations, social, economic, political, and educational, that are based on race. It takes its stand on biological grounds, namely that all men are one species, and on religious grounds, that all men have the Buddha-nature in them and are capable of attaining salvation. Here again, the elasticity of Buddhism makes it relatively easy for Buddhists to consider the discriminations due to race in the same light as those due to caste, more especially since such discriminations and prejudices are so analogous to each other.

Buddhism and War and Peace

The Buddha's position toward this is very clear and definite; he is against all violence and killing. Numerous passages may be found in the suttas stating this position. In one place, we read, "Putting away the killing of living things, Gautama, the recluse, holds aloof from the destruction of life. He has laid the cudgel and the sword aside." [43] The right livelihood stressed by the Buddha excludes the profession of a soldier. "A man is not just if he carries a matter by violence; no, he who distinguishes both right and wrong, who is learned and leads others not by violence, but by law and equity, . . . he is called just." [44] As another indication of his attitude, he said, "Not to a person with a sword in his hand, unless he is sick, will I preach the dhamma," and "I allow you, O monks, all kinds of brassware, except weapons." To the Buddha, violence never settles any dispute, for it only leads to further violence. "A man may spoil another, just so far as it may serve his ends, but when he's spoiled by others he, despoiled, spoils yet again." [45]

In this advocation of non-violence and non-killing, the Buddha was not alone, for during his time, non-killing was one of the conditions necessary for the higher life. However, there existed at the same time another doctrine, that of the special duty appropriate to each man. In a society of different groups there existed different duties. While a householder or an ascetic should not kill, it was the duty of the soldier to kill. The Buddha had to take cognizance of this condition, as illustrated in the following story. It appears that some soldiers under Bimbisara, king of Magadha, were talking to each other about the evil karma they were accumulating by their acts of war, and they decided to join the *sangha* to lead the holy life. By so doing they felt that they could avoid evil deeds. Having thus decided, they went to the monks and were ordained. When this incident was reported to King Bimbisara, he went to the Buddha and said that there were unbelieving kings who had to be kept at a distance by soldiers. Now if soldiers were to join the *sangha*, his army would be depleted and there would be no defenders left. Such a situation would be disastrous not only to the kingdom but also to the *sangha*. He therefore begged the Buddha not to receive soldiers into the *sangha*. The Buddha assented, and laid down the rule that no one in the royal service should be ordained. By this friendly compromise with the king, the Buddha acknowledged the necessity of the existence of armies whose duty was to kill. However, the Buddha also enunciated a number of rules to guarantee that the monks' relation to the army was cut to a minimum.

A group of six monks went to see an army in battle, and they were severely criticized by the laity for their action. This led the Buddha to state that it is an offense of expiation whenever a monk goes to see an army fight, unless there is a very good reason for so doing. In order to regain his good standing in the *sangha*, a monk charged with such an offense has to appear before the entire community of monks and confess his wrong-doing, after which the *sangha* would then grant him absolution. At another time, some monks staying with the army went to see a sham battle, and one of the monks was wounded by an arrow. This led the Buddha to lay down another rule, that if there is some reason for monks to stay with an army, that monk should not stay for more than three nights, and that if a monk should stay with an army for two or three nights, he should not go out to see a sham battle or to witness the troops pass in review.

The injunction of the Buddha against monks taking up arms to fight and kill has not been always kept in countries outside India. In Tibet during the twelfth and thirteenth centuries, the huge monasteries frequently organized armies of monks to defend their considerable wealth and to seize the wealth of others. Similar conditions also occurred in Japan. There have also been instances of Buddhist kings waging war against neighbors. The king of Upper Burma, after his conversion to Theravada Buddhism, invaded Lower Burma in 1057-8 just to obtain some Buddhist scriptures from the latter region. Thailand, even though professing Buddhism as the state religion, repeatedly invaded Burma and

Cambodia during the thirteenth and fourteenth centuries and destroyed the magnificent city of Angkor Wat. As revenge for these invasions, Burma, another Buddhist kingdom, attacked Thailand during the eighteenth century and systematically looted the Thai capital of Ayuthia. However, over the span of some twenty-five hundred years, even the most industrious historical research has failed to uncover more than the few examples mentioned above, nor do we find in Buddhist history anything like the horrors of the Inquisition, when so many innocent victims were put to the sword because of religious hatred. In Buddhism, there is only one sword, the sword of wisdom, and only one enemy, ignorance, which is destroyed by the sword of wisdom.

It is sometimes argued that the pages of Christian history are stained by warfare because Christianity spread among warlike tribes, while Buddhism spread among peaceable people. This is not entirely true. For instance, there were no more fierce warriors than the Mongols, the scourge of central Asia and eastern Europe during the middle ages, but when they were conquered by Buddhism, their zeal for warfare and conquest was extinguished. The same could be said of the Tibetans, bold, warlike, and fierce until they were converted to Buddhism.

Undoubtedly the Buddhist emphasis against warfare and the stress on non-violence and non-killing of living beings have much to do with curbing the warlike and aggressive tendencies of its converts. Instead of enmity and hatred, Buddhism preaches compassion, love, and sympathy for all living creatures. "Hatred does not cease by hatred at any time: hatred ceases by love, this is an old rule." In this manner the Buddha rebukes those who preach antagonism and ill-will. In another passage, we read, "Let us live happily, then, not hating those who hate us . . . free from hatred among those who hate. Let us live happily, then, free from greed among the greedy." Behind all the hostility, according to the Buddha, lies the greatest of all evils, greed or craving, craving for more power, more prestige, more wealth, more territory. The whole burden of the Buddha's message is directed toward the destruction of this craving. If we can destroy this greed or craving in individuals or in nations, the root cause of private struggles and public wars will be eradicated. In a world divided into hostile camps, each one filled with suspicion, hatred, and ill-will toward the other, this is the message of the Buddha on the overriding problem of war and peace.

Notes

1. F. L. Woodward and E. M. Hare, *Gradual Sayings*, London, Oxford University Press, 1932, 1.128.

2. H. Warren, *Buddhism in Translations*, Cambridge, Harvard University Press, 1947, 60-61.

3. Lord Chalmers, *Further Dialogues of the Buddha*, London, Oxford University Press, 1926, 53-54.

4. E. Hultzsch, *Inscriptions of Asoka*, Oxford, Clarendon Press, 1925, 164.

5. *Dhammapada* v. 183, *Sacred Books of the East*, Oxford, Clarendon Press, 1881, 10.50.

6. Mrs. Rhys Davids, *Psalms of the Early Buddhists*, London, H. Frowde, 1913, 2.143.

7. *Divyavadana*, Cambridge, 1886, 355.

8. Pe Maung Tin, *The Path of Purity*, London, Oxford University Press, 1929, 2.223.

9. F. W. Woodward, *Kindred Sayings*, London, Oxford University Press, 1924, 3.15.

10. E. J. Thomas, *Early Buddhist Scriptures*, London, Kegan Paul, Trench, Trubner, 1935, 30.

11. *The Path of Purity*, 2.273-274.

12. R. A. E. Hume, *The Thirteen Principal Upanishads*, London, Oxford University Press, 1931, 83.

13. S. Z. Aung, *Compendium of Philosophy*, London, Luzac, 1956, Introduction, 9.

14. *Vinaya* 2.239, translated in I. B. Horner, *The Book of the Discipline*, London, Luzac, 1952, 5.335.

15. T. W. Rhys Davids, *The Questions of King Milinda*, in *Sacred Books of the East*, Oxford, Clarendon Press, 1890, 35.114.

16. *Kindred Sayings*, 4.267.

17. Warren, *Buddhism in Translations*, 117-123.

18. S. Z. Aung and Mrs. Rhys Davids, *Points of Controversy*, London, Oxford University Press, 1915, 323.

19. D. T. Suzuki, *Outlines of Mahayana Buddhism*, London, Luzac, 1907, 223-224.

20. T. Stcherbatsky, *The Conception of Buddhist Nirvana*, Leningrad, Academy of Science of the U.S.S.R., 1927, 103.

21. D. L. Snellgrove, *The Hevajra Tantra*, London, Oxford University Press, 1959, 1.52.

22. T. W. Rhys Davids, *Dialogues of the Buddha*, London, Oxford University Press, 1910, 2.85.

23. *Op. cit.*, 1.281-282.

24. Warren, *Buddhism in Translations*, 395-401.

25. Richard Gard, *Buddhism*, New York, George Braziller, 1961, 179-185.

26. R. C. Majumder (ed.), *The Age of Imperial Unity*, Bombay, 1951, 76.

27. R. Mookerji, *Asoka*, London, 1928, 201-202.

28. G. P. Malalasekera, *The Pali Literature of Ceylon*, London, Royal Asiatic Society of Great Britain and Ireland, 1928, 295.

29. Fung Yu-lan, *History of Chinese Philosophy*, Princeton, Princeton University Press, 1953, 2.181.

30. M. Anesaki, *History of Japanese Religion*, London, Kegan Paul, Trench, Trubner, 1930, 61.

31. H. Dumoulin, *History of Zen Buddhism*, New York, Random House Inc., 1963, 168.

32. Malalasekera, *The Pali Literature of Ceylon*, 103.

33. L. Barnett, *The Path of Light*, London, John Murray, 1947, 44-45.

34. *Op. cit.*, 28.

35. Rhys Davids, *Dialogues of the Buddha*, 1.54.

36. D. L. Snellgrove, *Buddhist*

37. Walpola Rahula, *History of Buddhism in Ceylon*, Colombo, 1956, 278-279.

38. James Legge, *A Record of Buddhistic Kingdoms*, Oxford, 1886, 79.

39. Harry Williams, *Ceylon, Pearl of the East*, London, 1950, 345-346.

40. H. G. Quaritch Wales, *Siamese State Ceremonies*, London, B. Quaritch, 1931, 205.

41. H. Fielding Hall, *The Soul of a People*, London, 1903, 160-163.

42. Lafcadio Hearn, *Glimpses of Unfamiliar Japan*, Boston, 1894, 1.132-137.

43. Rhys Davids, *Dialogues of the Buddha*, 1.3-4.

44. *Sacred Books of the East*, 10.64.

45. *Kindred Sayings*, 1.110.

Himalayas, New York, 1957, 262-274.

Glossary

abhidhamma—higher subtleties of the dhamma, metaphysics, name given to one portion of the Pali canon, consisting of seven works.
abhisheka—initiation in the mandala or mystic circle.
alaya-vijnana—storehouse consciousness, where all ideas and impressions experienced by mankind since beginningless time are stored.
Amitabha—presiding Buddha of the Western Paradise or the Pure Land. Name means Infinite Light.
anatta—absence of permanent self or soul.
arhat—one who is worthy of offerings, one who has put an end to rebirth, the goal of the monastic discipline in Theravada Buddhism.
aryans—name of a race of people who poured into India sometime during 3000-2000 B.C.
asava—something that flows; the cankers or intoxicants that defile the mind.
atman—breath, self, soul, inner essence of man.
avasa—colony of monks living together within a prescribed area to pass the rainy season.
Avalokitesvara—the bodhisattva who is the personification of compassion; Kuan-yin in Chinese, Kannon in Japanese. The name has been variously translated. The Lord of Compassionate Glances, The Lord Who is Seen, As for the Chinese kuan-yin, it is taken to mean, The One Who Hears the Voices of the World.
Bhagavan—The Blessed One, an epithet of the Buddha.
bhakti—emotional devotion to a compassionate deity.
bodhisattva (Sanskrit) *bodhisatta* (Pali)—a being who is destined for enlightenment.
Brahma—the supreme absolute in the Upanishads.
Brahma—the chief of the gods in the Brahma world.
brahman—priestly class, the highest of the four castes.
dhamma (Pali) *dharma* (Sanskrit)—the teachings of the Buddha, law, truth, elements of existence.
Gautama—name of clan to which the Buddha belonged.
Hinayana—Lesser Vehicle.

indeterminate questions—a series of questions which the Buddha refused to elucidate, saying that they did not conduce to nirvana.
Jains—followers of Jainism, a religion founded by Nigantha Nataputta, a contemporary of the Buddha.
jhana (Pali) *dhyana* (Sanskrit)—contemplation, meditation, trance, ecstasy.
kalpa—an aeon, a long period of time.
Kanishka—name of Kushan king who rules over northern India during the first and second century A.D.
kamma (Pali) *karma* (Sanskrit)—deed or act and the consequence arising from that deed.
karuna—compassion.
kathina—robe ceremony.
Madhyamika—School of the Middle Way, founded by Nagarjuna.
Mahasanghika—name of Buddhist school that arose after the first schism in the monastic community. Name means the Great Assembly.
Mahavastu—The Great Story, title of a biography of the Buddha in Sanskrit.
Mahayana—the Great Vehicle.
mandala—mystic circle or diagram, cosmogram.
Manjusri—a bodhisattva who is the personification of wisdom.
mantra—mystic syllables, the correct pronunciation of which generates great powers.
Mara—the tempter in the Buddhist tradition.
metta—loving friendship.
mudra—movement or gesture of the hands, fingers, or body.
nirvana—enlightenment, emancipation, salvation, the goal of the Buddhist discipline.
pabbajja—the procedure of leaving the household life to the houseless state.
Pali—the sacred language of Theravada Buddhism.
panna (Pali) *prajna* (Sanskrit)—wisdom, insight.
parinirvana—the great nirvana, the death of a Buddha.
patimokkha—the basic rules that govern the conduct of monks, 227 in the Pali canon, 250 in the Chinese, and 253 in the Tibetan.
pema—sexual affection.
pitaka—basket, name given to each of the three divisions of the canon.
Rig-Veda—Laudatory Verses, earliest of the Vedas.
Sakyamuni—sage of the Sakya tribe.
samadhi—concentration.
samana—a recluse.
samsara—the cycle of rebirth.
sangha—the community of monks.

shudra—lowest of the four castes, comprising the laborers and workers.

Siddhartha—given name of the Buddha, meaning, he who has accomplished his objectives.

sila—moral conduct.

skandha—the five aggregates, material body, feeling, perception, predispositions, and consciousness that make up the individual.

sramanera—a novice.

sutta (Pali) *sutra* (Sanskrit)—a sermon or discourse of the Buddha. The word means that which is strung together.

sunya, sunyata—void, empty, vacuity, emptiness. An element is said to be sunya or empty when it is devoid of its self-nature, that is, it has to depend upon causes and conditions for its existence.

tanha—craving, hankering.

Tantrism—Esoteric School of Buddhism.

Tathagata—epithet of the Buddha. The word has been translated as Thus Come or Thus Gone, and appears to mean, He Who has Attained Enlightenment.

Theravada—Doctrine of the Elders, name given to the aspect of Buddhism which is based on the Pali canon.

tipitaka—the Three Baskets, a term used to designate the Buddhist canon. The three divisions or baskets of the canon are vinaya or the rules of discipline, sutta or the discourses of the Buddha, and abhidhamma, the higher subtleties of the dhamma.

Upanishads—a body of sacred literature in Sanskrit that emphasizes philosophical and mystical speculations about the truths in the Vedas.

upasampada—the full ordination of a monk.

uposatha—the fortnightly assembly of the monks.

Veda—sacred literature of the Hindus.

Vijnanavada—the School of Ideation Only, founded by the brothers Asanga and Vasubandhu.

vinaya—the rules of discipline that govern the conduct of monks and the affairs of the monastic community.

zazen—sitting in meditation, practiced by Ch'an or Zen Buddhists in China and Japan.

Selected Bibliography

Chapter II

Brewster, E. H., *The Life of Gotama the Buddha*, London, 1926.

Foucher, A., *La Vie du Bouddha*, Paris, 1949.

Oldenberg, H., *Buddha*, Berlin, 1881; English Translation, London, 1882.

Rockhill, W. W., *The Life of the Buddha*, London, 1884.

Thomas, E. J., *The Life of the Buddha*, London, 1949.

Chapter III

Conze, E., *Buddhism: Its Essence and Development*, Oxford, 1953.

Coomaraswamy, A. K., *Buddha and the Gospel of Buddhism*, N.Y., 1916.

Dutt, N., *Early Monastic Buddhism*, 2 vols., Calcutta, 1941-1945.

Eliot, C., *Hinduism and Buddhism*, 3 vols., London, 1954.

Horner, I. B., *Early Buddhist Theory of Man Perfected*, London, 1936.

La Vallée Poussin, L. de, *The Way to Nirvana*, Cambridge, 1917.

Lamotte, E., *Histoire du Bouddhisme Indien*, Louvain, 1958.

Pratt, J. B., *The Pilgrimage of Buddhism*, N.Y., 1928.

Rahula, Walpola, *What the Buddha Taught*, N.Y., 1962.

Sangharakshita, Bhikshu, *A Survey of Buddhism*, Bangalore, 1960.

Stcherbatsky, T., *The Central Conception of Buddhism*, London, 1923.

Tachibana, S., *The Ethics of Buddhism*, London, 1926.

Thomas, E. J., *History of Buddhist Thought*, London, 1933.

Warren, H., *Buddhism in Translations*, Cambridge, Mass., 1947.

Chapter IV

Bhattacharyya, B., *An Introduction of Buddhist Esoterism*, Oxford, 1932.

Conze, E., *Selected Sayings from the Perfection of Wisdom*, London, 1955.

Conze, E., *The Prajna Paramita Literature*, Hague, 1960.

Dasgupta, S. B., *Introduction to Tantric Buddhism*, Calcutta, 1950.

Dayal, H., *The Bodhisattva Doctrine in Buddhist Sanskrit Literature*, London, 1932.

Dutt, N., *Aspects of Mahayana Buddhism*, London, 1930.

Grousset, R., *In the Footsteps of the Buddha*, London, 1932.

Hamilton, C. H., *Wei Shih Erh Shih Lun*, New Haven, 1938.

Lessing, F., *Yung Ho Kung*, Stockholm, 1942.

Mallmann, Marie-Therese de, *Introduction a l'histoire d'Avalokite-svara, Paris, 1948.

Murti, T. R. V., The Central Philosophy of Buddhism, London, 1955.

Snellgrove, D. L., The Hevajra Tantra, 2 vols., London, 1959.

Snellgrove, D. L., Buddhist Himalayas, N.Y., 1957.

Stcherbatsky, T., Madhyanta-vibhanga, Discourse on Discrimination Between Middle and Extremes, Leningrad, 1936.

Stcherbatsky, T., The Conception of Buddhist Nirvana, Leningrad, 1927.

Suzuki, D. T., Studies in the Lankavatara Sutra, London, 1930.

Suzuki, D. T., Outlines of Mahayana Buddhism, London, 1907.

Tucci, G., Tibetan Painted Scrolls, 3 vols., Rome, 1949.

Chapter V

Dutt, S., Early Buddhist Monachism, London, 1924.

Gard, R. (ed.), Buddhism, N.Y., 1961.

Horner, I. B., The Book of Discipline, 6 vols., London, 1938-1967.

Chapter VI

Chatterji, B. R., Indian Cultural Influence in Cambodia, Calcutta, 1928.

Coedes, G., Les Etats Hindouises d'Indochine et d'Indonesie, Paris, 1948.

Gokhale, B. G., Buddhism and Asoka, Baroda, 1948.

Malalasekera, G. P., Dictionary of Pali Proper Names, 2 vols., London, 1937-1938.

Mookerji, R., Asoka, London, 1928.

Rahula, Walpola, History of Buddhism in Ceylon, Colombo, 1956.

Ray, N. R., Theravada Buddhism in Burma, Calcutta, 1946.

Wells, K. E., Thai Buddhism, Its Rites and Activities, Bangkok, 1934.

Chapter VII

Bagchi, P. C., India and China, Bombay, 1950.

Chan, W. T., The Platform Sutra, N.Y., 1963.

Chan, W. T., Religious Trends in Modern China, N.Y., 1953.

Chang, C. C., The Practice of Zen, N.Y., 1959.

Dumoulin, H., The Development of Chinese Zen, N.Y., 1953.

Dumoulin, H., History of Zen Buddhism, N.Y., 1963.

Legge, J., The Travels of Fa-hien, Oxford, 1886.

Petzold, B., The Chinese Tendai Teaching, Eastern Buddhist, 4. (1927-28).299-347.

Reischauer, E. O., Ennin's Travels in T'ang China, N.Y., 1955.

Suzuki, D. T., Essays in Zen Buddhism, 3 vols., London, 1927-1934.

Takakusu, J., Essentials of Buddhist Philosophy, Honolulu, 1947.

Waley, A., The Real Tripitaka, N.Y., 1952.

Wright, A. F., Buddhism in Chinese History, Stanford, 1959.

Zurcher, E., The Buddhist Conquest of China, Leiden, 1959.

Fung, Y. L., History of Chinese Philosophy, 2 vols., Princeton, 1952-53.

Chapter VIII

Anesaki, M., History of Japanese Religion, London, 1930.

Anesaki, M., Nichiren, The Buddhist Prophet, Cambridge, Mass., 1940.

Bunce, W., *The Religions of Japan*, Tokyo, 1955.

Eliot, C., *Japanese Buddhism*, London, 1935.

Morgan, K. (ed.), *The Path of the Buddha*, N.Y., 1956; Chapter VII, Buddhism in Japan.

Reischauer, A. K., *Studies in Japanese Buddhism*, N.Y., 1917.

Chapter IX

Bell, C., *Portrait of the Dalai Lama*, London, 1946.

Bell, C., *The Religion of Tibet*, London, 1931.

Dalai Lama, *My Land and My People*, N.Y., 1963.

Hoffman, H., *The Religions of Tibet*, N.Y., 1961.

Shen, T. L., and Liu, S. C., *Tibet and the Tibetans*, Stanford, 1953.

Snellgrove, D. L., *Buddhist Himalayas*, N.Y., 1957.

Tucci, G., *Tibetan Painted Scrolls*, 3 vols., Rome, 1949.

Chapter X

Aung, S. Z., and Mrs. Rhys Davids, *Points of Controversy*, London, 1915.

Barnett, L., *The Path of Light*, London, 1947.

Conze, E., *Selected Sayings from the Perfection of Wisdom*, London, 1955.

Conze, E., *The Prajna Paramita Literature*, Hague, 1960.

Cowell, E. B., and others, *The Jataka Stories*, 7 vols., London, 1895-1907.

Horner, I. B., *Middle Length Sayings*, 3 vols., London, 1954-1959.

Kern, H., *The Lotus Sutra*, Sacred Books of the East, vol. 21, Oxford, 1884.

Law, B. C., *History of Pali Literature*, 2 vols., London, 1937.

Malalasekera, G. P., *The Pali Literature of Ceylon*, London, 1928.

Pe Maung Tin, *The Path of Purity*, 3 vols., London, 1923-1931.

Radhakrishnan, S., *The Dhammapada*, London, 1950.

Rhys Davids, T. W., *Dialogues of the Buddha*, 3 vols., London, 1899-1921.

Rhys Davids, T. W., *The Questions of King Milinda*, 2 vols., Sacred Books of the East, vol. 34-35, Oxford, 1890-1894.

Mrs. Rhys Davids, C. A. F., and Woodward, F. L., *Kindred Sayings*, 5 vols., London, 1917-1930.

Suzuki, D. T., *The Lankavatara Sutra*, London, 1932.

Winternitz, M., *History of Indian Literature*, vol. 2, Calcutta, 1933.

Woodward, F. L., and Hare, E. M., *Gradual Sayings*, 5 vols., London, 1932-1936.

Chapter XI

Coomaraswamy, A. K., *Elements of Buddhist Iconography*, Cambridge, 1935.

Bhattacharyya, B., *The Indian Buddhist Iconography*, London, 1925.

Dutt, S., *The Buddha and Five After Centuries*, London, 1957.

Foucher, A., Etudes sur l'Art bouddhique de l'Inde, *Maison Franco-Japonaise*, Tokyo, 1928, pp. 7-50.

Foucher, A., *L'Art Greco-bouddhique du Gandhara*, 2 vols., Paris, 1905-1923.

Lohuizen-de Leeuw, J. E., *The Scythian Period*, Leiden, 1949.

Rowland, B., *Art and Architecture of India*, Baltimore, 1953.

Chapter XII

Ashikaga, E., Festival for the Spirit of the Dead, *Western Folklore*, 9.3.(1950). 217-228.

Fielding Hall, H., *The Soul of a People*, London, 1903.

Hearn, L., *Glimpses of Unfamiliar Japan*, Boston, 1894.

Legge, J., *The Travels of Fa-hien*, Oxford, 1886.

Quaritch Wales, H. G., *Siamese State Ceremonies*, London, 1931.

Rahula, W., *History of Buddhism in Ceylon*, Colombo, 1956.

Reischauer, E. O., *Ennin's Travels in T'ang China*, N.Y., 1955.

Williams, H., *Ceylon, Pearl of the East*, London, 1950.

Chapter XIII

Malalasekera, G. P., and Jayatilleke, K. N., *Buddhism and the Race Question*, Paris, 1958.

Moore, C., Buddhism and Science, in Yamaguchi, S. (ed.), *Buddhism and Culture*, Kyoto, 1960, pp. 89-125.

Story, F., *Buddhism Answers the Marxist Challenge*, Rangoon, 1952.

Index

abhidhamma, 215, 223-224
Abhayagiri, 123
aggregates (skandha), 44, 45, 72
Amitabha, 69-71, 159, 180-181, 204, 231, 247-248
Amoghavajra, 89
Ananda, 24, 25, 26, 82
Anathapindada, 99
anatta, 44-46, 47
Anawrahta dynasty, 125, 126, 128
Angkor Wat, 129, 131, 246, 281
Anuradhapura, 123, 124
Aris in Burma, 125
arhat, 53-56, 62
Aryans, 1, 10
Asanga, 77, 79
Asita, 18
Asoka, 14, 15, 28, 30, 212; conversion of, 112; pious tours, 113; promotion of Buddhism, 113; nature of his Buddhism, 113-115; contacts with Greek world, 116; missionary efforts, 116, 117, 135
Asokan inscriptions, 213
Atisha, 195, 197
atman, 5, 6
Avalokitesvara, 68, 70, 125, 170, 204, 205, 248
avasa, 90
Avatamsakasutra, 161, 163, 231, 234
Ayuthia, 129

Barlaam, 219-220
bhakti, 62, 241
Bharhut, 17, 28, 213, 236, 238, 239
birth stories, 34, 216, 217, 218
Bodhicaryavatara, 233-234

bodhisattva (bodhisatta), 13, 62, 67ff, 79, 109, 170, 233
Body of Communal Enjoyment, 66
Body of Essence, 65
Body of Transformation, 66
Bon religion in Tibet, 189, 191, 192
bon dance in Japan, 264-267
Book of Discipline, 215
Borobudur, 133, 246
Brahma (supreme absolute), 5, 6, 7
Brahma (chief of gods), 23
brahman, 7, 10, 11, 20
Buddha, date of, 14, 15; biography, 16-17; concept of, 63ff, 238, 240, 241; education, 19; renunciation, 20; enlightenment, 21; first sermon, 24; nirvana, 26; relics of, 26, 27, 55; bodies of, 63-66
buddha-nature, 164-165, 174, 185
Buddhaghosa, 123, 227, 228
Buddhism, alliance with Taoism, 137-138; and race, 276ff; and science, 274ff; and war, 279ff; contributions to Chinese culture, 166ff; decline in India, 133; elasticity of, 268-269; gentry Buddhism, 138-139; introduction into Ceylon, 117; Burma, 124-125; Thailand, 128-129; Cambodia, 130-131; China, 136; Japan, 171; Tibet, 190; religious warfare in, 280-281; persecution in China, 146, 156; persecution in Tibet, 194-195
Buddhist art, symbolism in, 236; aniconic feature, 237, spread of, 245ff
Buddhist Association of China, 273